6+1 Proposals for Journalism

6+1 Proposals for Journalism

Safeguarding the Field in the Digital Era

EDITED BY

Sofia Iordanidou and Chrysi Dagoula

Bristol, UK / Chicago, USA

First published in the UK in 2022 by
Intellect, The Mill, Parnall Road, Fishponds, Bristol, BS16 3JG, UK

First published in the USA in 2022 by
Intellect, The University of Chicago Press, 1427 E. 60th Street,
Chicago, IL 60637, USA

A catalogue record for this book is available from the British Library.

Copy editor: Newgen
Cover designer: Tanya Montefusco
Cover image: iStock by Getty Images. Photo by Shanina.
Production manager: Laura Christopher
Typesetting: Newgen

Hardback ISBN 978-1-78938-649-3
ePDF ISBN 978-1-78938-650-9
ePub ISBN 978-1-78938-651-6

To find out about all our publications, please visit
www.intellectbooks.com
There you can subscribe to our e-newsletter, browse or download our current
catalogue, and buy any titles that are in print.

This is a peer-reviewed publication.

Contents

CONTENTS

Illustrations

Figures

Tables

Case studies

Foreword

Charilaos Platanakis

The threats and challenges for journalists as individuals and journalism as a profession have intensified and transformed due to the shift into a global economy and digital technologies to such an extent that state regulation cannot protect their autonomy any longer. The digital modes of news distribution have overcome the modes of news production, solidifying the state monopoly and control of the past. As a result, the journalist, or even the editor, has been marginalized by the involvement of tech companies, such as Google and Facebook, in the circulation and promotion of news, while profit-driven advertising has cancelled out the seemingly liberal plurality of the openly competitive media sphere. Consequently, the primary influence of publicity has shifted from the quality of news production to algorithmic mechanisms (without transparency or integrity) that promote news/articles based primarily on readers' customer behaviour and advertisers' powerful purchasing monopolies.

The impact on readers is immense since it reinforces distorted beliefs and behaviours, notwithstanding the liberal anticipation of media pluralism, an effect that is strengthened further by the grouping of like-minded individuals on social media. Ethical implications of such a one-dimensional perspective disallow an empathic understanding of alternative views and beliefs, demonize anything 'different' and undermine the respect for human dignity and rights. In the political domain, such an attitude gives rise to populism by vindicating different political stands, downplaying them as indications of a conspiracy of conspicuous interests, internal and external, which jeopardizes open and deliberative democracy. Still, the cure from that threat should take journalism on board, as it did in the past, by allowing pluralistic and free press to reveal the convoluted nature of our world and the different perspectives of it and by emphasizing the benefits of joint deliberation and cooperation in a sincere and open dialogue that would establish a digital community of respect for the other instead of parallel, isolated, digital monologues.

The digital era of journalism has put journalists in an unprecedented, precarious position with insecure working conditions. The reposting of news by digital companies that focus only on news distribution, often without acknowledgement or reimbursement, is a clear case of unfairness that denies journalists their surplus value. Consequently, it deprives journalists of the resources that would contribute to their economic autonomy, both as individuals and as a professional group, in order to invest in their continuous training and meet the new challenges of the digital era, resulting into the improvement of the standards of the news they could produce. The need for continuous training is now more important than ever and makes the proposal of this volume for the taxation of big digital companies (i.e. Google, Apple, Facebook, Amazon) all the more important; something like this would give journalists the necessary resources for economic independence and life-long education, allowing them to perform their free and pluralistic role in our society. Such a proposed taxation would translate into a fair compensation for the squandered profits of journalists who would thus regain dignity of work and improve the standards of their professional activities in the new challenging era.

Only by addressing these two fronts in a synergic manner would media regain their civic role, allowing for an open liberal society to become democratic rather than chiefly capitalist based. Media literacy has a crucial part to play in enabling both journalists and readers to engage in participatory journalism. Redistribution of the profit of big digital companies to journalists, along with crowdfunding, would involve all stakeholders in the communicative sphere of the media. And if the Condorcet's jury theorem holds, civic participation would also bring us closer to the truth.

Introduction

Chrysi Dagoula

Can you imagine what a world without journalism, or what a world without news would look like? One response to these questions, and one that arguably points to the most alarming consequences of such a world, is to be found in the *Washington Post* masthead slogan 'democracy dies in darkness'. First adopted and incorporated into the newspaper's logo in 2017, it has been described as 'the most widely debated and commented upon newspaper slogan' (Farhi 2017: para. 1) in modern times. As such, the slogan lets us know what we can expect from a world without journalism. At its most extreme, this is a place where our ability to know what is going on in the world in any factual way is completely undermined. In fact, the role of journalism when it comes to shining a light on what goes on in society is exactly what is at risk in a world without news. As that light goes out and matters of common concern to members of society remain obscure, any formation of a well-informed citizenry as a basic democratic requirement ensuring that people can effectively participate in and influence matters that concern them becomes impossible.

Broadcasting an urgent appeal for the importance of standing up and fighting for journalism, the *Washington Post* engaged the famous actor Tom Hanks to convey the message regarding the essential public service journalism performs during the 2019 Super Bowl (one of the most watched televised events in the United States):

> When we go off to war. When we exercise our rights. When we soar to our greatest heights. When we mourn and pray. When our neighbours are at risk. When our nation is threatened. There's someone to gather the facts. To bring you the story. No matter the cost. Because knowing empowers us. Knowing helps us decide. Knowing keeps us free.
>
> (Anon 2019: n.pag.; Judkis 2019)

Lending further support to the claim that journalism is a societal necessity, Alan Rusbridger writes that 'anyone growing up in a western democracy had believed that it was necessary to have facts. Without facts, societies could be extremely dark places' (2018: x). Nevertheless, it is an undeniable fact that recent years have been very challenging for journalism. According to Rusbridger, 'we are, for the first time in modern history, facing the prospect of how societies would exist without reliable news – at least as it used to be understood' (2018: xix). In fact, he adds we have been handed the challenge 'of rethinking almost everything societies had, for centuries, taken for granted about journalism' (2018: xxi).

Rusbridger's argumentation echoes that of Bowman and Willis (2003: vi) who wrote that 'journalism is in the process of redefining itself, adjusting to the disruptive forces surrounding it'. Here Bowman and Willis were primarily referring to the impact of technological developments and their financial effects on journalism. Almost two decades later, discussions about journalism and predictions about its future have not altered as much as one would have expected due to the massive technological and financial changes that occurred in the media landscape, particularly in Western democracies. Instead, the same or very similar concerns remain today. We are still debating the major impacts of new technologies and platforms and how these have transformed the vertical world of journalism into a *horizontal* one (Rusbridger 2018). This transformation essentially captures the shift where production tools and news distribution channels are no longer only accessible to and handled by professional journalists but a wide range of actors. We are also still searching for financially sustainable business models for online news – what van der Wurff (2012: 231) refers to as 'the twenty-first-century Holy Grail (of news businesses)'.

Financial uncertainty and technologically driven changes are two of the major manifestations of what can be understood as the crisis of journalism, alongside with other manifestations that are related to constraints to free and independent journalism. For instance, the 2020 Press Freedom Index, compiled by the press freedom organization Reporters Without Borders, 'alerts us to the fact that geopolitical, technological, democratic and economic stresses combined with dwindling public trust in journalistic institutions not only reflect the "converging crises affecting the future of journalism" but also that these well-known challenges are now 'compounded by a global public health crisis' (CFOM 2020: para. 2).

In addition, as Callison and Young suggest, these two manifestations encompass a broader range of 'multiple overlapping crises' (2020: 2) that extend to questions about 'how journalists know what they know; who gets to decide what good journalism is and when it is done right; whether journalists are experts, and what role they should (and do) play in society?' (2020: 2). Arguably, the causes of the crisis of journalism must be understood as complex and interrelated and as connected to the power relations that are inherent in the journalistic profession.

2

Focusing on the US context, Victor Pickard, identifies the structural commercial collapse of journalism as one of these deeper causes of the journalistic crisis. In fact, he points to the 'especially toxic commercialism that prioritizes profit over democratic imperatives' (2020: 1) and refers to three systemic failures of journalism: (1) the emphasis on entertainment over information during electoral coverage; (2) the extensive amount of disinformation circulating on social media platforms; and (3) the slow-but-sure structural collapse of professional journalism (2020: 2–4). All these failures are, according to the author, central to the emergence of a 'misinformation society', where the electorate is 'increasingly served sensationalistic news coverage, clickbait, and degraded journalism instead of informative, fact-based, policy related news' (2020: 5). Ergo, Pickard emphasizes the need to *reinvent* journalism. This should be done he argues, firstly, by addressing the 'supply-side problems' (2020: 5), namely how journalism is produced and distributed.

While Pickard focuses on the American news media environment, the crisis narrative he discusses is pertinent to a range of media environments across the globe. To add to this understanding and explore how the crisis of journalism is manifest in the context of Europe, while at the same time discussing how these challenges might be addressed, we invited scholars, journalism professionals and experts that work in European countries to offer their perspective on a selection of areas linked to the crisis of journalism.

To this end, this book is divided into seven concrete proposals that aim to address journalism's precarious state. The proposals gathered in this book are based on outcomes from the Advanced Media Institute's Conference entitled 'Media, Polis, Agora: Journalism & Communication in the Digital Era' which was held in Thessaloniki (Greece) in September 2018. The rewarding discussions between academics and media professionals that took place during the conference resulted in the recognition of seven key manifestations of journalism's crisis and the identification of steps that we need to take to safeguard journalism. These areas cover topics related to the financial situation for journalism (including for instance discussions on current employment conditions, the dominance of 'web giants' and crowdfunding as a financing model); the need for professional and academic training for journalists and the ways in which journalism can benefit from closer collaboration between professional practitioners and academia; efforts to enhance audiences' media and information literacy; and the issue of media regulation (as, for example, via the establishment of the role of 'media ombudsman'). Adopting a positive, solution-focused frame, we confront these issues as opportunities for renewal.

The point of departure for these discussions is the Greek context, but the book also engages with other European countries. Greece offers an interesting case study not only due to the fact that the financial crisis that officially started in 2009 and was (and still is) clearly interlinked to the crisis of journalism in Greece but also because the manifestations of this crisis were (and still are) significant and wide-spread across various societal strata in the country. The example of Greece provides the starting point for a dialogue on differences and similarities with other national contexts as we feel that the Greek context reflects hopes and fears encountered in various countries in Europe.

Book outline

Part I: Funding journalism in the digital era

Proposal 1: 'Web Giants'

In the first chapter of the book, Nikos Smyrnaios approaches the topic of web giants theoretically, arguing that journalistic practices are increasingly determined by external logics (outside the media environment) and that journalism increasingly becomes more dependent on oligopolistic tech firms and on advertising. Smyrnaios focuses on two key traits of current media systems on a European level, namely, the online advertising models and the concentration of the means of information dissemination by a small group of companies. Smyrnaios also highlights that contemporary journalistic practices are conditioned by the infrastructure of digital journalism and the ways these are shaped by particular economic and technical strategies. Smyrnaios argues that a more in-depth critical analysis of the political economy of online journalism is needed.

In Chapter 2, Michael Panayiotakis explores how taxation of web corporations could benefit journalism and could help independent media outlets to survive. Panayiotakis argues for the development of a funding scheme that involves a monetary transfer from dominant corporations to journalistic initiatives through the means of taxation. For this purpose, he evaluates various tax initiatives in Europe and beyond and questions whether proposals for increased taxation of tech giants 'carry a missionary hue' or whether they might be a feasible solution to address current financial struggles. In the process of assessing how a potential capital reallocation could lead to a financial strengthening of journalistic production, the author investigates regulation approaches, such as the European Copyright Directive.

Proposal 2: Other types of funding

Apart from the adoption of particular policies, the authors of the next proposal emphasize the need to find alternative means of funding journalism that balance the effects of technological and societal changes. They refer to exemplary ventures by individual journalists or media initiatives with only one exception and how these should be supported, either by charitable foundations and/or funds for innovation or through crowdfunding or crowdsourcing (by financing from the audience or cooperative structures). In Chapter 3, Minos-Athanasios Karyotakis, Evangelos Lamprou, Matina Kiourexidou and Nikos Antonopoulos, focus on crowdfunding, crowdsourcing and crowdcreation of journalism in Greece and Cyprus. Their research reveals that most media organizations in these two countries do not employ such means of funding. Considering those findings in relation to the overall business context in Greece and Cyprus as demonstrated by Mavrouli and Fouska in Chapter 5, it could be argued that not much action is taken to develop and adopt new funding models that could help confront the financial challenges that media organizations come up against.

Contrary to these national tendencies, Kathryn Geels (Chapter 4) finds that a diversity of business models is being adopted across Europe where new revenue streams are emerging from financial models based on membership, subscriptions, donations, products, grant funding, commercial collaborations and crowdfunding. Exploring the concept of 'community engagement', Geels presents a snapshot of innovative community-driven news organizations from nine European countries and studies their business and legal structures as well as their various and projected revenue streams. The chapter provides a practical and informative guide to the issue of funding models for journalism, valuable to both professionals and academics.

Part II: Journalists' working conditions

Proposal 3: Employment conditions

The next two chapters focus on the experiences of media professionals by exploring employment conditions in Greece and Bulgaria and by discussing ways in which the financial conditions for journalistic outlets and their employees can be improved. Hence, Chapter 5 tackles an issue that has caused journalists much distress over the last years: job security. Eleni Mavrouli and Despina Fouska examine the correlation between the digitization of journalism in Greece and how this process has affected media employees' working conditions. Through a series of semi-structured interviews with professional journalists working primarily for digital media, they paint a rather discouraging picture that indicates higher demands for speed and profit, more insecurity, longer working hours and lower wages. The authors encourage researchers to trace the roots of this problem, seek explanations by examining journalists' perceptions of their work and raise awareness about the situation as a pathway to improving those conditions.

Lada Trifonova Price's chapter (Chapter 6) on media workers in Bulgaria, points to another significant correlation: insecure employment conditions and a country's political and economic context. Importantly, Trifonova Price highlights that the crisis of journalism might have severe repercussions not only for the functioning of a society but also for its democratic status. By portraying the situation for journalism in Bulgaria, including conditions of rising unemployment, low wages and a rather difficult social state of affairs, Trifonova Price argues that joint European action and policy is needed which, through collaboration between media organizations and journalists, will put media freedom and pluralism on the agenda and that can enable the adoption of concrete legal mechanisms. Such policy, Price argues, will not only improve working conditions within the borders of the European Union but also will also benefit media organizations and journalists in non-European fragile democracies that do not have self-sustaining financial mechanisms to support free and independent journalism.

Proposal 4: 'Media Ombudsman'

On the topic of regulation, the next proposal includes only one chapter (Chapter 7), which delves into the topic of journalistic ethics and how these could be protected, especially by taking into account the diversity of actors that are involved in journalism today, and the variety of platforms on which journalism is currently undertaken. In this chapter, Vasilis Sotiropoulos proposes the establishment of a media ombudsman as a means for industry self-regulation to address ethics violations. Sotiropoulos regards a media ombudsman as an institution that can personify the rules of professional ethics and that could have an advisory capacity or provide recommendations upon invitation. Accounting for the processes surrounding and successful examples of such systems of ethical regulation the author suggests that the effective application of journalistic professional ethics can only function through an internal mediator especially in situations where ethical considerations tend to be neglected or sidestepped.

Part III: Journalism education

Proposal 5: Technology and education

The precarious financial situation and other effects that are related primarily to the impact of technological disruption (such as the involvement of non-journalistic actors in journalistic processes and production) creates a competitive environment in which journalists and media employees need to continuously prove their value to remain employed. Lida Tsene (Chapter 8) argues that to remain competitive and sustainable, professional journalism needs to continuously review the list of necessary professional journalistic skills and to consider lifelong education as necessary means to evolve and stay relevant. Drawing on a variety of examples, Tsene makes a case for improved journalist training, arguing that the most valuable investment for media organizations is to invest in their personnel and not (only) in innovative equipment or technologies. This way, Tsene adds to the academic discourse highlighting that investing in technologies is not an end in itself but that the focus should be on how journalists can make use of these technologies to serve society.

The next chapter (Chapter 9), written by Chrysi Dagoula, focuses specifically on Twitter and showcases the need to generate advantages for journalistic practice from the possibilities that new technologies bring. The author examines Twitter as a journalistic tool which can enable journalistic processes but which also presents journalism with significant challenges. Based on empirical research on the journalistic use of Twitter during election reporting in the United Kingdom, the author discusses journalists' and media organisations' limited success when it comes to effectively using Twitter as a journalistic tool. As a consequence, the chapter endorses Hermida's (2016) suggestion that social media is both a blessing and a curse in the sense that it can create further anxieties among already stressed journalism professionals.

Proposal 6: Academia and professionals

An analysis about education as a condition for safeguarding journalism's future would not be complete without a discussion about the role of academia. The authors of the sixth proposal argue for a closer collaboration between academics and media professionals – and for the need to connect theory and practice. In Chapter 10, Valia Kaimaki starts from the premise that the gap between professionals and academics is a matter of disciplinary boundaries and the fact that exchange requires communication across disciplines and professional capacities. However, Kaimaki argues that journalism can be considered a unique case as the academic study of journalism largely coincides with vocational training. Kaimaki approaches the issue from two sides: first, she explores the inside context which sheds light on the specific challenges that journalists and academics face. Secondly, she positions the discussions more broadly by examining the effect of the social context on the development of a gap or disconnect between the two. Illustrating this gap and the related tension between academics and professionals Kaimaki uses Bourdieu to highlight the urgent need to create a bridge between the two for the benefit of both.

Focusing on the issue of the safety of journalist practitioners, as captured in the UN Action Plan on the Safety of Journalists and the Issue of Impunity, Sara

Torsner's contribution to this proposal (Chapter 11) showcases that tackling the problem necessitates multi-stakeholder involvement by academia, civil society organizations, media professionals and institutions and UN agencies. Using work undertaken at the Centre for the Freedom of the Media (CFOM), University of Sheffield, to illustrate this point, Torsner assesses the value of an academic contribution to policy development and discusses the significance of multi-stakeholder engagement and exchange for the development of policy agendas to address pressing societal problems. Importantly, Torsner proposes ways for how to build mutually beneficial relationships – or partnership – between academic and non-academic actors that will ultimately facilitate a better understanding of the challenges journalism faces (in this case, related to safety) but also a better understanding on how to tackle current knowledge gaps.

Proposal 7: Media literacy

The last proposal of the book is dedicated to the topic of media and information literacy. Amid discussions on information disorder, media literacy is considered one of the most important mechanisms to confront misinformation. However, as Joëlle Swart argues in Chapter 12, media literacy interventions might also backfire. Swart presents various examples as, for instance, the fact that cultivating a high awareness about privacy online might lead to the emergence of passive media users that do not engage publicly with news. Explaining these issues, Swart highlights the current challenges related to media education and argues for a user-centric approach that takes into account the practices and the experiences of media users themselves. The author engages with this problem through in-depth interviews with young people from the Netherlands and suggests that, in the process of empowering users, an emic approach to media literacy is the key for a more nuanced and layered understanding of the topic. In the final chapter of the book (Chapter 13), Sofia Papadimitriou and Lina Valsamidou emphasize the pedagogical use of media in school classrooms. They focus on particular practices in Greece and Cyprus to showcase methods for the effective implementation of critical thinking in classrooms. Those practices, that are enabled by international collaborations, aim to empower students to become informed and active citizens.

Conclusion

In this volume, we navigate across a broad range of topics related to journalism. The authors of this volume raise issues that could be regarded as problems – as reasons for worry. But those issues could also be considered as harbouring a potential for solutions – as proposals for how to move forward and reinvent journalistic outputs and practices for the age 'of sharing, interactivity and innovation' (Beckett 2018: 52). This understanding moves beyond narratives that focus on the crisis of journalism toward narratives that can facilitate headway and evolution. The authors we invited to contribute to this book, experts in their field, have helped us develop the dialogue we aimed to build by connecting national contexts; exploring differences and similarities; sharing insights from their respective field of expertise (academic or non-academic); looking into specific cases and examples; showcasing good, even inspiring, practices; delving into the challenges as well as opportunities; and allowing us to gain a deeper understanding on intricate topics. The authors were also instrumental in helping us to build the book as guide based on concrete proposals. Taking into account that we live 'in a complex world full of change and uncertainty' where 'the public appetite for news has grown' (Beckett 2018: 53), we hope that these proposals will be useful to people interested in media and in the future of journalism.

REFERENCES

Anon. (2019), 'Democracy dies in darkness', *The Washington Post*, 3 February https://www.washingtonpost.com/graphics/2019/national/democracy-dies-in-darkness/. Accessed 11 October 2020.

Beckett, Charlie (2018), 'The power of journalism: Back to the future of news', in C. Foster-Gilbert (ed.), *The Power of Journalists*, London: Haus Curiosities, pp. 51–60.

Bowman, Shayne and Willis, Chris (2013), *We Media We Media: How Audiences Are Shaping the Future of News and Information*, Reston: The Media Center at the American Press Institute.

Callison, Candis and Young, Mary Lynn (2020), *Reckoning: Journalism's Limits and Possibilities*, New York: Oxford University Press.

CFOM (2020), 'World press freedom day 2020', The Centre for Freedom of the Media, https://bit.ly/3lAeyEH. Accessed 11 October 2020.

Farhi, Paul (2017), 'The Washington Post's new slogan turns out to be an old saying', *The Washington Post*, 24 February, https://www.washingtonpost.com/lifestyle/style/the-washington-posts-new-slogan-turns-out-to-be-an-old-saying/2017/02/23/cb199cda-fa02-11e6-be05-1a3817ac21a5_story.html. Accessed 11 October 2020.

Hermida, Alfred (2016) 'Social media and the news', in T. Witschge, C. W. Anderson, D. Domingo and A. Hermida (eds), *The Sage Handbook of Digital Journalism*, London: SAGE publications, pp. 81–94.

Judkis, Maura (2019), 'The Washington Post airs its first Super Bowl spot', *The Washington Post*, 1 February, https://www.washingtonpost.com/lifestyle/style/the-washington-post-creates-its-first-super-bowl-spot-narrated-by-tom-hanks/2019/02/01/f1984a3a-263a-11e9-ad53-824486280311_story.html. Accessed 11 October 2020.

Pickard, Victor (2020), *Democracy Without Journalism?* New York: Oxford University Press.

Rusbridger, Alan (2018), *Breaking News: The Remaking of Journalism and Why It Matters Now*, Edinburgh: Canongate.

Van der Wurff, Richard (2012), 'The economics of online journalism', in E. Siapera and A. Veglis (eds), *The Handbook of Global Online Journalism*, Chichester: Wiley-Blackwell, pp. 231–50.

PART I

FUNDING JOURNALISM IN THE DIGITAL ERA

PROPOSAL 1

'WEB GIANTS'

1

Internet Giants' Dominance and the Perils of Heteronomy for Digital Journalism

Nikos Smyrnaios

Introduction

The emergence of participatory and social media in the mid-2000s is believed to have led to the empowerment of journalists and their publics with consequences that are intrinsically positive for society. Part of the research in digital journalism and participatory practices, especially from the United States, takes up this idea (Gillmor 2004; Jenkins 2006). In brief, the emergence of social media has allegedly strengthened the autonomy of not only journalists but also that of the public against the power of big organizations, for example, states or corporate media and the economic and political constraints they entail. Autonomy is a central idea in the modern concept of the individual in the West. It finds its origins in the philosophy of Kant, and it implies the capacity of giving oneself one's own law (Foessel 2011). By contrast, heteronomy is an external or transcendent law that imposes itself on the subject (Castoriadis 1991). On the social scale, according to Bourdieu (1996), the autonomy of a social field, for example, champ social, like that in journalism consists of specific rules and interests that are distinct from those of other social spaces, such as the rules of business. Within a field, the most autonomous individuals are recognized by their peers based on field-specific values rather than by agents from other social spaces.

However, a careful examination of the new conditions in the exercise of journalism reveals that while a process of empowerment is probably under way, for the vast majority of actors (publishers, journalists and audiences) what is happening is exactly the opposite: the production and consumption of online information follow trends that are rather akin to heteronomy. In other words, journalistic practices, as well as those of the public, are increasingly determined by external logics and evaluated by agents from social spaces other than journalism

(Durand 2004). These logics of sociotechnical and economic nature are related to the constraints imposed by digital production, dissemination and monetization of information. The increasing dependence on oligopolistic tech firms and advertising, the commercial exploitation of user data, the increasing pressure for productivity and standardization of journalistic work and the manipulation and propaganda that are instrumentalizing social media are some of the features that make the internet a vector of heteronomy. Among them, I propose to question in this chapter, through the lens of critical political economy, the consequences of two strong features that characterize digital journalism: the advertising dependence of online news and the concentration of the means for the distribution of online news in the hands of a few internet multinational companies. Indeed, the centrality and concomitance of these two traits, namely the online advertising model and the concentration of the means for information dissemination, are primordial characteristics of the contemporary media system that introduces elements that are external to the journalistic field as far as the definition of norms and dominant practices is concerned. As a result, they greatly influence the nature and quality of information in the digital public space.

Advertising dependence of the internet

As with all complex sociotechnical issues, the economic fundamentals of the internet strongly influence the uses and purposes of journalism. The fact that many of the goods and services available online are funded by advertising largely defines their nature and the material conditions of their production and marketing. In other words, online news, a large part of which is freely available and financed by advertising, cannot be considered irrespective of the business models of the companies that produce and disseminate it and the constraints they induce. Indeed, if – from a strictly economic point of view – advertising produces positive effects for the public by sustaining the production of content in the form of free informational and cultural goods, then from the point of view of the public sphere, things are different. The business model of a particular media outlet has profound repercussions on its functioning and on the values and interests that it has to defend. The critique of television by Bourdieu (1996) is based explicitly on an analysis of the harmful effects of the advertising model: according to the author, instead of producing the pluralism promised by its promoters, the privatization of television and its exclusive financing from advertising has generated standardization in a market where channels are subject to the pressure of maximizing their audience. The result is self-censorship which sometimes does not hamper the interests of the most powerful advertisers but, above all, in choosing the subjects to be discussed, the content produced, the privileged genres and the target audiences, does restrict mainly in terms of their economic efficiency. As Julien Duval (2004) shows in his empirical study on economic journalism, for example, the increased dependence on advertising funding pushes media organizations to maximize the satisfaction of advertisers to the detriment of a part of their audience. Tim O'Reilly (2016), who was behind the tech-savvy Web 2.0 concept, made the same point about Facebook as part of the 2016 US presidential campaign.

Criticism of the advertising-dependent media can be summed up in the fact that they thus become heteronomous. The two-sided market model involves a theoretical convergence of interests between the public and advertisers (the former gets free content, while the latter has to target their potential clients). However, in many cases, these interests, considered from a political point of view and not simply from an economic one, are actually conflicting. While McDonalds' interest is to maximize its sales through advertising, society has a general interest to limit the adverse health effects of junk food. Except that when commercial media are faced with this type of opposition, they tend to fall in line with the interests of advertisers or at least avoid opposing them. In other words, they tend to favour private interests to the detriment of the general public.

Across the internet, the dependence of news websites on advertising also imposes pressure to maximize their audience. This is a classic media problem, but it seems to intensify online. Thus, the reinforcement of clickbait sees the multiplication of contents whose main objective is to attract maximum views by making use of ridiculous, even deceptive, titles, and sensational and emotional information elements that jeopardize the quality or accuracy of news (Blom and Hansen 2015). This frenzied search for audience has reached new peaks in recent years with the emergence and massification of 'fake news', i.e., deliberately misleading content whose stated purpose is to flatter public prejudices, whether racist, sexist or conspirator, to generate clicks and advertising revenue (Allcott and Gentzkow 2017). Moreover, from the perspective of Bourdieu, this intense competition to channel the attention of internet users leads in many cases to a 'circular circulation of information' – a certain homogenization of the subjects treated and the discursive frameworks mobilized (Smyrnaios et al. 2010). The logic of productivity, immediacy, and comprehensiveness that dominates large-audience sites whose business models rely heavily on advertising resources, accentuate their reliance on third parties such as news agencies and public relations consultants. Consequently, the information that is freely and easily available to the large numbers of internet users is, in fact, redundant and of lesser quality than that which can be found in the written press or among the independent journalistic ventures and alternative media.

Finally, the effectiveness of advertising on the internet depends on its ability to target users very finely, according to their socio-demographic characteristics and their preferences. What matters in this model is not so much the size of the audience targeted by a promotional message but rather its quality. In other words, internet advertisements must be able to attract the attention of the consumer in a saturated information environment, through behavioural, contextual and socio-demographic targeting. This is done in particular via a very dense network of information exchange between internet users through multiple tracking devices. Obviously, this ubiquitous tracing of users produces phenomenal amounts of data and pushes the boundaries of surveillance (Tubaro et al. 2014). Now it is enough to 'be online' to produce a lot of data over which users have no control and which are commercially exploited. In this context, journalists are forced to choose topics and treatment angles with a high potential for 'engagement' in the form of likes, shares or retweets (thus emotionally charged topics and angles), which are likely to increase the economic value of the information. These editorial choices are therefore well dictated by heteronomous logics aiming to satisfy the algorithms of internet platforms (social media, search engines, aggregators, etc.) to increase the commercial potential of content.

Consequences on journalistic practices

This economy of low-cost production of information, a corollary of the advertising model, deepens the general deterioration of the working conditions of journalists: precariousness, flexibility, circumvention of collective agreements, increased productivity requirements, lowering of social protection and increasing power in the hands of managers. Even if precariousness and flexibility do not always become constraints but values claimed among freelance journalists (Pilmis 2010), the fact remains that they are being exploited by publishers more often than not (Accardo 1998). This exploitation involves increasing the added value extracted from freelance work and no longer through direct subordination (i.e., formal employees) but rather through a subcontracting relationship with the aim of lowering production costs. From this point of view, journalism has been 'uberized' before the gig economy even existed. Indeed, the media take advantage of the unpaid labour time that freelancers need in order to prepare an article and propose it to a publisher and capture the totality of the intellectual property of precarious journalists (Cohen 2012). In France, it is common to see freelancers paid only for copyright, which reduces the costs of media production (about 8 per cent of charges against more than 50 per cent on wages), and also a decline in journalists' worker rights (no paid holidays, unemployment allowance nor health insurance). The increase in the number of freelancers in recent years is concomitant with the proliferation of free access news sites, based on low-cost production models. The same process is used to justify the total abnegation required by employers in digital start-ups (Ross 2003). In the online news sector, traces of this logic can be found in certain journalistic start-ups, where it is expected that the employees place the general interest of the firm above their own (Damian-Gaillard et al. 2009). In this context, management uses emotional leverage to pressure journalists. The proliferation of small, specialized or local information news websites broaden the trend toward various structural forms (cooperative, non-profit, etc.), which are sometimes distant from the classical capitalist business model and at the margins of the journalistic field.

At the same time, under the influence of advertising, the precariousness and abnegation demanded from online journalists go hand in hand with a movement of rationalization and intensification of their activity. In some online newsrooms, one can observe rationalization processes similar to those underway in customer call services, such as the standardization of work, the quantification of objectives, the formalization of procedures and the omnipresence of supervision (Woodcock 2016). Indeed, the pre-eminence of the advertising model and the search for maximum audience is associated with a sustained pace of publication that, in turn, increases the productivist pressure in newsrooms and the stress of journalists (Boczkowski 2004). The practice of 'shovelware', which consists of the quick production and publishing of second-hand information compiled from various sources and also tasks such as search engine optimization, community management or audience acquisition, requires a series of repetitive and very dense informational operations. Although they sometimes involve complex arbitrations, these actions are framed by sophisticated content management and audience measurement software that formulates production and narrows the journalist's room for intervention.

This logic of heteronomy due to the advertising model is reinforced by the concentration of means of information dissemination in the hands of a few multinational internet companies that impose their will on publishers and journalists.

Ownership of the means of distribution of news

The democratization of the means of cultural production is anterior to the internet, but the latter has democratized the means of massive dissemination of content (Napoli 2010). Indeed, what differentiates the current situation is the ability of individuals to reach a (potentially) mass audience through platforms like YouTube or Facebook. However, if these means of dissemination are now within the reach of a growing part of the population – a fact with undeniable positive effects for the pluralism of the public space – their property remains largely in the hands of private multinational and financialized companies. Tech firms, such as Google and Facebook, control infomediation platforms, defined as the set of business segments and digital devices that allow internet users to come in contact with all types of online information but also with other internet users (Smyrnaios 2018). They can thus change the rules of the game (algorithms, conditions of use, moderation rules) to maximize the value from these proposed services, including when these modifications are against the interests of the users.

This trend is not new. Since the beginnings of connected computing in the 1980s, news has been one of the essential components of online consumer services. Whether it is the Minitel in France or Prodigy and CompuServe in the United States, online service providers have always taken care of including offers in their news content by professional media to increase the value of their services. The advent of the web has only reinforced this trend, although changing the balance of power; in the early 2000s, Google imposed its will on media publishers because of its online search facility, which then appeared to be the main path to online content. This led to the launch of Google News in 2002 without any consultation with media publishers, who bore the will of the Californian firm and had to adapt accordingly (Smyrnaios 2015). Nevertheless, the rise of mobile internet has changed the scene. The product of professional journalists' work is more than ever a major audience attraction. But, alongside Google, there is also a small number of players who control the bulk of content distribution channels, including mobile media. Apple, Facebook, Twitter and Snapchat are now Google's competitors in the distribution of news over mobile internet (Smyrnaios and Rebillard 2019).

However, Google's search engine and Facebook's Newsfeed are still the most powerful distribution channels of online news. Both are based on algorithms that exploit 'the automatic aggregation of uncertain, scattered and random judgments of the crowd of internet users' (Cardon 2013: 74) in an industrial way. For Google's PageRank, these judgments take the form of hypertext links that link web pages to each other. This linking process, which still plays a major role in the search engine's algorithm, is now complemented with a multitude of other signals produced by the online activity of a huge crowd of humans and computers (freshness and originality of information, source credibility, reader interactions, sharing on social media, HTML attributes, etc.). In addition, Google also offers many specialized infomediation services that try to simulate the social logics that prevail in specific areas (Google News, Google Shopping, Google Scholar, Google Play, etc.). Facebook, for its part, prioritizes the appearance of information in the news feed of its users on the basis of algorithms that take into account the many links within its platform (likes, shares, comments, user networks) but also qualities attributed to the content (format, popularity, novelty, etc.). In both cases, it is a question of 'defining metrics intended to describe the relational forms of the social' (Cardon 2013) to hierarchize and assemble information into coherent sets that produce an effective and enjoyable 'user experience', while maximizing the income of infomediation platforms. Incidentally, these infomediaries set up an 'organizational architecture of visibility' produced by software that defines what we can perceive, or not, among the immensity of possibilities (Bucher 2012). This architecture imposes a certain number of usage constraints and technical affordances and is the subject of a specific social appropriation process by the public according to various determinants: socio-economic and cultural characteristics, objectives pursued, contexts of usage, etc.

Faced with these powerful actors, publishers of news sites are in an ambiguous position that can be summarized by the concept of 'coopetition'. They establish with the infomediaries a semi-competitive, semi-cooperative relationship, characterized by a mutual but unequal dependence that makes it difficult to define a coherent strategy. Indeed, publishers need Facebook, Google or Apple to access the extremely large audiences who use their services. But, at the same time, these oligopolistic multinational corporations capture a very large share of the revenue generated by online journalism to the detriment of publishers who finance its production. For example, Google and Facebook alone account for more than half of Britain's online advertising market. The balance of power between infomediaries and publishers, therefore, appears to be very unequal. The proof is that many publishers are forced to adopt specific work methods and even make editorial choices according to the criteria imposed by tech giants. Journalists, for their part, are obliged to adapt their everyday practices in order to maximize the impact of the content they produce in terms of audience and advertising value (Sire 2015). This trend is all the stronger as some services, such as Facebook and Twitter, have become unavoidable in the daily routines of journalistic work.

Social media: Essential but ambiguous tools for journalists

Two features particularly visible in the field of digital journalism are in line with the use of social media by journalists. First, the rise of desk journalism, based primarily on reprocessing existing materials rather than on field reporting (Paterson and Domingo 2008). In this context, social media are reprocessing and multiplying unoriginal content (Messner et al. 2011). They also allow journalists to approach sources in social spheres that are remote or hermetic to them. Another evolution of journalism, in line with the rise of social media, is the new and complicated (for journalists) exercise of explanation and self-justification (Datchary

2010). If audience critique is mainly exercised in the perimeter of news sites and editorial spaces (comments, blogs, official accounts in social media, etc.), it can also overflow and reflect on less institutionalized spaces such as the personal profiles and social media pages of journalists. From this arises a growing confusion between professional and private time and space, a tendency accentuated in the case of journalists by the nature of the news, which is diffuse and omnipresent. In social networks, both public and private spaces, journalists successively assume the role of a professional, a citizen, a 'buddy', a client, etc. The audience they acquire, sometimes measured in thousands of people, indirectly serves the organization that employs them. Thus, the sense of humour and repartee, the quick and synthetic thinking or the rich and eclectic culture of a cognitive worker such as a journalist are all traits of their personality that can be valued on Twitter or Facebook in terms of popularity or 'influence'. The latter can be captured by the employer in the form of audience, visibility or credibility. Management of the relationship with the public and with peers becomes more complex and leads to the implementation of various strategies that can range from the refusal to engage in dialogue to intensive affective labour – in other words emotional investment in the creation and maintenance of personal relationships with a part of the public and sources (Siapera and Iliadi 2015). It indeed affects personality traits, more or less authentic, that are expressed, formatted, measured, interpreted and marketed on these platforms through 'self-quantification' (Pharabod et al. 2013).

As these logics gain momentum, organizations' strategies for capturing the externalities that flow from the digital identity of the journalists-as-cognitive-workers become more and more pressing, eventually taking the form of an 'injunction to participate' in newsrooms (Asdourian et al. 2015). However, the tendency of journalists to combine professional activity and social life within social media regularly generates tensions between, on the one hand, media directorates concerned with the good image of their respective organizations and, on the other hand, journalists defending the principle of their free expression online. While managerial injunctions aim to make the use of social media networks conditional on the promotion of media organizations, journalists resist and try to negotiate individual spaces of freedom. Twitter and Facebook thus become new fields in which this historic power tug of war on the issue of journalistic autonomy is played out (Lemieux 2010).

This 'permanent connectivity' of online journalistic work, often required and sometimes imposed by the very nature of this professional activity, increases the tendency to 'dispersion', understood as having to do several things at the same time, to be solicited relentlessly (Datchary 2011). Employees are exposed to an environment characterized by last-minute changes, permanent interruptions and arbitrations and an extreme variety of tasks that can be standardized and streamlined. This is a typical characteristic of journalistic activity, accentuated on the web by the acceleration of production rates and by the complexity of the information environment in which this production takes place. These situations require special skills to manage the unpredictable (Pilmis 2014), while being sources of psychic, cognitive and physical fatigue. In addition, the ability of workers to manage this dispersion is not always recognized as a professional competence in its own right nor valued as such. The pluri-activity of cognitive workers such as journalists is reinforced by the intensive use of digital technologies that generate a multitude of informational stimuli. 'Permanent connectivity' within social media (instant messaging, Twitter, Facebook, Skype, etc.) and the management of different types of content require the use of specialized software. Mastery of these techniques as well as the 'creative' management of dispersion can be a source of personal satisfaction and even pleasure. But they can also generate frustration, especially as the tension grows between the ideal of investigative journalism and the reality experienced by the majority of journalists who are caught in rationalized production processes (Degand 2011).

Conclusion

Recall that the radical break of the internet from the previous configuration of the media landscape is a banality. It is evident that many examples of quality journalism, even of social criticism and resistance against dominant ideology, have been able to develop by exploiting the technical and economic advantages of the internet. From the point of view of the public, a multitude of unprecedented content in human history is accessible at any time and with disconcerting ease. The diversity of points of view and the pluralism of opinions are thus favoured from this situation. Nevertheless, the habits of the public remain sociologically, technically and economically determined. Few of us are fully exploiting the possibilities offered and are completely free from the commercial constraints imposed on us. In the same way, journalistic practices are massively conditioned by the economic and technical strategies that form the infrastructure of digital journalism. These strategies incorporate logics of exploitation and alienation for the cognitive workers who are journalists, editors and all the other trades that produce online news. They reinforce journalistic heteronomy and thus pose threats to society and democracy. The debates triggered not only by online misinformation but also the populism of the commercial media in the era of the referendum on Brexit and of Trump's election are proof of that. It is imperative to confront them as such, both theoretically and empirically, by deepening a critical analysis of the political economy of online journalism, in the broader context of a critique of the 'digital age'.

REFERENCES

Accardo, Alain (ed.) (1998), *Journalistes précaires, journalistes au quotidien*, Bordeaux: Le Mascaret.

Allcott, Hunt and Gentzkow, Matthew (2017), 'Social media and fake news in the 2016 election', working paper no. 23089, Cambridge, MA: NBER.

Blom, J. N. and Hansen, Kenneth Reinecke (2015), 'Clickbait: Forward-reference as lure in online news headlines', *Journal of Pragmatics*, 76, pp. 87–100.

Boczkowski, Pablo (2004), 'The processes of adopting multimedia and interactivity in three online newsrooms', *Journal of Communication*, 54:2, pp. 197–213.

Bourdieu, Pierre (1996), *Sur la télévision*, Paris: Raisons d'agir.

Bucher, Taina (2012), 'Want to be on the top? Algorithmic power and the threat of invisibility on Facebook', *New Media & Society*, 14:7, pp. 1164–80.

Cardon, Dominique (2013), 'Dans l'esprit du PageRank. Une enquête sur l'algorithme de Google', *Réseaux*, 177, pp. 63–95.

Castoriadis, Cornelius (1991), *Philosophy, Politics, Autonomy: Essays in Political Philosophy* (trans. D. A. Curtis), New York: Oxford University Press.

Cohen, Nicole S. (2012), 'Cultural work as a site of struggle: Freelancers and exploitation', *tripleC*, 10:2, pp. 141–55.

Damian-Gaillard, Beatrice, Rebillard, Franck and Smyrnaios, Nikos (2009), 'La production de l'information Web: quelles alternatives? Une comparaison entre médias traditionnels et pure players de l'Internet', *New Media and Information Conference*, Athens, 6–9 May.

Datchary, Caroline (2011), *La dispersion au travail*, Toulouse: Octarès.

Degand, Amandine (2011), 'Le multimédia face à l'immédiat: Une interprétation de la reconfiguration des pratiques journalistiques selon trois niveaux', *Communication*, 29:1, https://journals.openedition.org/communication/2342, Accessed 28 October 2021.

Durand, Pascal (ed.) (2004), *Médias et censure: Figures de l'orthodoxie*, Liège: Éditions de l'université de Liège.

Duval, Julien (2004), *Critique de la raison journalistique: Les transformations de la presse économique en France*, Paris: Seuil.

Foessel, Michaël (2011), 'Kant ou les vertus de l'autonomie', *Études*, 3, pp. 341–51.

Gillmor, Dan (2004), *We the Media: Grassroots Journalism by the People, for the People*, Sebastopol: O'Reilly.

Jenkins, Henry (2006), *Fans, Bloggers, and Gamers: Exploring Participatory Culture*, New York: New York University Press.

Napoli, Philip M. (2010), 'Revisiting "mass communication" and the "work" of the audience in the new media environment', *Media, Culture and Society*, 32:3, pp. 505–16.

O'Reilly, Tim, (2016), 'Media in the age of algorithms', *Medium*, 11 November, https://www.oreilly.com/radar/media-in-the-age-of-algorithms/. Accessed 26 May 2021.

Pharabod, Anne-Sylvie, Nikolski, Vera and Granjon, Fabien (2013), 'La mise en chiffres de soi', *Réseaux*, 1:177, pp. 97–129.

Pilmis, Olivier (2010), 'Fonder l'attractivité d'activités indignes. La critique artiste au secours des pigistes', in C. Lemieux (ed.), *La subjectivité journalistique*, Paris: Éditions de l'EHESS, pp. 169–85.

Pilmis, Olivier ((2014), 'Produire en urgence. La gestion de l'imprévisible dans le monde du journalisme', *Revue française de sociologie*, 55:1, pp. 101–26.

Ross, Andrew (2003), *No-collar: The Humane Workplace and Its Hidden Costs*, New York: Basic Books.

Siapera, Eugenia and Iliadi, Ioanna (2015), 'Twitter, journalism and affective labour', *Sur le journalisme-About Journalism*, 4:1, pp. 76–89.

Sire, Guillaume (2015), *Google, la presse et les journalistes: Analyse interdisciplinaire d'une situation de coopétition*, Bruxelles: Bruylant.

Smyrnaios, Nikos (2015), 'Google and the algorithmic infomediation of news', *Media Fields*, 10, http://mediafieldsjournal.squarespace.com/google-algorithmic-infomedia/. Accessed 28 October 2021.

Smyrnaios, Nikos (2018), *Internet Oligopoly: The Corporate Takeover of Our Digital World*, Bingley: Emerald Publishing.

Smyrnaios, Nikos, Marty, Emmanuel and Rebillard, Franck (2010), 'Does the long tail apply to online news? A quantitative study of french-speaking news websites', *New Media & Society*, 12:8, pp. 1244–61.

Smyrnaios, Nikos and Rebillard, Franck (2019), 'How infomediation platforms took over the news: A longitudinal perspective', *The Political Economy of Communication*, 7:1, pp. 30–50.

Tubaro, Paola, Casilli, Antonio and Sarabi, Yasaman (2014), *Against the Hypothesis of the End of Privacy*, New York and Heidelberg: Springer.

Woodcock, Jamie (2016), *Working the Phones: Control and Resistance in Call Centres*, London: Pluto Press.

2

Taxing the Internet Oligopoly and Helping Independent Media Survive: A Summary of Recent International Developments and Proposals

Michael Panayiotakis

Introduction

One of the 6+1 proposals that have emerged from the Advanced Media Institute's Media, Polis, Agora meeting in Thessaloniki in September 2018 was that part of the value produced (that accrues to the 'web giants') should be reallocated to enhancing quality – through taxation or other processes. Such a proposal might have sounded overly optimistic, maybe even carrying a missionary hue, but it reflected a vigorous discussion taking place on national and international levels that is in parts converging to the same conclusion: Without some sort of monetary transfer from these web giants to a scheme of funding for journalism and the media, the latter will continue to deteriorate. With it, much of what is now called 'the content industries', the companies and individuals feeding the algorithms and the networks that drive the profitability of the web giants, will also decline. At a minimum, simply taxing the US-based internet oligopolies would somewhat level the playing field and weaken the leverage these companies have over the media.

Taxing times

The development and expansion of the political economy of digital media is currently at a critical juncture, brought on by a confluence of political and economic factors on both sides of the Atlantic. These comprise the increasing discomfort of large states, including the European Union, from having US-based multinational companies owning a very large chunk of their citizens' data – especially given the importance of massive data gathering in AI; the deleterious effects of the internet's oligopolistic structure and its algorithmic practices on almost every business model that concerns media and content in general, and thus the (real and perceived) losses of content industries to the tech giants; as well as their centrality in the emerging surveillance economy and the threat that the large internet monopolies (especially Google/Facebook) pose in their roles as a market-driven universal editor-in-chief of public information and knowledge.

Oligopolies appear to form in every aspect of internet function and maintenance – from Google and Facebook's domination on web advertising globally[1] to the national and regional ISP markets (Bode 2018), mass media and cloud services. This trend is not unique to the internet, but it is very prominent in the sector, especially in areas such as social media and search, where the 'first mover' advantage is especially important. Evading the constraints of serious regulation is a competitive sport for all multinational companies (Cobham and Janský 2018), and Google, Amazon, Facebook, Apple (GAFA), the four largest web-based multinationals, are among its champions (Meijer 2019). A report by the not-for-profit Fair Tax Mark published in December 2019, examined the amount of taxes paid by what they call 'the Silicon Six' (Facebook, Apple, Amazon, Netflix, Google and Microsoft). The report claims that for these six companies, over a period of ten years, 'the gap between the current tax provisions and the cash taxes actually paid was $100.2bn' (Fair Tax Mark 2019).

Another part of the issue is the domination of local digital ad markets by Facebook and Google (with Amazon catching up slightly in the past couple of years [Colburn 2019]), which damages media companies' budgets, subverts professional journalism and drains much needed resources from a media sector undergoing multiple crises. This duopoly also competes unfairly with the local advertisers who, unlike large multinational companies, cannot tax evade.

A third part of the economic threat, widely perceived as such outside the United States (with the exception of China and Russia to an extent, countries that have their own national internet giants and restrict or ban GAFA access to their national population), concerns the data that these US-based multinational corporations harvest from their interactions with non-American users. These are used as raw material for training expert systems and researching AI, thus depriving non-American economies of a critical lever that could aid them to compete in the transition toward the Fourth Industrial Revolution.

Faced with this triple economic quandary, it is no wonder that the discussion on how to regulate, reign in and redirect a portion of these profits to content creators and to the public coffers, by taxing these internet behemoths – and not only in the United States – is gaining importance as an issue in national and international deliberations and negotiations. One part of the agenda concerns various schemes of taxation for the GAFA and another making them pay for the content that is circulated, recovered and shared through their platforms.

The European Copyright Directive

The least promising of these schemes to redirect profits from the GAFA oligopoly is the European Union Copyright Directive (EU 2019/790). Although ostensibly an attempt to return to content creators some of the profits that Google and Facebook make using various forms of their copyrighted or otherwise licensed content, the directive was, according to its critics, either ineffective by design or downright counterproductive for the creators, empowering in the medium- and long-term the very internet oligopolies it was supposed to regulate.[2] Indeed, the whole exercise seems like a rear-guard action aimed to give some, temporary, bargaining leverage to EU content oligopolies rather than creators (Xnet 2018).

A perfect example of the problematic nature of this directive is what has happened in relation to voted version of draft article 11/article 15 of the European Union Copyright Directive (EU 2019/790).[3] The article allows talk of a 'link tax' that would require online platforms to purchase a license if they were to link to other sites or even to quote from articles; in the end of 2018, it ignited quite a debate over the wisdom or even the legal footing of such a move. This is also discussed in the report on *Strengthening the Position of Press Publishers and Authors in the Copyright Directive* (Bently et al. 2017).

Opponents to this proposal were fast to point at the five-year-old decision of Spain to impose fees on aggregator sites pruning news from already published/uploaded material: Google's reaction, at that time, was to pull out their Google News operation from the Spanish market, leading to, empirically accurate, comments about killing the very goose that laid golden eggs (Masnick 2015). Even more instructive has been the experience of the German approach of the *Leistungsschutzrecht fuer Presseverleger*, which intended to use some sort of centrally managed clearing house to impose fees and collect on internet content providers. That initiative, which ended in a law passed at the Bundestag on May 2013, received high-profile attention since it was a central issue for the then Christian Democratic Union of Germany/Free Democratic Party Coalition (CDU/FDP), Government; Chancellor Merkel indicated Germany would push for such an approach at a European level (Merkel 2011). The result of this effort was far less than glorious: several German publishers followed a low-profile path, signing zero-cost licensing agreements with Google so that their content would continue to be used by Google News. This meant that they considered such a display to be of higher indirect importance than any fee.[4]

Google has indeed reacted as forecast, announcing in September 2019 that it was considering a removal of descriptions and thumbnails of EU news sites from its search results (Lee 2019), threatening to cancel Google News services in the European Union altogether, and in fact, Google News did indeed remove all but the title and the URL address of French news articles. This led to a vigorous reaction from the French government and publishers which accused Google of ignoring 'the spirit and the letter' of the EU copyright directive (Willsher 2019). In November unions representing press publishers and Agence France-Presse (AFP) lodged a complaint to *Autorité de la concurrence*, the French competition authority, which in April 2020 was accepted and 'interim measures in the context of the urgent interim measures procedure' were adjudicated. The Autorité found that 'when Google's practices went into effect, the related rights law likely constituted an abuse of a dominant position and caused serious and immediate harm to the press sector' (Autorité de la concurrence 2020: n.pag.).

It thus required Google 'within three months, to conduct negotiations in good faith with publishers and news agencies on the remuneration for the re-use of their protected contents' (Autorité de la concurrence 2020: n.pag.). Google appealed the interim measures, and by September 2020, negotiations with French publishers had failed (Kayali and Larger 2020). As of this writing, Google's appeal will be decided by the Paris Court of Appeal on 8 October. On 1 October 2020, Google announced its 'News Showcase' initiative, through which it pledges a $1 billion investment in European news media (Brittin, Matt 2020). This was seen as subterfuge from Google by the EU publishing industry, which through its News Media Europe website, pointed out that the 'Google News Showcase launched today is no substitute for the EU publishers right' (News Media Europe 2020).

Facebook, however, has sought to reassure European governments that it accepts the necessity of paying significantly more taxes in the European Union than it currently does. In February 2020, Facebook founder and CEO Mark Zuckerberg stated that he would be 'happy to pay more tax in Europe' (Anon, 2020a). As these developments were occurring, the EU Commission was involved in a targeted consultation with all stakeholders on article 17 of the copyright directive (European Commission 2020). The results were considered a step in the right direction by internet freedom activists but were condemned as a negation of the Copyright Law by publishers and some EU governments.[5] In January 2020, the United Kingdom announced that since it was leaving the European Union, it did not intend to implement the EU's copyright law.

Tax initiatives

Meanwhile, on the front of regulation and taxation, the situation has progressed intermittently in the European Union. European Commission 26 April 2018 proposals for a regulation on online intermediation services (European Commission COM/2018/238 final),[6] following on the trail of J.-Cl. Juncker's 13 September 2017 State of the Union priorities over the online economy, focused mainly on transparency and on conflict resolution as well as on creating an observatory on the online platform economy, referred only tentatively (recital 20) to the extent of value creation. It seemed that the debate was maturing at a European level. See for example the Commission Communication on Online platforms of 25 May 2016 (European Commission COM [2016] 288 final) (European Commission 2016).[7] However, in early 2019, due to objections from Ireland and the Scandinavian countries, the failure of the EU digital tax scheme proposed by France and Spain, among other countries, transferred the issue of a pan-European digital sales tax to the Organisation for Economic Co-operation and Development (OECD) (Valero 2019) to set a global standard. This brought back the legislative initiative to individual EU nations.

Developments were sped up when France made it known that its government was working on a national tax of up to 5 per cent on the GAFA group to be applied on digital providers with a turnover – in this line of business – of more than €750 million worldwide and €25 million in France. This tax will have a retroactive effect from 1 January 2019 and is expected to generate some €500 million in revenue – to be used mainly for social purposes (activities originating from the 'Gilets Jaunes' protests).[8] The tax does not set aside EU efforts to deal with the issue but is clearly intended as a sign of restlessness over Brussels' pace. The American reaction was furious, with Donald Trump threatening the European Union and France early on with a tariff war in retaliation (Davison 2019). This was underscored in December 2019 by the results of an investigation by the Office of the US Trade Representative which claimed that 'France's digital services tax (DST) discriminates against US companies', recommending that the United States 'take action' against the DST to fight the 'growing protectionism of EU member states' (United States Trade Representative 2019). Following up on this report, the Trump administration threatened tariffs of over $2.4 billion on French products like cheese, wine, handbags, etc. After a meeting between Presidents Emmanuel Macron and Donald Trump in Davos in January 2020, the French government agreed to 'delay collecting a new tax on multinational technology firms until the end of 2020' (Anon. 2020b: n.pag.).

The urgency of the taxation issue became even more pronounced as the COVID-19 pandemic spread around the world, causing a global depression and becoming a pillar of the European Union's scheme to finance its pandemic recovery plans (Stolton 2020). However, the discussions/negotiations held under the auspices of the OECD were thrown into disarray in mid-June 2020 when the United States suspended talks with European countries on the issue. According to the *Financial Times*, 'In a letter to four European finance ministers seen by the Financial Times, US Treasury secretary Steven Mnuchin warned that discussions had reached an "impasse"'. He said the US was unable to agree even on an interim basis on changes to global taxation law that would affect leading US digital companies' (Fleming et al. 2020).

The move was followed by an announcement by the Trump administration of the imposition of 25 per cent tariffs on $1.3 billion (€1.1 billion) worth of French goods to begin in 2021 due to the pandemic. France reiterated its intention of imposing the digital tax on Google by the end of 2020 (Okello 2020). Austria followed a similar path by announcing in late 2018 (Fingas 2018) and passing through a first vote in Parliament in September 2019 a bill imposing a 5 per cent tax on advertising revenue on digital companies that met a set of criteria. The law came into effect on 1 January 2020. Following Austria, the Czech Republic pledged it would introduce an even higher tax rate of 7 per cent on 'revenues from online advertising, the sale of user data, and intermediation services', targeting only companies with a global turnover of €750 million or more and with sales in the Czech Republic of at least €1.9 million per year (Patricolo 2019: n.pag.). The rate was lowered to 5 per cent in June 2020 after internal negotiations,[9] and the law is expected to be passed by parliament within the year. Italy and Spain also legislated digital services taxes of 3 per cent on revenue on 1 January 2020 (Sylvers and Schechner 2019) for Italy and on 1 October 2020, for Spain[10] despite protestations and threats by the United States.

Meanwhile in the United Kingdom, a digital services tax has been in effect since 1 April 2020, which imposes a 2 per cent levy on 'the revenues of search engines, social media platforms and online marketplaces which derive value from UK users' (HM Revenue and Customs 2019: n.pag.). Even more ambitiously, the Labour Party, in opposition, has pledged to implement 'an independent fund for public interest journalism paid for by tech giants' (Labour Party 2018: n.pag.). Similar initiatives are being discussed in Belgium and a host of other EU countries. A recent decision by the European Union General Court on 27 June 2019, 'overturned a 2016 commission decision that Hungary's tax on advertising revenue violated EU state aid rules, because it captures companies based on the size of their turnover' (Stojaspal and Gottlieb 2019: n.pag.). Though not a final judgment, the decision is considered a positive sign regarding the legality of aforementioned individual EU country-members' digital sales tax initiatives.

Beyond Europe, the idea of taxing the American-based internet oligopolies is spreading. Similar legislative initiatives have been implemented or are being set in New Zealand (Prescott-Haar et al. 2019), India (Seth 2019), Turkey, Israel and many more countries, in what seems to be an expanding trend.[11] Australia released in July 2020 a draft mandatory code of conduct that would force Google and Facebook to remunerate news media for use of their content (McGuirk 2020b). Facebook reacted by threatening to disallow use of news on its platform in Australia (Easton 2020). The Australian government pledged to amend the draft legislation in order to allay some of the concerns of the duopoly (McGuirk 2020a) but made clear that it intended to proceed with implementation regardless of Facebook's actions (Kaye 2020). The indications that we might be on a cusp are multiplying, and measures to tax the big internet oligopolies are perhaps policies whose time has come, especially given the effect on internet media that the COVID-19 pandemic had. So as far as what the future might hold, the key is probably in the United States.

Plans to save journalism

Unsurprisingly, an equally, if not more, important part of the discussion on taxing the digital giants is taking place in the United States. These are discussions in the vein of what James Curran has called 'public reformism', that is, the effort 'to enhance the democratic performance of the media through concerted action' (Curran 2011). A number of authorities, technical, economic and political, have advocated the imposition of a digital sales tax on the internet oligopolies and the whole issue of regulation, including taxation, of these companies was prominently featured in the presidential primary debates of the Democratic Party.

The respected media activist NGO Free Press has tabled a proposal to impose a small tax on *targeted* advertising. The proceeds of such a tax would be diverted to a 'new, multibillion-dollar Public Interest Media Endowment funded by taxing the purveyors of targeted advertising', created by the US Congress. As they explain, 'Rather than attempting to police content, the endowment would direct tax revenues to fund independent and non-commercial news outlets'. This tax would be 'levied against targeted advertising to fund the kinds of diverse, local, independent and non-commercial journalism that's gone missing and to support new news-distribution models, especially those that do not rely on data harvesting for revenue' (Karr and Aaron 2019: n.pag.). The authors suggest three options through which such a Public Interest Media Endowment could be funded through this tax:

> Option 1: A 2 percent targeted-ad tax on all online enterprises that earn more than $200 million in annual digital-ad revenues would yield more than $1.8 billion for the endowment, based on 2018 ad sales [...]. Commercial online publishers and platforms making $200 million or less in digital-ad revenues would not be subject to the tax [...]
>
> Option 2: A lower tax rate levied on all advertising revenues, including offline placements, which increasingly draw on similar data profiles gleaned from online activity [...] a 1 percent tax rate would yield approximately $2 billion for the endowment.
>
> Option 3: A tax equal to 1.5 percent of taxable income levied on any platform with an annual taxable income of $1 million or greater if more than 60 percent of such income is derived from the sale of advertisements presented to patrons or users. Based on 2018 revenues, this would yield close to $2 billion.

This proposal took on additional significance when it was endorsed in August 2019 by US Democratic presidential candidate and Senator Bernie Sanders in an op-ed, he published in the Columbia Journalism Review (Sanders 2019).

At the heels of the Free Press plan, Paul Romer, the 2018 recipient of the Nobel Prize in economics, published an op-ed in the *New York Times* (Romer 2019: n.pag.), in which he too proposed a tax that would be 'applied to revenue from sales of targeted digital ads, which are the key to the operation of Facebook, Google and the like', as a way to restrict the harmful practices of these oligopolies, though not as a way to make funds available for independent journalism.

Bernie Sanders's endorsement of such a plan was significant, especially when one considers the pledge, in the same vein, of the UK Labour party. The idea of not simply *taxing* the web giants but also taxing them *to fund journalism* itself (and other forms of content creation possibly) is gaining ground, despite the losses of both these agendas on both sides of the Atlantic. There is the overarching concern that independent, investigative and honest journalism is indispensable for the proper functioning of democracy. Internet oligopolies are undermining the prospects of market-funded journalism. So, a tax derived from the duopoly that drains most of the value produced by creators, organizations and collective entities could and should be the bedrock on which some plan ensuring the public provision of the necessary independent quality journalism should be built. The need for such an institution arguably predates even the internet and the total disruption of the ad-based, worldwide dominant business model the mass media relied on, but at this point, it might prove to be the only available life raft for keeping independent media alive and viable.

There are of course many other options beyond an endowment plan, such as the Free Press organization proposals. In particular, the taxation of the internet giants could provide the basis for a commons-based journalism, in which journalists and media organizations would agree to contribute to and reuse content from journalistic commons to be eligible for remuneration either through some automatic allocation mechanism or through, this is, a voucher system. The University of Westminster's Communication and Media Research Institute recently published a policy report titled 'The Online Advertising Tax as the Foundation of a Public Service Internet' (Fuchs 2018: n.pag.) which is, and their author has indicated as much, in the same vein as the Labour proposals. Beyond suggesting the creation, at both the national and European level, of internet platforms run by public service media – funded by a digital sales tax on the major digital advertisers – it includes commons-centric proposals, such as a Participatory Media Fee. In this scheme:

> Each household or individual receives a particular sum of money per year [...] that must be donated to non-profit civil society online platforms or other non-profit media and cultural organisations that advance the common good, do not use advertising, are non-commercial and non-profit, are not associated with powerful organisations, and do not have a discriminatory purpose. Participatory budgeting and state power are combined in the model of the participatory media fee: the state taxes corporations and then passes on the achieved income via participatory budgeting to citizens, who donate their public sphere cheque to civil society platforms.

Similar ideas, involving 'a public interest journalism fund that would directly subsidize news organizations to conduct investigative journalism' and would receive funding from a sales tax on the digital ad duopoly, have been floated in Australia as well (Eltham 2017: n.pag.).

Conclusion

If all of this looks like a promising path, one should turn to the reaction by the duopoly itself. In mid-January Facebook announced plans to put $300 million into journalism projects focused 'on local journalism [that] is one of the areas that needs the most help' (Ingram 2019: n.pag.). By delving deeper into this initiative, one sees that the indicated sum would be spent over three years and that the local journalism focus 'is derived from consultations with media partners and users' (Ingram 2019: n.pag.).

However, Google has always groomed much better relations with the media, through a series of journalism grants it distributes around the world, what one author calls 'Google's "operating system" for journalism' (Fanta 2018: n.pag.). In addition 'beyond its immediate business interests, Google also runs a 150-million-euro programme to promote innovation in journalism. The Digital News Initiative (DNI) was launched in 2015, at a time when many publishers in Europe were fiercely criticising Google as disruptor of journalism's business model'. This is in tune with the fact that, as the author notes, 'the company is shifting from being a mere search engine to becoming a central node for the production and distribution of news' (Fanta 2018: n.pag.). In that sense, Google is fortifying itself against regulation with a massive and well-funded PR campaign, aimed at its foremost critics: the media (Bell 2019). The Google News Showcase is part of this Google tradition of co-optation through funding to avoid regulation.

So, one can easily see that, however promising the trek toward the reallocation of the value produced by 'web giants' to enhance quality in journalism, that very trek is riding at the razor's edge. The proposals for a new publicly funded – but not necessarily state-dictated – model for independent and investigative journalism are there, and they all depend on the premise of taxing the internet giants. The 'publicly funded, but not necessarily state dictated, model for independent and investigative journalism' part should be emphasized. This is a case of what Binakuromo Ogbebor (2020) has described as non-governmental public reformism. Neither the Participatory Media Fee (which is basically a voucher system in which the state has no direct say on the organizations that could receive money) nor the Public Interest Media Endowment (which would be along the lines of the successful and independent National Endowment for the Arts model) would be state controlled. So, in essence the state, in both cases, would be the 'collector' of funds, though in both cases it would not have a direct role in distributing them. But, the ability to enforce transparency rules and deontological regulations on government institutions, at least in most democracies, is greater than the ability to enforce the same on unaccountable and profit-oriented multinational, monopolistic, private entities with an enormous lobbying budget.

For technical reasons, through the sheer force of the size of GAFAM industries, or because of trade rules and compromises, this might prove much more difficult to implement successfully. Such a failure will mean a certain further decline of journalism around the world and/or the takeover of the media industries by Facebook and – especially – Google. There is no clear alternative to these trends, unless one is willing to introduce public funding of a public good that the market cannot provide for, even without the GAFA tax revenue – at least initially. This would imply, however, developments on a social and economic level that are well beyond the scope of this paper to analyse.

NOTES

1. Google accounted for 31.1 per cent of worldwide ad spending in 2019, and Facebook for another 20.2 per cent. These percentages are larger if one excludes China, which has its own internet monopolies and severe restrictions on Google and Facebook's activity (Enberg 2019).

2. See, for example, the statement made by the Federal Data Protection Commissioner of Germany, Ulrich Kelber, titled 'Copyright reform also poses risks to data privacy rights', where he points out that draft article 13/Directive article 17 leads to a further concentration of data at the hands of the current internet oligopolies (Kelber 2019).

3. Directive (EU) 2019/790 of the European Parliament and of the Council of 17 April 2019 on copyright and related rights in the Digital Single Market and amending Directives 96/9/EC and 2001/29/EC (text with European Economic Area [EEA]relevance).

4. For a discussion on the Spanish and German precedents, see 'Copyright, online news publishing and aggregators: A law and economics analysis of the EU reform' (Colangelo and Torti 2019).

5. 'In its consultation paper, the Commission is going against its original objective of providing a high level of protection for rightsholders and creators and to create a level playing field in the online Digital Single Market', said 23 trade bodies representing publishers, music industries and film and TV producers in a joint letter to EU digital chief Thierry Breton and seen by Reuters (Chee 2020).

6. See also: European Commission (2018), *Proposal for a Regulation of the European Parliament and of the Council on Promoting Fairness and Transparency for Business Users of Online Intermediation Services*, Brussels: COM 238 final (European Commission 2018).

7. See also: European Commission (2016), *Online Platforms and the Digital Single Market Opportunities and Challenges for Europe*, COM 288 final.

8. See also: Conseil de ministers, 'Création d'une taxe sur les services numériques et modification de la trajectoire de baisse de l'impôt sur les sociétés', 3 March, https://www.gouvernement.fr/conseil-des-ministres/2019-03-06/creation-d-une-taxe-sur-les-services-numeriques-et-modificat. Accessed 26 May 2021.

9. See also: Kafkadesk (2020), 'Czech Republic agrees to lower "GAFA tax" on digital giants', 13 June, https://kafkadesk.org/2020/06/13/czech-republic-agrees-to-lower-gafa-tax-on-digital-giants/. Accessed 26 May 2021.

10. See also: Bloomberg Tax (2020), 'Spain's senate votes to advance taxes on stock trades, big tech', 1 October, https://news.bloombergtax.com/daily-tax-report/spains-senate-votes-to-advance-taxes-on-stock-trades-big-tech. Accessed 26 May 2021.

11. For a detailed review of the digital sales tax in the EU and beyond, see 'A Review of the proposals for taxation of profits of businesses in the digitalized economy' (Ndibe 2019).

REFERENCES

Advanced Media Institute (2018), *AMIRetreat 2018: 6+1 Proposals for Journalism*, Thessaloniki: Advanced Media Institute.

Anon. (2020a), 'Facebook boss "happy to pay more tax in Europe"', BBC, 14 February, https://www.bbc.com/news/business-51497961. Accessed 26 May 2021.

Anon. (2020b), 'France agrees to delay new tax on tech giants', BBC, 21 January, https://www.bbc.com/news/business-51192369. Accessed 26 May 2021.

Autorité de la concurrence (2020), *Related Rights: The Autorité Has Granted Requests for Urgent Interim Measures Presented by Press Publishers and the News Agency AFP (Agence France Presse)*, Paris: Autorité de la concurrence. 9 April, https://www.autoritedelaconcurrence.fr/en/press-release/related-rights-autorite-has-granted-requests-urgent-interim-measures-presented-press. Accessed 26 May 2021.

Bell, Emily (2019), 'Do technology companies care about journalism?', *Columbia Journalism Review*, 27 March, https://www.cjr.org/tow_center/google-facebook-journalism-influence.php. Accessed 3 October 2019.

Bently, Lionel, Kretschmer, Martin, Dudenbostel, Tobias, Carmen, Maria del, Calatrava Moreno and Radauer, Alfred (2017), *Strengthening the Position of Press Publishers and Authors and Performers in the Copyright Directive*, Brussels: European Parliament's Policy Department for Citizens' Rights and Constitutional Affairs, http://www.europarl.europa.eu/RegData/etudes/STUD/2017/596810/IPOL_STU(2017)596810_EN.pdf. Accessed 1 October 2019.

Bode, Karl (2018), 'The cable industry is quietly securing a massive monopoly over american broadband', Techdirt, 20 March, https://www.techdirt.com/articles/20180314/09251639423/cable-industry-is-quietly-securing-massive-monopoly-over-american-broadband.shtml. Accessed 2 October 2019.

Chee, Foo Yun (2019), 'Apple says $14 billion EU tax order "defies reality and common sense"', *Reuters*, 16 September, https://www.reuters.com/article/us-eu-apple-stateaid-idUSKBN1W1195. Accessed 2 October 2019.

Chee, Foo Yun (2020), 'Europe's creative industry slams EU Commission for rewriting copyright rules', *Reuters*, 10 September, https://uk.reuters.com/article/uk-eu-copyright/europes-creative-industry-slams-eu-commission-for-rewriting-copyright-rules-idUKKBN2613DT. Accessed 2 October 2020.

Cobham, Alex and Janský, Peter (2018), 'Global distribution of revenue loss from corporate tax avoidance: Re-estimation and country results', *Journal of International Development*, 30, pp. 206–32.

Colangelo, Giuseppe and Torti, Valerio (2019), 'Copyright, online news publishing and aggregators: A law and economics analysis of the EU reform', *International Journal of Law and Information Technology*, 27:1, pp. 75–90.

Colburn, Colin (2019), 'Google, Facebook, and Amazon: From duopoly to triopoly of advertising', *Forbes*, 4 September, https://www.forbes.com/sites/forrester/2019/09/04/google-facebook-and-amazon-from-duopoly-to-triopoly-of-advertising/#785874536343. Accessed 4 October 2019.

Curran, James (2011), *Media and Democracy*, London and New York: Routledge.

Davison, Laura (2019), 'Google, Facebook unite with Trump to protest French tech tax', *Bloomberg*, 19 August, https://www.bloomberg.com/news/articles/2019-08-19/google-facebook-unite-with-trump-to-protest-french-tech-tax. Accessed 2 October 2019.

Easton, Will (2020), 'An update about changes to Facebook's services in Australia', *Facebook*, 31 August, https://about.fb.com/news/2020/08/changes-to-facebooks-services-in-australia/. Accessed 30 September 2020.

Eltham, Ben (2017), 'We should levy Facebook and Google to fund journalism – here's how', *The Conversation*, 17 May, http://theconversation.com/we-should-levy-facebook-and-google-to-fund-journalism-heres-how-77946. Accessed 4 October 2019.

Enberg, Jasmine (2019), 'Digital ad spending 2019 global', *eMarketer*, 27 March, https://www.emarketer.com/content/global-digital-ad-spending-2019/. Accessed 2 October 2019.

Fair Tax Mark (2019), *The Silicon Six and Their $100 Billion Global Tax Gap*, Manchester: Fair Tax Mark, https://fairtaxmark.net/wp-content/uploads/2019/12/Silicon-Six-Report-5-12-19.pdf. Accessed 30 September 2020.

Fanta, Alexander (2018), 'The publisher's patron: How Google's news initiative is re-defining journalism', *European Journalism Observatory*, 28 September, https://en.ejo.ch/digital-news/the-publishers-patron. Accessed 3 October 2019.

Fingas, Jon (2018), 'Austria plans its own tax for tech giants like Apple and Google', *Endgadget*, 30 December, https://www.engadget.com/2018/12/30/austria-digital-tax/. Accessed 3 October 2019.

Fleming, Sam, Brunsden, Jim, Politi, James and Giles, Chris (2020), 'US upends global digital tax plans after pulling out of talks with Europe', *Financial Times*, 17 September, https://www.ft.com/content/1ac26225-c5dc-48fa-84bd-b61e1f4a3d94. Accessed 30 September 2020.

Fuchs, Christian (2018), *The Online Advertising Tax as the Foundation of a Public Service Internet*, London: University of Westminster Press.

HM Revenue and Customs (2019), *Introduction of the New Digital Services Tax*, London: HM Revenue & Custom, https://www.gov.uk/government/publications/introduction-of-the-new-digital-services-tax/introduction-of-the-new-digital-services-tax. Accessed 30 September 2020.

Ingram, Matthew (2019), 'Facebook says it plans to put $300M into journalism projects', *Columbia Journalism Review*, 19 January, https://www.cjr.org/the_new_gatekeepers/facebook-journalism-funding.php. Accessed 4 October 2019.

Karr, Timothy and Aaron, Craig (2019), 'Confronting the news crisis', *Free Press*, https://www.freepress.net/sites/default/files/2019-02/Beyond-Fixing-Facebook-Final.pdf. Accessed 4 October 2019.

Kayali, Laura and Larger, Thibault (2020), 'Google and French publishers fail to reach deal on fees for news content', *Politico*, 2 September, https://www.politico.eu/article/google-and-publishers-fail-to-reach-deal-on-licensing-fees-for-news-in-france/. Accessed 1 October 2020.

Kaye, Byron (2020), 'ACCC dares Facebook to block news content', *IT News*, 18 September, https://www.itnews.com.au/news/accc-dares-facebook-to-block-news-content-553496. Accessed 1 October 2020.

Kelber, Ulrich (2019), *Reform des Urheberrechts birgt auch datenschutzrechtliche Risiken*, Bonn and Berlin: Der Bundesbeauftragte.

Labour Party (2018), 'Empower those who create and consume media over those who Want to Control or Own It – Jeremy Corbyn', https://www.gov.uk/government/publications/introduction-of-the-new-digital-services-tax/introduction-of-the-new-digital-services-tax. Accessed 1 October 2019.

Lee, Timothy B. (2019), 'Google takes hard line, refuses to pay French news sites despite new law', *Ars Technica*, 29 September, https://arstechnica.com/tech-policy/2019/09/despite-new-law-google-refuses-to-pay-to-link-to-french-news-sites/. Accessed 3 October 2019.

Masnick, Mike (2015), 'Study of Spain's "Google Tax" on news shows how much damage it has done', *Techdirt*, 29 July, https://www.techdirt.com/articles/20150725/14510131761/study-spains-google-tax-news-shows-how-much-damage-it-has-done.shtml. Accessed 1 October 2019.

McGuirk, Rod (2020a), 'Australia to amend law making Facebook, Google pay for news', *Associated Press*, 17 September, https://apnews.com/article/australia-media-social-media-legislation-archive-1adc33ea0c0124978d122199c2698317. Accessed 1 October 2020.

McGuirk, Rod (2020b), 'Australia to make Google and Facebook pay for news content', *Associated Press*, 23 July, https://apnews.com/article/australia-international-news-media-legislation-technology-5edf987c499302471a6694ef19b2d456. Accessed 2 October 2020.

Meijer, Bart (2019), 'Google shifted $23 billion to tax haven Bermuda in 2017: Filing', *Reuters*, 3 January, https://www.reuters.com/article/us-google-taxes-netherlands-idUSKCN1OX1G9. Accessed 3 October 2019.

Merkel, Angela (2011), 'Rede von Bundeskanzlerin Angela Merkel anlässlich des Zeitungskongresses des Bundesverbandes Deutscher Zeitungsverleger e.V', Berlin: Die Bundeskanzlerin.

Ndibe, Chukwuebuka Stanley (2019), *A Review of the Proposals for Taxation of Profits of Businesses in the Digitalized Economy*, Master of Laws Research Papers Repository, 5, Western Ontario: University of Western Ontario.

News Media Europe (2020), 'Google News Showcase launched today is no substitute for the EU publishers right', *News Media Europe*, 1 October, http://www.newsmediaeurope.eu/news/google-news-showcase-launched-today-is-no-substitute-for-the-eu-publishers-right/. Accessed 2 October 2020.

Ogbebor, Bina (ed.) (2020), 'Conclusion', *British Media Coverage of the Press Reform Debate*, Cham: Palgrave Macmillan, pp. 212–13.

Okello, Christina (2020), 'France to levy digital tax despite US decision to walk out of talks', *RFI*, 18 June, https://www.rfi.fr/en/france/20200618-france-push-on-with-digital-tax-desp ite-us-provocation. Accessed 1 October 2020.

Patricolo, Claudia (2019), 'Czech Republic moves forward with digital tax', *Emerging Europe*, 6 September, https://emerging-europe.com/business/czech-republic-moves-forward-with-digi tal-tax/. Accessed 1 October 2019.

Prescott-Haar, Leslie, Sunde, Stefan and Day, Sophie (2019), 'New Zealand digital services tax update', *MNE Tax*, June 11, https://mnetax.com/new-zealand-digital-services-tax-update-34291. Accessed 3 October 2019.

Romer, Paul (2019), 'A tax that could fix big tech', *New York Times*, 6 May, https://www.nyti mes.com/2019/05/06/opinion/tax-facebook-google.html. Accessed 4 October 2019.

Rushe, Dominic (2019), 'Amazon made an $11.2bn profit in 2018 but paid no federal tax', *The Guardian*, 15 February, https://www.theguardian.com/technology/2019/feb/15/ama zon-tax-bill-2018-no-taxes-despite-billions-profit. Accessed 1 October 2019.

Sanders, Bernie (2019), 'Op-Ed: Bernie Sanders on his plan for journalism', *Columbia Journalism Review*, 26 August, https://www.cjr.org/opinion/bernie-sanders-media-silicon-val ley.php. Accessed 4 October 2019.

Seth, Rohan (2019), 'India's upcoming digital tax: How will big tech cope?', *The Diplomat*, 21 August, https://thediplomat.com/2019/08/indias-upcoming-digital-tax-how-will-big-tech-cope/. Accessed 2 October 2019.

Stojaspal, Jan and Gottlieb, Isabel (2019), 'Digital tax challenges just got a little tougher in Europe', *Bloomber Tax*, 18 June, https://news.bloombergtax.com/daily-tax-report-intern ational/digital-tax-challenges-just-got-a-little-tougher-in-europe. Accessed 3 October 2019.

Stolton, Sam (2020), 'Commission mulls digital tax to fund Europe's multi-billion euro recovery', *Euractiv*, 27 May, https://www.euractiv.com/section/digital/news/commission-mulls-digital-tax-to-fund-europes-multi-billion-euro-recovery/1471387/. Accessed 29 September 2020.

Sylvers, Eric and Schechner, Sam (2019), 'Italy follows France in levying a digital tax', *Wall Street Journal*, 24 December, https://www.wsj.com/articles/italy-follows-france-in-levying-a-digital-tax-11577209660. Accessed 1 October 2020.

United States Trade Representative (2019), *Report on France's Digital Services Tax Prepared in the Investigation under Section 301 Investigation*, Washington, D.C.: Office of the United States Trade Representative, https://ustr.gov/sites/default/files/Report_On_France%27s_D igital_Services_Tax.pdf. Accessed 30 September 2020.

United States Trade Representative (2019), *Conclusion of USTR's Investigation Under Section 301 into France's Digital Services Tax*, Washington, D.C.: Office of the United States Trade Representative, https://ustr.gov/about-us/policy-offices/press-office/press-releases/2019/december/conclusion-ustr%E2%80%99s-investigation. Accessed 1 October 2020.

Valero, Jorge (2019), 'The EU's digital tax is dead, long live the OECD's plans', *Euractiv*, 11 March, https://www.euractiv.com/section/economy-jobs/news/the-eus-digital-tax-is-dead-long-live-the-oecds-plans/. Accessed 1 October 2019.

Willsher, Kim (2019), 'France accuses Google of flouting EU copyright law meant to help news publishers', *Los Angeles Times*, 17 October, https://www.latimes.com/business/story/2019-10-17/france-accuses-google-ignoring-copyright-law. Accessed 1 October 2020.

Xnet (2018), 'The EU call it copyright, but it is massive internet censorship and must be stopped', *Open Democracy*, 25 October, https://www.opendemocracy.net/en/can-europe-make-it/civilised-societies-don-t-call-it-censorship-but-copyright/. Accessed 5 October 2019.

PROPOSAL 2

OTHER TYPES OF FUNDING

3

Crowdfunding, Crowdsourcing and Crowdcreation in Greek and Cypriot Media Websites

Minos-Athanasios Karyotakis, Evangelos Lamprou,
Matina Kiourexidou and Nikos Antonopoulos

Introduction

One of the many changes that have occurred in the field of journalism over the last years is the involvement of citizens in news production, a development which has challenged some of the traditional values of journalism and led to the emergence of new concepts, such as crowdsourcing. Crowdsourcing is a process of obtaining information and services from many organizations or individuals. The notion of crowdsourcing includes crowdcreation (or user-generated content) and crowdfunding (asking the crowd to provide funding). This study adds to the existing literature of crowdsourcing, crowdcreation and crowdfunding by focusing closely on Greek and Cypriot news websites and by examining how these websites use crowdsourcing features. The findings demonstrate that the majority of the news websites in Greece and Cyprus do not include crowdsourcing features (crowdfunding and crowdcreation) on their websites.

Crowdfunding, crowdsourcing and crowdcreation

Crowdsourced journalism is related to the term 'crowdsourcing', a broad term that includes several forms of online participation and contribution. It is actually an open call for contributing online ideas, talent, opinions, viewpoints and knowledge. The notion of crowdsourced journalism is closely associated with the participation of the public in news production. There are several ways of contributing to this process such as by submitting new information, opinions, sending footage, correcting the provided journalistic content or giving a different aspect of a news story. This new approach tends to become common practice in the field of digital journalism. The practices mentioned above offer the public the opportunity not only to participate effectively but also to shape what they read daily. A typical case of crowdsourced journalism is when the news organization asks for the public to help in investigating an issue (Aitamurto 2011; 2016; Mitchell and Lim 2018; Bruns 2011). For instance, in the field of data journalism, journalists rely on getting data from the public (Appelgren and Nygren 2014), and as Bradshaw offers an indicative example: 'One project which crowdsourced water prices, for example, asked users to also submit a scan of their bill' (2015: 206). Additionally, several scholars have pointed out that the crowdsourcing processes can transform further the way journalism, news media and the online industry work (Milioni et al. 2012: 22; Aitamurto 2019: 13; Pilloni 2018: 2).

Another essential aspect of crowdsourcing is that it does not just ask from the public to contribute by providing content but also by offering their expertise on the covered topics. This contribution can happen through a public invitation by the news organization. To produce a better result, the readers/users begin a dynamic interaction with the journalists, exchanging information. However, one of the central problems is connected with this type of interaction is that the audience might not remain engaged after the provision of information, and their participation in the news production process. As a result, news companies have to invent new methods for maintaining this beneficial relationship (Gopalkrishnan and Nylund 2014: 2–3), for instance, by involving the public in the comment sections of their news websites. To do so, news organizations use different platforms for the users to comment as the content of the comments can result in improving the popularity of a website (Karyotakis et al. 2019: 8). Nevertheless, in several cases, news organizations cannot find the appropriate method to secure the constant participation of the audience (Gopalkrishnan and Nylund 2014: 8–9; Karyotakis et al. 2019: 9–10).

According to Howe (2009), crowdsourcing also includes the applications of crowdcreation and crowdfunding. Crowdcreation, concerns the contribution of user-generated content (UGC) (Geiger et al. 2011: 1; Ståhlbröst and Lassinantti 2015: 29). User comments for instance are considered one of the most effective ways for producing UGC as the public can easily add content on the webpage of the relevant news article such as videos, photos, information or hyperlinks. The acceptance of user comments is not considered a new approach in the field of journalism and are similar to the practice of Letters to the Editor, which was popular in the pre-digital era. Through this process, the readers of the newspapers could express their opinion against or in favour of a published news article. Nevertheless, Letters to the Editor are not considered as dynamic a communication process as the online commenting, in which the barriers to commenting and participating are few (McCluskey and Hmielowski 2012: 314–15). Nowadays, in contrast to Letters to the Editor, almost every contribution is published immediately, and every individual can read the comments. Consequently, the UGC helps in provoking insightful discussions and attracting more interest from the professionals and the public than before (Bergström and Wadbring 2015).

A useful tool in the process of crowdcreation is the function of hashtag (a keyword or a sentence led by the symbol '#'), which offers an easy way of distributing UGC on specific topics. The use of the hashtag is considered a crowdsourcing process as it provides a gateway to large volumes of data but also helps news companies coordinate their content and information more efficiently (Bruns and Highfield 2012; Bruns et al. 2016). By clicking on the hashtag word or sentence, each individual can track the related information and follow a topic or issue. Hashtags are considered helpful for covering news, and they have been used extensively in more recent events such as the war in Syria (#syria) for sharing information (Habel et al. 2018: 1614). Hashtags are also used by news organizations for reporting breaking news, such as the tsunami and the earthquake in Japan in 2011, in which the hashtag #tsunami was used to share relevant information and news. According to Antonopoulos and Veglis (2013: 134–35), there is a large variety of forms of hashtags (or show tags). News companies use hashtags on their websites to indicate the most read or visited news articles. Therefore, the news websites can suggest to users the issues that seemed to be the most important, resulting in improved usability and more users via this interactive feature.

Another form of crowdsourcing is crowdfunding, in which the public (or crowd) is asked to provide financial support to the crowdsourcer (Aitamurto 2019: 2). As Aitamurto suggests, through crowdfunding, the audience can provide news organizations with financial support. The direct effect is that news organizations will rely less on the elites that might want to influence the news production (Aitamurto 2011: 440–42; 2019: 7–8).

There are various online platforms through which journalists can start campaigns and gain financial support from their audience, such as Kickstarter, Indiegogo, FundRazr or RocketHub. One of the main goals of these initiatives is to fund investigative news pieces (investigative journalism demands time to research topics related, e.g., to corruption, crimes, political elites, etc.) and retain editorial independence or to have a more decentralized editorial model (Aitamurto 2011: 443; 2019: 7–8). The independence of the editorial is not a new issue for the field of journalism. Several studies have revealed that the notion of independence is an essential part of the journalists who consider their profession a public service (Deuze 2005; Hunter 2015: 275–76; George et al. 2019: 10–14).

The case of Greece and Cyprus

There are three distinct issues in Greece's and Cyprus' media landscape, that are connected to editorial independence and the subsequent seeking of alternative sources of funding. In both countries, there are strong ties between media and political elites (Iosifidis and Papathanassopoulos 2019: 2–5; Milioni et al. 2015). As a result, the state tends to intervene and to set the agenda. For example, in Greece, the Public Service Broadcaster (ERT) remains until today an organization where political power thrives by firing and hiring, according to their preferences, the top executives of the organization. According to Iosifidis and Papathanassopoulos (2019: 2–5), the transactions between the media and political establishment of Greece tend to affect the media system of the country, resulting in dependent coverage in several Greek media companies. Moreover, the unprecedented decline of newspapers' sales led the parent companies to invest in the online presence of these publications. This development created a more concentrated news industry (Iosifidis and Papathanassopoulos 2019: 2–5).

Moreover, the size of media market in these countries plays an important role. In Cyprus, for instance, the population was 1,266,676 million people in July 2020, according to the Central Intelligence Agency (n.d.). Therefore, as Surugiu and Radu (2009) explain, throughout the process of digitization, private television stations chose not to invest in new technologies from the start due to the high cost of the investment. Instead, they waited for the new technologies to be established, before changing their model. In the end, the citizens had to support these changes by consuming the products (Surugiu and Radu 2009: 8).

Lastly, another major problem is that the public in Greece does not seem to want to pay for online news. According to the annual Digital News Report of Reuters Institute (2016; 2017; 2018; 2019),the percentage of the Greek citizens that pay for online news in Greece was between 6–7 per cent of the country's online population but jumped to 11 per cent in 2020. This might be a result of the low trust levels in media organizations – as Greece has one of the lowest trust levels in the mainstream media of the examined countries in the Reuters' reports. Although there are no data for Cyprus from the Reuters' reports, the partly shared media system with Greece, due to the leading role of some prominent Greek media companies in Cyprus, suggests that similar problems might occur.

The study

By taking into consideration the importance of crowdsourcing for journalism and the news industry, this study examined the crowdsourcing approaches employed by Greek and Cypriot news media news websites. The study sample consisted of the most popular news websites of Greece (n=175) and Cyprus (n= 128) in 2019, according to the rankings of alexa.com. The cognitive walkthrough method was used to inspect usability issues in technological interactive systems. The walkthrough method is based on systematic observation and investigation of technologies and technological products providing insights about them, such as usability features, properties of the examined technology or product and operational problems (Light et al. 2018; Fernandez et al. 2011). Furthermore, the classification of the news websites was developed in accordance with the methodology used by Antonopoulos and Veglis in a previous study (2012), according to which the news websites were classified into three categories: (1) portals (those websites that have exclusive online presence); (2) newspapers (traditional newspaper websites); (3) mass media (websites that are part of a group that has more than just one medium online, such as television, radio, etc.).

To identify the crowdsourcing characteristics of the news websites in Greece and Cyprus, the following aspects were researched: whether news websites ask their readers to correct the content on published news articles; whether readers are asked to offer information/content or ideas for a forthcoming issue or a news article; and whether there is evident usage of hashtags in their homepages to demonstrate most visited articles and trends. Consequently, the following research questions were asked:

RQ1: To what extent do news media websites ask users for corrections on their journalistic content?

RQ2: To what extent do news media websites ask for information or ideas for a forthcoming issue or a news article?

RQ3: To what extent do news media websites use forms of hashtags in their homepages to demonstrate most visited articles and trends?

RQ4: To what extent do news websites from Greece and Cyprus have an option of crowdfunding on their website?

Similarities and differences of the websites

For this study, the most visited websites of Greece and Cyprus were analysed according to the rankings of alexa.com for the year 2019. Alexa.com provided

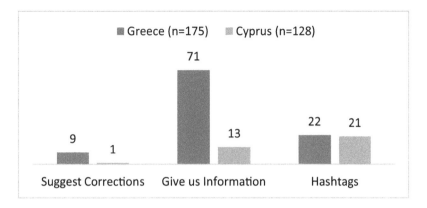

FIGURE 1: The results for the Greek and Cypriot news websites.

the 500 most popular websites for those countries. However, those rankings included many websites that could not be considered news websites, as they were used for commercial purposes, and therefore they were excluded from the study's sample. Furthermore, the researchers could not access some of the news websites due to the General Data Protection Regulation (GDPR). Subsequently, the number of examined news websites were n=175 for Greece and n= 128 for Cyprus.

From the 175 examined Greek news websites, only nine (5.14 per cent) asked the public to provide corrections regarding the content of the news website. Noteworthy is the difference between suggestions for information/content and corrections of the published content by users/readers, as there were far more news websites, 71 (40.57 per cent), that asked for corrections. Finally, the Greek news websites using hashtags for coordinating the provided content were 22 (12.57 per cent).

The most frequently occurring category regarding Cypriot news websites was the use of hashtags, with 21 Cypriot news websites (16.4 per cent) using hashtags to signal their most popular content to readers. A smaller number of thirteen (10.15 per cent) Cypriot news websites requested information, whereas only one news website (0.78 per cent) out of 128 asked the public about suggesting corrections regarding its content (Figure 1).

Regarding the more specific observation about crowdfunding, in 2019, there were only twelve Greek news websites and twelve Cypriot news websites that featured direct crowdfunding on their website. It is worth noting though that in 2018, there were more news websites in Greece (n=16) and Cyprus (n=13) that featured methods of direct crowdfunding by the public (Figure 2).

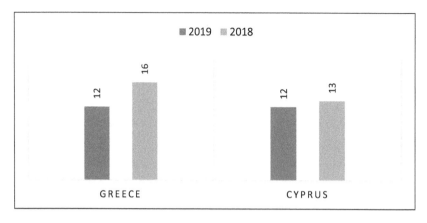

FIGURE 2: The results for the Greek and Cypriot news websites that offer direct crowdfunding method(s) for the years 2018 and 2019.

Crowdfunding as a vital tool for journalism's viability

The participation of the public in the news production process via footage, photos, ideas, opinions, etc. is supposed to be common practice for crowdsourced journalism (Aitamurto 2016: 281–84). Despite the importance of crowdsourcing in journalism to promote a dynamic relationship with the public, most news websites in both Greece and Cyprus do not seem to consider crowdsourcing features on the websites as crucial for their sustainability and operation, especially when it comes to crowdfunding. Similarly, asking for corrections on their published news content does not seem to be important for them either. In Greece, there were only nine websites that asked the audience to send them corrections, whereas in Cyprus, there was only one website, which was asking for corrections (RQ1). For the second research question (RQ2), the results were quite different. Almost half of the Greek news websites asked for information from the public. Contrary to Greece, fewer Cypriot news websites follow this practice, as from the overall sample of 128 news websites, only thirteen promoted the request of information from the public.

As far as the RQ3 is concerned, hashtags (or show tags) are powerful tools for disseminating content and were introduced initially on Twitter. Similar to Twitter, news websites can include a category of the most viewed (or read) or the most popular of articles published on the website, suggesting to users' specific articles that are more popular and interesting than others. However, most news websites do not use the function of hashtags; the number of them in both countries is almost the same (Greece=22 and Cyprus=21). Finally, the response to the last research question of this study (RQ4) revealed that there used to be more news websites in 2018 that had a direct feature for receiving money from the public. In 2019, this number dropped from sixteen to twelve in Greece and from thirteen to twelve in Cyprus. The decline is not significant, but it shows a tendency toward abandoning requests for money from the public. Perhaps, this change is related to the unwillingness of audiences to pay money for online news, as the Digital News Reports from 2016–19 have shown.

Finally, this study questions show how news websites in Greece and Cyprus operate and whether they can leverage crowdfunding features. In the last years, the attacks against journalists by political elites have risen dramatically, and many news organizations try to keep their independence by being more open to the participation of their readers and by becoming more accountable to them (George 2019; George et al. 2019). Under such conditions, crowdfunding is considered a vital tool for gaining financial support so as not to have to give in to the demands of the market forces. Also given that in the Greek and Cypriot case, the media system of countries is being shaped by the interplay between the media and political elites; this may be the crucial problem of the Greek and Cypriot news media online system, also considering the unwillingness to embrace the beneficial features of crowdsourcing. A reason why the audience may not want to invest money in news websites is because they feel that they might not have a say in the way they operate and produce news. This argument is consistent with other relevant studies of the field (Carvajal et al. 2012; Hunter 2015; 2016). The majority of the examined news websites did not seem to strongly embrace the researched crowdsourcing features. Perhaps, a solution to the discussed problems could be public reformism (Curran 2011) that 'seeks to improve the standard and viability of journalism through concerted action, such actions as could enhance the democratic performance of the media' (Ogbebor 2020: 212).

Regarding the limitations of the study, the news websites of Greece and Cyprus included, were based on the ranking of alexa.com (top sites in Greece and Cyprus for 2019). New research based on different ranking may offer more insightful aspects of the crowdsourcing features of the news websites in Greece and Cyprus by employing other quantitative and qualitative approaches.

REFERENCES

Aitamurto, Tanja (2011), 'The impact of crowdfunding on journalism: Case study of spot.us, a platform for community-funded reporting', *Journalism Practice*, 5:4, pp. 429–45.

Aitamurto, Tanja (2016), 'Crowdsourcing as a knowledge-search method in digital journalism', *Digital Journalism*, 4:2, pp. 280–97.

Aitamurto, Tanja (2019), 'Crowdsourcing in journalism', in J. F. Nussbaum (ed.), *Oxford Research Encyclopaedia of Communication*, Oxford: Oxford University Press.

Antonopoulos, Nikos and Veglis, Andreas (2012), 'Technological characteristics and tools for web media companies in Greece', *16th Panhellenic Conference on Informatics*, PCI: 44–50, Athens, October.

Antonopoulos, Nikos and Veglis, Andreas (2013), 'The evolution of the technological characteristics of media websites', *Asian Conference on Media and Mass Communication*, Osaka, November, pp. 130–46.

Appelgren, Ester and Nygren, Gunnar (2014), 'Data journalism in Sweden: Introducing new methods and genres of journalism into 'Old' Organizations', *Digital Journalism*, 2:3, pp. 394–405.

Bergström, Annika and Wadbring, Ingela (2015), 'Beneficial yet crappy: Journalists and audiences on obstacles and opportunities in reader comments', *European Journal of Communication*, 30:2, pp. 137–51.

Bradshaw, Paul (2015), 'Data journalism', in L. Zion and D. Craig (eds), *Ethics for Digital Journalists: Emerging Best Practices*, New York and London: Routledge, pp. 202–19.

Bruns, Axel (2011), 'Gatekeeping, gatewatching, real-time feedback: New challenges for journalism', *Brazilian Journalism Research*, 7:2, pp. 117–36.

Bruns, Axel and Highfield, Tim (2012), 'Blogs, Twitter, and breaking news: The produsage of citizen journalism', in R. A. Lind (ed.), *Produsing Theory in a Digital World: The Intersection of Audiences and Production in Contemporary Theory*, New York: Peter Lang Publishing Inc., pp. 15–32.

Bruns, Axel, Moon, Brenda, Avijit, Paul and Münch, Felix (2016), 'Towards a typology of hashtag publics: A large-scale comparative study of user engagement across trending topics', *Communication Research and Practice*, 2:1, pp. 20–46.

Carvajal, Miguel, García-Avilés, José A. and González, José L. (2012), 'Crowdfunding and non-profit media: The emergence of new models for public interest journalism', *Journalism Practice*, 6:5&6, pp. 638–47.

Central Intelligence Agency (n.d.), 'Europe: Cyprus', https://www.cia.gov/library/publications/the-world-factbook/geos/print_cy.html. Accessed 8 October 2020.

Curran, James (2011), *Media and Democracy*, London: Routledge.

Deuze, Mark (2005), 'What is journalism? Professional identity and ideology of journalists reconsidered', *Journalism: Theory, Practice & Criticism*, 6:4, pp. 442–64.

Fernandez, Adrian, Insfran, Emilio and Abrahão, Silvia (2011), 'Usability evaluation methods for the web: A systematic mapping study', *Information and Software Technology*, 53:8, pp. 789–817.

Geiger, David, Seedorf, Stefan, Schulze, Thimo, Nickerson, Robert C. and Schader, Martin (2011), 'Managing the crowd: Towards a taxonomy of crowdsourcing processes', *Proceedings of the Seventeenth Americas Conference on Information Systems*, Detroit, Michigan, 4–7 August, AMCIS 2011 Proceedings, pp. 1–12.

George, Cherian (2019), 'Journalism in a climate of hate', *Journalism*, 20:1, pp. 106–09.

George, Cherian, Zeng, Yuan and Mazumdar, Suruchi (2019), 'Navigating conflicts of interest: Ethical policies of 12 exemplary Asian media organisations', *Journalism*, 22:6, pp. 1279–95.

Gopalkrishnan, Asha and Nylund, Mats (2014), 'Crowdsourcing in media', *Arcada Working Papers*, 4, pp. 1–12.

Habel, Philip, Moon, Ruth and Fang, Anjie (2018), 'News and information leadership in the digital age', *Information, Communication & Society*, 21:1, pp. 1604–19.

Howe, Jeff (2009), *Crowdsourcing: Why the Power of the Crowd Is Driving the Future of Business*, New York: Crown Business.

Hunter, Andrea (2015), 'Crowdfunding Independent and Freelance Journalism: Negotiating Journalistic Norms of Autonomy and Objectivity', *New Media & Society*, 17:2, pp. 272–88.

Hunter, Andrea (2016), '"It's like having a second full-time job": Crowdfunding, journalism and labour', *Journalism Practice*, 10:2, pp. 217–32.

Iosifidis, Petros and Papathanassopoulos, Stylianos (2019), 'Media, politics and state broadcasting in Greece', *European Journal of Communication*, 34:4, pp. 345–59.

Karyotakis, Minos-Athanasios, Lamprou, Evangelos, Kiourexidou, Matina, and Antonopoulos, Nikos (2019), 'SEO practices: A study about the way news websites allow the users to comment on their news articles', *Future Internet*, 11:9, pp. 188.

Light, Ben, Burgess, Jean and Duguay, Stefanie (2018), 'The walkthrough method: An approach to the study of apps', *New Media & Society*, 20:3, pp. 881–900.

McCluskey, Michael and Hmielowski, Jay (2012), 'Opinion expression during social conflict: Comparing online reader comments and letters to the editor', *Journalism*, 13:3, pp. 303–19.

Milioni, Dimitra, L., Vadratsikas, Konstantinos and Papa, Venetia (2012), '"Their two cents worth": Exploring user agency in readers' comments in online news media', *Observatorio*, 6:3, pp. 21–47.

Milioni, Dimitra, Spyridou, Lia-Paschalia and Vadratsikas, Konstantinos (2015), 'Framing immigration in online media and television news in crisis-stricken Cyprus', *Cyprus Review*, 27:1, pp. 155–85.

Mitchell, Scott S. D. and Lim, Merlyna (2018), 'Too crowded for crowdsourced journalism: Reddit, portability, and citizen participation in the Syrian Crisis', *Canadian Journal of Communication*, 43:3, pp. 399–419.

Ogbebor, Binakuromo (2020), *British Media Coverage of the Press Reform Debate: Journalists reporting Journalism*, Cham: Springer Nature.

Pilloni, Virginia (2018), 'How data will transform industrial processes: Crowdsensing, crowdsourcing and big data as pillars of Industry 4.0', *Future Internet*, 10:3, p. 24.

Reuters Institute for the Study of Journalism, University of Oxford (2016), *Digital News Report 2016*, https://reutersinstitute.politics.ox.ac.uk/sites/default/files/research/files/Digital%2520News%2520Report%25202016.pdf. Accessed 20 June 2019.

Reuters Institute for the Study of Journalism, University of Oxford (2017), Digital News Report 2017, https://reutersinstitute.politics.ox.ac.uk/sites/default/files/Digital%20News%20Report%202017%20web_0.pdf. Accessed 20 June 2019.

Reuters Institute for the Study of Journalism, University of Oxford (2018), Digital News Report 2018, http://media.digitalnewsreport.org/wp-content/uploads/2018/06/digital-news-report-2018.pdf. Accessed 20 June 2019.

Reuters Institute for the Study of Journalism, University of Oxford (2019), Digital News Report 2019, https://reutersinstitute.politics.ox.ac.uk/sites/default/files/2019-06/DNR_2019_FINAL_0.pdf. Accessed 20 June 2019.

Reuters Institute for the Study of Journalism, University of Oxford (2020), Digital News Report 2020, https://reutersinstitute.politics.ox.ac.uk/sites/default/files/2020-06/DNR_2020_FINAL.pdf. Accessed 8 October 2020.

Ståhlbröst, Anna and Lassinantti, Josefin (2015), 'Leveraging living lab innovation processes through crowdsourcing', *Technology Innovation Management Review*, 5:12, pp. 28–36.

Surugiu, Romina and Radu, Raluca-Nicoleta (2009), 'Introducing new technologies in media companies from Romania, Portugal, Spain and Cyprus. A comparative approach', *Revista Română de Jurnalism si Comunicare*, 3:4, pp. 93–102.

4

Funding Journalism: Toward New Revenue Streams and Diversity of Business Models

Kathryn Geels

Introduction

During the last decade, various strategic bodies working in news media (including funders, research organizations and academic institutes) across Europe, and further afield in the United States and Asia, have undertaken mapping and research of innovation and trends of business models and revenue streams in journalism. As news organizations shift away from relying predominantly on advertising and also move from establishing themselves as traditional for-profit companies, there is an ever-increasing need and desire from publishers to exploit alternative revenue streams and business models in order to better serve and grow their audiences/communities and to be resilient for the long term. There is also an increasing need for publishers to more effectively identify and diversify which new revenue streams are a good fit for their organization and to be more strategic at implementing them. This chapter aims to demonstrate a variety of funding and revenue streams that are increasingly being exploited by news organizations in Europe, with a focus on those pertinent to journalism that prioritizes a desire to better serve communities and to be resilient for the long term. The funding and revenue streams described in the chapter are relevant to news organizations that are for-profit or non-profit.

Key considerations and terminology

This chapter draws on research, literature, mapping, methodologies, case studies and examples from European academic bodies, philanthropic initiatives, news organizations and individuals with expertise in the relevant fields. Some reference is made to initiatives beyond Europe, where there is significant crossover and similarities in trends and examples between the different geographies. Key considerations are provided to guide readers to better understand concepts around business model innovation and exploitation of different revenue streams particularly relevant to approaches to journalism that can help news organizations better serve their communities.

Community engagement

In the context of journalism, community engagement falls under several constructs and definitions. It comprises 'engaged journalism', which can be understood as journalism that puts community engagement (geographical or topical) at the centre of a news organization's ownership, reporting, distribution, impact and revenue, viewing journalism as a conversation and as a utility that empowers communities (Engaged Journalism Accelerator 2019: n.pag.). It includes participatory journalism, which captures the idea of collaborative and collective, in which people inside and outside news organizations are engaged in communicating not only to but also with one another and building a multifaceted community (Singer et al. 2011: 2). It also includes reciprocal journalism, which looks to how journalists might develop more mutually beneficial relationships with audiences across three forms of exchange – direct, indirect and sustained (Lewis et al. 2013: 1). Community engagement through journalism not only increases people's confidence in journalists and journalism organizations, resulting in people being more civically engaged, but also leads to people willingly financing journalism (Green-Barber and Garcia McKinley 2019: 4–5), which, in turn, can help news organizations be more sustainable (Goligoski and Hansen 2018a: 23–25).

Here it is useful to make a distinction between 'viable' 'sustainable' and 'resilient' in relation to the financial and business development trajectory that news organizations can assess themselves as a baseline, and as they look to progress towards resilience.

- A viable organization can be defined as: 'An organization that is fulfilling a demand or perceived need for content.'
- A sustainable organization can be defined as: 'An organization that is able to sustain a flow of content (meeting a demand for or perceived need for content over time) and draws on revenue that covers some or all human resources and overheads.'
- A resilient organization can be defined as: 'An organization that is able to sustain a flow of content and make profit or grow/scale, is able to adapt to and thrive among wider changes within the ecosystem and can exploit new market opportunities' (Geels forthcoming: n.pag.).

These delineations by Geels, acknowledged by a growing number of journalism stakeholders, build on previous ideas and mapping about publishers' (in particular, hyperlocal) business models, financial trajectories and related interdependencies. The distinctions made by Geels, particularly between sustainable and resilient organizations, also build on the idea that competitive advantage (the products, services, capabilities or other attributes of an organization that sets it apart from, or makes it superior to, its competitors) being sustainable (that is, over a long period of time) is a naïve concept and rather that competitive advantage is transient. With transient or temporary advantages, it is considered that the existing model, capabilities or assets of an organization will come under pressure, resulting in a need for reconfiguration renewal or launching of a 'new wave' (McGrath 2013: 30–36).

It is also useful to note a distinction between the terms 'community' and 'audience'. These terms are widely used interchangeably across the news media industry; however, there is a distinction made between them in certain contexts in this chapter, given the focus on community engagement. Therefore, a community can be described as a group of people that have a common interest, develop relationships and a shared identity with each other as well as with an organization or brand, and not only listen but also contribute (both financially and non-financially) (Spinks 2017: n.pag.). This is opposed to what is considered a more traditional role of an audience, which can be deemed as an anonymous crowd of mostly passive journalism consumers (Bode 2019: n.pag.).

In addition, it is useful to describe the difference between the terms 'business model', 'revenue stream', 'revenue model' and 'business structure'. Although there is not a single definition of what a business model is, there are core components that can help to describe the value proposition of any news organization:

- Value creation (what value an organization is creating – not only through its services and products but also through its processes, skills, values, organizational culture, network of partners or its community and other benefits that it is providing to its users or stakeholders).
- Value capture (the ability of an organization to create revenue or profit from its transactions with its users or stakeholders).
- Value delivery (how an organization produces, delivers and communicates value to its users or stakeholders).

In simpler terms, a business model explicitly states how an organization functions to generate profitable and relevant revenue streams. Revenue streams are individual sources of income for an organization that constitute an organization's revenue model/revenue structure – which is the framework or strategy for generating revenue through each revenue stream (Günzel and Holm 2013: 6–8).

In regard to ownership, this is constituted by the business/legal structure of an organization, who is responsible for profits and losses, how much tax is paid, who is in control of the organization and its activities and the purpose of the organization (Caramela 2018: n.pag.). The number of business and legal structures across different countries in Europe is vast; therefore they will not be covered in detail in this chapter. However, specific examples, case studies and Table 1 in this chapter highlight some of the different business/legal structures used by European news organizations, innovating their business models and revenue streams and taking a community engagement approach to their journalism.

Types of funding and revenue streams

This section describes seven different funding and revenue streams that are increasingly being exploited by news organizations in Europe: memberships, subscriptions, donations, products, grant funding, commercial collaborations and crowdfunding. The section also includes two case studies and other examples to help readers better understand different applications and opportunities of each stream. Although advertising is still an effective revenue source for many news organizations – such as those that produce printed newspapers and magazines and those that have strong relationships with local businesses – it is not being detailed in this chapter. This is because this chapter aims to highlight revenue streams relevant to approaches taken by news organizations that prioritize community engagement.

Membership

Membership offers publishers the opportunity to reflect a desire to have their community vested in their organization beyond merely a transactional relationship. As well as serving as a revenue stream (e.g., via monthly or annual payments from users), a membership model can help news organizations deepen their relationship and engagement with users. This can result in better insights into users' demographics, interests and needs (and, therefore, an improved ability to meet users' needs), the ability to establish new or tap into existing communities and develop loyalty over time.

Financial membership contributions assist organizations in becoming financially sustainable, covering operating costs, implementing specific projects and bringing in additional staff. Non-financial contributions, such as providing time, skills or professional expertise to support operational or editorial activities, can help organizations enhance content production and distribution, create more transparency and democratize processes and objectives (Goligoski and Ho 2018: n.pag.). There are various ways of rewarding financial and non-financial support to members. Including providing them with special access or privileges to content, events, and meetings, connecting them with other members, helping them raise their voices or meet their own goals, and giving them more visibility and public-facing appreciation.

Key ingredients that news organizations should look to have before launching a membership model include a loyal, engaged community; previous dialogue with the community about the need to raise money; deep user research into community needs, preferences and habits; and readiness, capacity and strategic insight within the organization to launch and develop a membership model (Goligoski and Hansen 2018b: 14). Researcher and co-founder of the Media Innovation Studio (MIS) at the University of Central Lancashire Clare Cook developed a framework and toolkit for news organizations to better explore ways to convert audience relationships into revenues. It included prompts for organizations to use in order to assess different ingredients that they need and what their organization's and audience's readiness is in relation to reader revenues (Cook 2019: n.pag.).

Membership case study

Experimenting with messaging, pricing and design to boost memberships (Engaged Journalism Accelerator 2021a: n.pag.)

- ➤ The Local, founded in 2004, is an independent company and the largest English-language news network in Europe.

- ➤ It has twenty staff members working across six countries, a wide freelance network and a centralized business and commercial team based in Stockholm, Sweden.

- ➤ It operates ten news and lifestyle websites (nine editions are country-specific, and one is Europe-wide) serving an international community.

Initiating experimentation

- ➤ In November 2017, The Local moved from being solely advertising funded to incorporating membership as a revenue stream.

- ➤ It asked readers of the Swedish edition, followed by the German and French, to become members for €5 a month and has since launched membership across all nine countries.

- ➤ During twelve months, the team experimented with homepage messaging and pricing and design on membership pages to increase conversion of readers to members.

Continued

Membership case study

Experimenting with messaging, pricing and design to boost memberships (Engaged Journalism Accelerator 2021a: n.pag.)

➤ The Local used paywall provider Piano and lead generation tool Get Site Control to customize widget messaging and vary how and when target messaging appeared.

➤ Experiments included testing long versus short messaging, messaging with staff portraits versus without, emotive appeals versus transactional and A/B testing with different design and price messaging on the membership pages.

➤ At any one time, the team ran between two to four tests and monitored impressions, conversions and net revenue of each test in Piano.

➤ As well as homepage and membership page tests, the team used Google Analytics and Content Insights to understand which articles converted readers to membership.

Benefits of experimentation

✓ In August 2018, The Local had 4000 members, and by December 2018, it had 7000. By March 2021, it passed 40,000 members.

✓ Emotive wording worked better than transactional wording, resulting in an increase in conversion to membership.

✓ Adding journalists' names and headshots also improved the conversion to membership – seeing journalists' faces potentially added a level of accountability and trust.

✓ Content that effectively converted readers to members tended to be articles with tips and practical advice. Very few readers became members via sports coverage.

✓ Different pricing strategies were implemented for different country editions, based on editorial teams' local knowledge of readers' willingness to pay.

✓ The team identified that more of their focus needed to be on The Local products to create more value for members.

Challenges of the experimentation

✗ Everyone in the editorial team had access to the Google Analytics and Content Insights tools; however, not everyone used them regularly to help inform future content.

✗ Focusing on creating value for readers of different geographic editions did not go far enough. Therefore, The Local also has needed to invest time and resources after the initial experimentation phase into creating value for communities of interest.

Subscriptions

Subscriptions offer publishers the opportunity to ask users to pay for some or all content and services. Paying for content online is often associated with paywalls, yet it comes in many forms. There are many ways to set pricing plans for digital content, such as number of articles, time spent and access to additional content or services. News organizations also offer subscriptions for printed content, such as magazines. As well as subscribers paying for content purely as a transactional relationship, subscribers do also contribute as a means to benefit a wider cause or because they buy into the mission, goals or brand of the news organization (Kantar Media 2017: 8).

In research published in 2019 by the Reuters Institute for the Study of Journalism, it stated that subscriptions (along with membership) are a growing key priority for a range of organizations across the global news industry (Newman 2019: 5). However, news organizations also need to take into account the barriers to subscriptions before relying on them as a revenue stream. In countries or communities of interest, where there is little culture for paying for digital content, launching and growing a subscription model is challenging. Similarly, where the target audience (of the content) are users that do not have financial means to pay for content, news organizations may need to look to other user groups to pay instead – as a pay-it-forward concept. With regard to 'subscription fatigue' (whereby people can become frustrated with too many choices or requirements for pay-for content and services, and/or do not have the financial means to pay for more and more services), news organizations can look to bundle or aggregate their offering in partnership with another organization (news or other) as a way to add more value to subscribers (Fletcher et al. 2019: 13).

A useful example of a publisher innovating with a subscription model is Denmark-based journalism-education organization Koncentrat, which uses its platform to strengthen young people's civic engagement and for building trust in journalism through participation of schools in editorial development. With contributions from young people and teachers, it produces content focused on solutions journalism, with teaching materials developed alongside articles. In 2019, Koncentrat partnered with Denmark's leading publisher of primary education materials, Alinea, in which Koncentrat makes income from school subscriptions. Koncentrat entered the partnership to enhance efficiencies, raise awareness of its work and be more accessible and valuable to subscribers across its and Alinea's platform.

Donations

A donation model enables news organizations to receive financial contributions from people on an ad hoc or reoccurring basis. Unlike membership or subscription models, where there is predominantly an expectation to receive something in return for a financial contribution, donations are deemed as gifts (whereby people donate purely to support the organization or its wider mission). It is useful to note that across many countries in Europe, there are tax incentives to encourage donations to organizations with charitable status (European Fundraising Association 2018: 3). Organizations can set a minimum donation amount, such as €5 for mid- to low-level donors (regular donors) or €10,000 for high-level donor (major donors) or enable individual donors to choose.

News organizations can have mixed results from implementing a donation model. From Nesta's research in 2015–16 on hyperlocal revenue models in the United Kingdom and Europe, 35 hyperlocal news organizations from five countries were analysed, in which several indicated they used third-party sites such as PayPal, Flattr and J'aime L'info to enable readers to give donations. However, it was found that these generated very little revenue (Cook et al. 2016a: 46).

For Dutch news website *De Correspondent* and for the United Kingdom's Guardian Media Group (GMG), strategic appeals for donations have proven beneficial. In December 2013, *De Correspondent* was launched after €1.3 million was raised through crowdfunding and donations in support of a mission to produce in-depth journalism using an ad-free platform that actively engages readers. And in 2016, *The Guardian* (GMG's daily newspaper and website) launched its 'relationship strategy' with the goal of creating deeper relationships with readers by increasing reader revenues and reducing overall costs by 20 per cent. By April 2019, *The Guardian* had received over 340,000 one-off contributions from more than 300,000 contributors, helping it to meet its goals (*The Guardian* 2019: n.pag.). It is useful to note that, depending on an organization's business/legal structure, donations may be deemed as income and therefore taxable.

Products

News organizations incorporate product thinking and methodologies into their routines and daily work to create journalism that serves users' needs and solves their problems and to bring more value back into their organization. Product thinking is a holistic approach in which designing, creating and delivering a product puts the needs of users first, rather than the needs of the news organization, and weaves together editorial success, commercial success, functionality and efficiency (Sonderman 2016: n.pag.).

Products in journalism include editorial content (such as articles, videos and audio clips), commercial assets (including data and events), technologies (such as smartphone apps and software) and tangible resources (including merchandise and printed newspapers) that users interact with. Products can be audience facing (B2C) or client facing (B2B). News organizations develop new products and adapt existing products to monetize them and to deepen their relationship with users. One way to think about a journalism product is not so much about what the product is but how it is packaged, what processes are adopted to create it and how it is delivered to users (Bassan 2017: n.pag.).

An editorial product as simple as an email newsletter can be a powerful tool in engaging audiences and driving traffic to websites and other products. In 2015–16, Nesta ran the *Action Research in Audience Analytics* project with ten hyperlocal publishers. Newsletters were seen by several participants as a 'valuable opportunity to build a direct relationship with readers – and therefore a more loyal user base'. Participants also indicated that newsletters 'can help with advertising sales – overcoming the challenge provided by Ad Blockers and off-site consumption on social media' (MTM and Nesta 2016: 39, 40). Similarly, for traditional publishers, newsletters can help them to drive new subscriptions or keep current subscribers engaged. Based on reader research, *The Economist* learned more about its audience's motivations and frustrations. Recently revamping its newsletters has resulted in referral traffic from newsletters overtaking referral traffic from Twitter (Law 2019: n.pag.).

Regarding technology products, bespoke content management system (CMS) software (used to create and manage digital content, including web content) and customer relationship management (CRM) software (used by organizations to manage and develop more effective processes to build relationships with customers/ users) are a growing priority for many evolving news organizations. Publishers are developing their own CMS and CRM products to create efficiencies (including better integration and organization of conversations and communities), focus on more relevant metrics, better meet the needs of their users and ultimately grow revenue. There is also the opportunity, through open source or other licencing, for publishers to charge other news organizations to employ their software. And an opportunity to charge other organizations consultancy fees to help them employ the software or help them build their own.

Grant funding

News organizations can access grant funding through a range of different strategic bodies and initiatives and for working across a spectrum of innovation areas and with a variety of goals. These include:

- initiatives in which news organizations contribute to policy and research development, for example, European Commission 'calls for proposals';

- initiatives that provide news organizations with funding to develop or test certain technologies, such as the Google News Initiative's Digital News Innovation Fund;
- areas of social innovation, in which organizations can be funded to help solve or improve societal, health, education, community development or environmental challenges, such as the European Journalism Centre's European Development Journalism Grants; and
- areas of business and financial innovation, in which organizations can be funded to develop new processes, services, products, markets and business models, for example, Facebook's Local News Subscriptions Accelerator in Germany.

Grants are a key component of income generation for many small and emerging news organizations looking to develop their business model. For example, in a database of 189 community-driven European news organizations, at least 80 have grants listed as a revenue stream – complementary to other forms of income – with several other of the listed organizations having pursued grant funding in the past but without success (*Engaged Journalism Accelerator* 2021b: n.pag.). Grants are also used by emerging publishers as well as traditional publishers to develop new projects (sometimes collaborative and sometimes one-off) and test new ideas. A benefit of grant funding is that both for-profit and non-profit organizations can apply for it. Applications for funding are often competitive processes and organizations are required to demonstrate eligibility against criteria. Organizations also need to invest significant time and resources to apply for reporting purposes and often also for participation in a funding initiative, for example, where benefit to the grant recipient goes beyond funding alone, and they participate in a range of activities, such as events, mentoring, online forums, podcasts, blogs or interviews that complement the funding they receive.

Across Europe, innovation in journalism is fragmented, underfunded and generally focused on technology innovation, new forms of content distribution and one-off projects. Support for news organizations focused on internal culture change or developing new models for community engagement is limited. And where it does exist, it is not linked to long-term resilience of news organizations, or wider cultural or social impact. Nor does it come with enough support or structures for ongoing training, coaching or development within news organizations. There is a growing importance and need for funding across the industry in Europe, including a need for more diversity of the types of organizations and activities funded and in the organizations that provide funding. This is voiced by grant recipients (Bureau Local 2019: 2) as well as existing funders (Padania 2018: 9).

Commercial collaborations

News organizations are increasingly working with each other and corporate clients to enhance revenue opportunities and share resources and intelligence to further their mission. Collaborations can take place through content production, consultancy and commissioning. Collaborations between news organizations can work effectively both when there is direct and non-direct competition (for audiences, stories and resources). However, there is a need to unite over certain aspects of their work, such as shared missions and goals, adapting internal structures and aligning ways to chart and measure impact of their work (Graves and Jenkins 2019: 6).

The Local Democracy Reporting Service (LDRS), funded by the BBC as part of its 2017–27 Royal Charter commitment, is an example of this. The LDRS was launched in 2017 as a result of an initiative by the BBC to more effectively partner with representatives and news organizations from regional, local and hyperlocal news media in the United Kingdom. A working group was established for the BBC to understand the challenges and nuances of different news organizations working with local communities, producing public service journalism and trying to improve local democracy. The working group also provided the BBC with ideas as to how it could more effectively support the production and distribution of local public service journalism, including ways to directly benefit other news organizations and journalists producing this type of information. The Local News Partnerships (LNP) was developed as a result of the working group and comprises three projects – one being the LDRS.

The LDRS had an initial objective to create up to 150 new journalism jobs to 'help fill a gap in the reporting of local democracy issues across the UK' (BBC 2019a: n.pag.). The BBC funds the reporters, but they are employed by more than 10 supplier companies. There are more than 160 individual companies in the LNP that all benefit from the content produced by the LDRS reporters, and between them, they represent more than 1000 separate news organizations or newspaper titles. Within the first year, reporters working within the LDRS filed more than 54,000 stories covering matters of public interest, such as local council expenditure, and both the BBC and news organizations included in the service praised its effectiveness (BBC 2019b: n.pag.). As part of the *2019 Cairncross Review* – an independent review of the sustainability of the production and distribution of high-quality journalism in the United Kingdom, commissioned by the UK government – there were calls by some UK journalism stakeholders to expand the LDRS and also suggestions by others of ways to improve it, in particular, to make it more inclusive of a larger pool of smaller, independent news organizations (Cairncross 2019: 152–54).

In addition, misaligned missions or conflicts of interest can create barriers to collaborations proceeding between news organizations and corporate clients. News organizations need to put clear processes and principles in place so that the collaboration is feasible. The case study below highlights this. Greek publisher Solomon also works to reduce barriers in working with corporate clients through separating its publications service and studio service. The publications service comprises in-depth reporting and storytelling focusing on Greek policy and society and migration and refugees, whereas the studio enables Solomon to work with commercial clients to deliver services including photography, web design, filmmaking and fixing.

Commercial collaborations case study

Creating an 'ethical content studio' to generate revenue and further an organization's mission (*Engaged Journalism Accelerator* 2021c: n.pag.)

✓ Outriders is a not-for-profit organization in Poland with thirteen staff members.

✓ It was established in 2017 following a crowdfunding campaign, which raised approximately €19,500 from more than 630 people.

✓ It specializes in interactive, solutions-driven stories focusing on global issues including migration, technology and the environment.

Launching the *Studio*

✓ Soon after Outriders published its first stories in January 2018, several corporate and non-profit organizations approached the team asking for help to create media projects.

✓ Outriders' co-founder Jakub Gornicki developed the Outriders Studio (subsequently re-branded 'Outriders Mixer') and brought the team together to create rules and principles that all projects and clients must align with.

✓ The *Studio* was launched in December 2018 with the goal of building custom projects with commercial partners – aligned with the Outriders mission – in which all of the profit generated by the *Studio* is used to support journalism produced by the Outriders' team.

Benefits of the *Studio*

✓ Most projects delivered by the *Studio* comprise 'ready products' for partnerships with bigger media players.

✓ The team actively seeks media partnerships as part of the organisation's revenue- and membership-growth strategy.

✓ Many businesses have corporate social responsibility (CSR) budgets to use to explain their work and positive impact to the public. This presents a business opportunity for the *Studio*.

✓ The team looks at their resources-to-monthly-income ratios before taking on a project. For example, if an event production project takes two days of work but brings in 30 per cent of the monthly income, it is worthwhile to deliver.

✓ The team has a rule that *Studio* projects should not take more than 25 per cent of their resources at any time. This means they can continue producing their own stories and ensure Outriders remains a not-for-profit organization.

✓ In its first year, the *Studio* generated around 45 per cent of Outriders' overall income.

Challenges of the *Studio*

✗ As the work of the *Studio* is highly innovative, this has sometimes created barriers to increasing reach of prospective media partners.

✗ Several prospective clients have backed out of commissioning Outriders due to not being fully on board with the *Studio*'s rules and principles.

  ○ The team recommends ensuring each client is fully on board before committing much time or resource to discussions.

Crowdfunding

Crowdfunding is an effective way to generate income for a specific project or campaign and in a specific time period. News organizations can make use of several crowdfunding platforms, including Seedrs, Crowdfunder, Crowdcube and Kickstarter, or develop their own bespoke platform. There are four primary types of crowdfunding: donation-based, reward-based, lending-based and equity-based. Each aligns with different motivators of funders (people who contribute financially) and with different types of projects, products and services that will result from the crowdfunding. For example, reward- and donation-based crowdfunding aligns with cause-based projects that appeal to funders' personal beliefs and passions.

Equity- and lending-based crowdfunding aligns more so with funders' motivations of a financial return and with the creation of tangible or digital products (Massolution 2012: 19).

Community-driven organizations, in particular, can benefit from launching a crowdfunding campaign, such as through increasing volunteering and tapping into other non-financial contributions (with investors' interest in community projects nearly always going beyond financial returns). However, publishers also need to carefully consider the challenges of both launching a campaign (driving fundraising) and then transitioning their organization to a community business. For example, organizations need the right leadership and management skills in both phases and need to find effective ways of continuously keeping the community engaged (Baeck et al. 2018: 51–57).

Examples of recent successful crowdfunding campaigns in Europe include French publisher Rue89 Strasbourg, which in 2015 launched a crowdfunding campaign and collected more than €36,000. The funds were raised for the new website's design, to develop responsive design, to buy a video camera and to develop more editorial sections. The team also created Strasbourg Connect, a project to integrate social functions into the website (Cook et al. 2016b: 49). Also in 2015, UK-based constructive journalism magazine *Positive News* ran its #OwnTheMedia campaign and became the first crowdfunded global media cooperative, with 1525 owners from across 33 countries. It was also the first 'community shares' project launched by crowdfunding platform Crowdfunder, in partnership with the Community Shares Company (Positive News 2015: n.pag.).

Table 1 provides a snapshot of twelve innovative community-driven news organizations from nine European countries, including their business/legal structures, and existing and prospective revenue streams. All twelve organizations were grantees of the Engaged Journalism Accelerator.

Recommendations

For news organizations to better serve and grow their communities and to be resilient for the long term, they need to continually adapt to changes within the wider journalism ecosystem and pivot their business model and revenue streams accordingly. As well as applying concepts and principles from academic research and professional literature, there are practical resources that news organizations should exploit to make the most of the changing ecosystem. There are resources developed by a range of journalism institutions, such as Nieman Lab's 'business models hub' Nieman Lab 2021: n.pag); for-profit companies, such as Hearken's *Connecting Engagement to Revenue* guide (Hearken 2021: n.pag); philanthropic

Region	Country	Organization	Business/legal structure	Existing revenue streams (as at Quarter 4, 2019)	Prospective revenue streams (that each organization has considered prioritizing), not including grants
Eastern Europe	Hungary	Mérce merce.hu. Est. 2017	Registered non-governmental organization	Donations, grants	Expanding donations/micro-donations
	Romania	Decât o Revistă dor.ro. Est. 2009	Non-profit association	Subscriptions, events, consultancy, online shop, corporate sponsorship, advertising, sponsored content, grants, other	Licensed products, membership, subscriptions
	Ukraine	Tvoe Misto tvoemisto.tv. Est. 2014	Company	Donations, corporate sponsorship, advertising, sponsored content, grants	Membership, paid services, paywall
Southern Europe	Greece	Solomon wesolomon.com. Est. 2015	Not-for-profit organization	Donations, consultancy, advertising, grants, commercial content production	Membership, subscriptions, expanding commercial content production
	Spain	Civio civio.es. Est. 2011	Foundation	Memberships, donations, grants, products (e.g., CMS licensing), other	Expanding donations and memberships

Region	Country	Organization	Business/legal structure	Existing revenue streams (as at Quarter 4, 2019)	Prospective revenue streams (that each organization has considered prioritizing), not including grants
		Maldita maldita.es. Est. 2014	Not-for-profit association. Transitioning to a not-for-profit foundation since November 2020	Events, crowdfunding, grants, commercial content production	Membership and donations
Western Europe	Belgium	Médor medor.coop. Est. 2014	Cooperative with a social purpose	Memberships, subscriptions (including printed magazine), donations, advertising, grants	Expanding subscriptions
	Germany	Krautreporter krautreporter.de. Est. 2014	Company	Memberships	Expanding memberships
	United Kingdom	Bureau Local thebureauinvestigates.com/local. Est. 2017	Not-for-profit company limited by guarantee	Donations, consultancy, grants	- Bureau Learn: fee-based partnership for journalism education - Bureau Exchange: fee-based framework for sharing insights and learnings - Bureau Bridgemaker: fee-based springboard for impact and engagement with community partners

Region	Country	Organization	Business/legal structure	Existing revenue streams (as at Quarter 4, 2019)	Prospective revenue streams (that each organization has considered prioritizing), not including grants
		Clydesider clydesider.org. Est. 2016	Social enterprise limited by guarantee	Consultancy, advertising, sponsored content, grants, other	Crowdfunding, membership
		On Our Radar onourradar.org. Est. 2012	Not-for-profit company limited by guarantee without share capital	Consultancy, grants, products (e.g., CMS licensing), other	Expanding monetization of products, expanding consultancy, commissions and partnerships
Northern Europe	Denmark	Koncentrat koncentrat.alinea.dk. Est. 2018	Company	Subscriptions (with schools), events, grants, other	Expanding subscriptions, commercial partnerships

TABLE 1: Business structure and revenue stream examples.

and applied research programmes, such as the Membership Puzzle Project's tools including *The Membership Launch Handbook*, *Membership Models in News Database* and *Membership in Public Radio Database* (The Membership Puzzle Project 2021: n.pag); and by individual news organizations, such as Germany-based Krautreporter, which in October 2019 published a playbook to help other independent, community-driven publishers build a sustainable future (Fryszer 2019: 11–16).

With relevance to philanthropic and applied research programmes, they not only produce resources for news organizations to use and learn from but also provide financial and business support to individual news organizations, develop communities of practice and enable sharing of knowledge, expertise, skills and resources across these communities of practice. These mechanisms can further support news organizations to pivot their business model and exploit new revenue streams, and more effectively learn from and adopt similar approaches to more advanced or innovative publishers.

A further proposal that can support news organizations and add benefit to the wider journalism ecosystem is for more significant industry-wide research to be undertaken on the link between community engagement, trust, revenue and long-term resilience. Organizations and initiatives in the United States, including the *Trusting News Project*, the *Membership Puzzle Project*, American Press Institute, Hearken and the Center for Media Engagement at the University of Texas, have undertaken research into this link, but so far there are few clear answers, in part because 'trust' is a complex and multifaceted idea that is hard to measure.

Collective efforts across a wide range of European news organizations, journalism practitioners and researchers are needed to develop a clear framework and metrics, agree on key questions and obtain rich, standardized data within a longitudinal study. Expansion of the Journalism Trust Initiative (JTI), initiated by Reporters Without Borders (RSF), to incorporate ways for news organizations to assess revenue growth and long-term resilience against their compliance with the JTI indicators could be one approach. Another could be to actively learn from and apply frameworks from non-journalism initiatives, such as social impact investing and even the craft beer movement – for example, the approaches taken by UK brewery and bar chain BrewDog – about the opportunities of community engagement, increased revenue and sustainability (Alexander 2016: n.pag).

REFERENCES

Alexander, Jon (2016), 'In food as in life, we are more than just consumers', *Medium*, 10 May, https://medium.com/new-citizenship-project/in-food-as-in-life-we-are-more-than-just-consumers-62969212feaf. Accessed 20 May 2021.

Baeck, Peter, Bone, Jonathan, Boyle, Dave and Old, Rosalyn (2018), *Taking Ownership Community Empowerment through Crowdfunded Investment*, London: Nesta, https://media.nesta.org.uk/documents/Taking_ownership_v4.pdf. Accessed 21 October 2019.

Bassan, Valerio (2017), 'How product thinking can help the media industry thrive', *Medium*, 12 May, https://medium.com/journalism-innovation/how-product-thinking-can-help-the-media-industry-thrive-8d247422a955. Accessed 17 November 2019.

BBC (2019a), 'Local democracy reporting service', https://www.bbc.com/lnp/ldrs. Accessed 17 November 2019.

BBC (2019b), '"Journalism partnerships work" says the BBC, a year on from the launch of pioneering project in local news', https://www.bbc.co.uk/mediacentre/latestnews/2019/local-news-partnerships. Accessed 17 November 2019.

Bode, Kim (2019), 'Engaged journalism: Why newsrooms should put the needs of their communities first', *WAN IFRA*, 25 January.

Bureau Local (2019), *Let's Talk about Sustainability: The Bureau Local's Approach To Business Development*, London: Bureau Local, https://engagedjournalism.com/assets/pdf/Bureau-Local-business-development-guide-Engaged-Journalism-Accelerator-2019.pdf. Accessed 21 October 2019.

Cairncross, Frances (2019), *The Cairncross Review: A Sustainable Future for Journalism*, n.p.: Department for Digital, Culture Media and Sport (DCMS), https://assets.publishing.service.gov.uk/government/uploads/system/uploads/attachment_data/file/779882/021919_DCMS_Cairncross_Review_.pdf. Accessed 17 November 2019.

Caramela, Sammi (2018), 'How to choose the best legal structure for your business', *Business News Daily*, 18 June, https://www.businessnewsdaily.com/8163-choose-legal-business-structure.html. Accessed 17 November 2019.

Cook, Clare (2019), 'A new methodology to design reader revenues for journalism', *Medium*, 18 October, https://clare-cook.medium.com/a-new-methodology-to-design-reader-revenues-for-journalism-896940ce5cd5. Accessed 2 April 2021.

Cook, Clare, Geels, Kathryn and Bakker, Piet (2016a), *Hyperlocal Revenues in the UK and Europe*, London: Nesta, https://media.nesta.org.uk/documents/hyperlocal-revenues-in-the-uk-and-europe-report.pdf. Accessed 21 October 2019.

Cook, Clare, Geels, Kathryn and Bakker, Piet (2016b), *Hyperlocal Revenues in the UK and Europe*, London: Nesta, https://media.nesta.org.uk/documents/hyperlocal-revenues-in-the-uk-and-europe-report.pdf. Accessed 21 October 2019.

Engaged Journalism Accelerator (2019), 'About', https://engagedjournalism.com/ about. Accessed 17 November 2019.

Engaged Journalism Accelerator (2021a), 'How The Local uses homepage messaging to boost subscriptions', 11 March, https://engagedjournalism.com/resources/how-the-local-uses-homepage-messaging-to-boost-subscriptions. Accessed 2 April 2021.

Engaged Journalism Accelerator (2021b), 'Engaged journalism in Europe database', 20 January, https://engagedjournalism.com/resources/engaged-journalism-in-europe-database. Accessed 17 March 2021.

Engaged Journalism Accelerator (2021c), 'Outriders Poland engaged journalism content studio', 20 May, https://engagedjournalism.com/resources/outriders-poland-engaged-journalism-content-studio. Accessed 20 May 21.

European Fundraising Association (2018), *Tax Incentives for Charitable Giving in Europe*, Amsterdam: European Fundraising Association, https://efa-net.eu/wp-content/uploads/2018/12/EFA-Tax-Survey-Report-Dec-2018.pdf. Accessed 20 November 2019.

Fletcher, Richard, Kalogeropoulos, Antonis, Kleis Nielsen, Rasmus and Newman, Nic (2019), *Digital News Report 2019*, Oxford: Reuters Institute for the Study of Journalism, https://reutersinstitute.politics.ox.ac.uk/sites/default/files/inline-files/DNR_2019_FINAL.pdf. Accessed 21 October 2019.

Fryszer, Leon (2019), *The Engaged Journalism Playbook*, Berlin: Krautreporter, https://krautreporter-public-production.s3.eu-central-1.amazonaws.com/public/Krautreporter's+Engaged+Journalism+Playbook-d6c23.pdf. Accessed 20 May 2021.

Geels, Kathryn (forthcoming), *Pathways to Impact*, London: Kathryn Geels.

Graves, Lucas and Jenkins, Joy (2019), *Case Studies in Collaborative Local Journalism*, Oxford: Reuters Institute for the Study of Journalism, https://reutersinstitute.politics.ox.ac.uk/sites/default/files/2019-04/Jenkins_Collaborative_Local_Journalism_FINAL_1.pdf. Accessed 21 October 2019.

Green-Barber, Lindsay and Garcia McKinley, Eric (2019), *Engaged Journalism: Practices for Building Trust, Generating Revenue, and Fostering Civic Engagement*, n.p.: Impact Architects, https://s3-us-west-2.amazonaws.com/lindsaygreenbarber.com/assets/IA+Engaged+Journalism+Report+1.31.19.pdf. Accessed 17 November 2019.

Goligoski, Emily and Hansen, Elizabeth (2018a), *Guide to Audience Revenue and Engagement*, New York: Columbia University Libraries, https://www.cjr.org/tow_center_reports/guide-to-audience-revenue-and-engagement.php. Accessed 21 October 2019.

Goligoski, Emily and Hansen, Elizabeth (2018b), *Guide to Audience Revenue and Engagement*, New York: Columbia University Libraries, https://www.cjr.org/tow_center_reports/guide-to-audience-revenue-and-engagement.php. Accessed 21 October 2019.

Goligoski, Emily and Ho, Stephanie (2018), 'Participation pathways', *The Membership Puzzle Project*, 12 December, https://membershippuzzle.org/articles-overview/participation-pathways. Accessed 21 October 2019.

The Guardian (2019). 'Guardian Media Group announces outcome of three-year turnaround strategy', 1 May, https://www.theguardian.com/gnm-press-office/2019/may/01/guardian-media-group-announces-outcome-of-three-year-turnaround-strategy. Accessed 21 October 2019.

Günzel, Franziska and Holm, Anna (2013), 'One size does not fit all – Understanding the front-end and back-end of business model innovation', *International Journal of Innovation*

Management, 17:1, pp. 1–40, https://www.researchgate.net/publication/256056099_One_size_does_not_fit_all_-_Understanding_the_front-end_and_back-end_of_business_model_innovation. Accessed 17 November 2019.

Hearken (2021), 'Connecting engagement to revenue', https://wearehearken.com/gated-content-engagement-to-revenue/. Accessed 2 April 2021.

Kantar Media (2017), *Attitudes to Paying for Online News*, n.p.: Kantar Media, https://reutersinstitute.politics.ox.ac.uk/sites/default/files/2017-09/KM%20RISJ%20Paying%20for%20online%20news%20-%20report%20230817_0.pdf. Accessed 17 November 2019.

Law, Denise (2019), 'Focusing on our core digital products', *Medium*, 3 June, https://medium.com/severe-contest/focusing-on-our-core-digital-products-8dd1d7a80a20. Accessed 21 October 2019.

Lewis, Seth, Holton, Avery and Coddington, Mark (2013), 'Reciprocal journalism', *Journalism Practice*, 8:2, pp. 229–41, https://www.tandfonline.com/doi/abs/10.1080/17512786.2013.859840. Accessed 17 November 2019.

Massolution (2012), *Crowdfunding Industry Report: Market Trends, Composition and Crowdfunding Platforms*, Los Angeles: Massolution. file:///Users/geels/Downloads/CROWDFUNDING_INDUSTRY_REPORT_Market_Tren.pdf. Accessed 17 November 2019.

McGrath, Rita (2013), *The End of Competitive Advantage: How to Keep Your Strategy Moving as Fast as Your Business*, Boston: Harvard Business Review Press.

Membership Puzzle Project (2021), 'Tools', https://membershippuzzle.org/tools. Accessed 2 April 2021.

MTM and Nesta (2016), *Destination Local, Action Research in Audience Analytics, Project Evaluation and Learnings*, London: Nesta, https://www.nesta.org.uk/blog/action-research-in-audience-analytics-project-completion-and-evaluation/. Accessed 21 October 2019.

Newman, Nic (2019), *Journalism, Media and Technology Trends and Predictions 2019*, Oxford: Reuters Institute for the Study of Journalism, https://reutersinstitute.politics.ox.ac.uk/sites/default/files/2019-01/Newman_Predictions_2019_FINAL_2.pdf. Accessed 21 October 2019.

Nieman Lab (2021), 'Business models', https://www.niemanlab.org/hubs/business-models/. Accessed 2 April 2021.

Padania, Sameer (2018), *An Introduction to Funding Journalism and Media*, London: Ariadne, https://www.ariadne-network.eu/wp-content/uploads/2015/03/An-Introduction-to-Funding-Journalism-and-Media.pdf. Accessed 21 October 2019.

Positive News (2015), 'Positive news worlds global media cooperative', 8 July, https://www.positive.news/society/ownthemedia/positive-news-worlds-global-media-cooperative/. Accessed 21 October 2019.

Singer, Jane, Domingo, David, Heinonen, Ari, Hermida, Alfred, Paulussen, Steve, Quandt, Thorsten, Reich, Zvi and Vujnovic, Marina (2011), *Participatory Journalism: Guarding Open Gates at Online Newspapers*, Chichester: Wiley-Blackwell.

Sonderman, Jeff (2016), *Best Practices for Product Management in News Organizations*, Arlington: American Press Institute, https://www.americanpressinstitute.org/publications/reports/white-papers/product-management-best-practices/. Accessed 17 November 2019.

Spinks, David (2017), 'The difference between an audience and a community', *Medium*, 15 May, https://medium.com/@davidspinks/the-difference-between-an-audience-and-a-community-c4a38059a952. Accessed 17 November 2019.

PART II

JOURNALISTS' WORKING CONDITIONS

PROPOSAL 3

EMPLOYMENT CONDITIONS

5

Clicks über alles:
Digital Labour and Greek Digital Media

Eleni Mavrouli and Despoina Fouska

Introduction

Recently, the Greek media landscape has undergone significant changes for several reasons; some of them were triggered by the financial crisis (Iosifidis and Boucas 2015), coupled with the increasing penetration of technology in the daily practices of journalists and the inevitable demand for more profitable content as fast as possible. A direct consequence is that journalists in Greece are now asked to sacrifice the quality, values and ethics of the journalistic profession for the sake of 'clicks' and profit. This qualitative descriptive research aims to record the digital media status in Greece in respect to the changing working conditions of journalists working on information websites and how this affects the news product. It relies on 11 semi-structured interviews with professional journalists employed by Greek digital media. The results showed insecurity, stifling pressure for more speed and profit, low wages, exhausting working hours, labour alienation and working conditions similar to those of the forging industry. Such conditions have a critical impact on the quality of the news product and equally critical consequences for the journalists, who face the risk of deskilling. This first attempt to record the working conditions prevailing in digital media in Greece paints a particularly worrying picture of the future of journalism and highlights the need for further research into the changing working conditions in the media.

Media labour in Greece

Over the last years, the media landscape in Greece has undergone significant changes for several reasons; one of them is related to the economic crisis which applies to the media sector in much the same way as in different sectors of the contemporary labour market (Paulussen 2012: 59). A growing body of literature on the organization of labour in capitalist societies suggests that 'all work, including that of journalists, is increasingly subject to casualization, freelancing and other non-permanent contractual arrangements, flexibility and insecurity' (Örnebring 2010: 59). Relevant, in this context, is Richard Sennett's work on 'the culture of the new capitalism'(Sennett 1997: 162). 'New capitalism' refers to the changes induced to production within the capitalist system and to the working conditions by the globalization of the economy and the use of modern technology. According to Sennett, in new capitalism:

> The social guarantees of the welfare states of an earlier era are breaking down, capitalism itself has become economically flexible, highly mobile, its corporate structures ever less determinate in form and in time. These structural changes are linked to a sudden and massive outpouring of productivity, new goods like computers, new services like the global financial industries. As a result, though, the ways we work have altered: short-term jobs replace stable careers, skills rapidly evolve; [...] the new capitalism is impoverishing the value of work.
>
> (Sennett 1997: 161–62)

Therefore, a central element in new capitalism is the individualization of labour and thus the intensification of managerial control over the workforce.

The role of technology in new capitalism cannot be ignored. New digital technologies are often perceived as the main driver behind economic and organizational transitions in the workplace. Media scholar Henrik Örnebring (2010) also notes that journalists are tempted to view technology as a primary cause of organizational and professional changes in the newsroom. The focus on technology as a driving factor of change may be explained by the fact that the immediate, direct effects of the implementation of new technology in the newsroom are often more visible and tangible than the effects of other developments, such as commercialization. Yet, one must be cautious of the notion of technological determinism, that is, the notion that an autonomous technology (in both its development and use) shapes social relations (Kline 2015).

As digital-first news organizations have developed, insight into digital journalists' working conditions has come primarily from media accounts: overwork, high stress, burnout, job turnover and low pay (Peters 2010; Testa et al. 2014; Shade 2015). Journalists work frenetically to meet 'traffic quotas', work 24/7 via smartphones, email and group chat programmes and confront a constantly speeding-up pace of work, while having only little say in management decisions (Segal 2015: n.pag.). In *Media Work*, Mark Deuze (2007) suggests that career paths in media will increasingly be characterized in terms of casual and contingent employment, high demand for flexibility and convergence of previously distinct tasks and responsibilities (Deuze 2007, 2009; Deuze and Fortunati 2010). Although accelerated by the recession, this precarious employment situation is also the result of structural organizational changes in the media, driven by a market logic aiming to reduce costs while increasing productivity and maximizing profit (Altmeppen 2008). Typically, research on work and labour in journalism examines labour relations, conflict and struggle between workers and owners of media companies (Örnebring 2010; Rhomberg 2012). In this study, the focus is on labour-capital dynamics as they stem from specific corporate ownership models and practices (pressuring labour costs down and rationalizing production to increase profits) (Braverman 1974).

Today's media capitalism – that is, the way the media businesses are structured in terms of radical media political economy, of which a defining feature is to connect media to the production and maintenance of inequalities in the distribution of social power and resources (Hardy 2014) – is constituted not only by 'network media industries' (Winseck 2011: 6) but also by a network of external, digital-based corporations whose operating logics exert new pressures and forms of control on journalists. What Anderson (2013) calls the journalism ecosystem today involves not just a range of institutional players – journalists, media activists, bloggers, social media users, hackers and developers – but companies ranging from corporate giants, such as Google and Facebook, to companies that build and sell news apps, social media management tools and analytics services that have an enormous influence on 'the conditions under which news is created and circulates' (Ananny and Crawford 2015: 195).

Smyrnaios (2015) identifies Facebook, Google and other social media corporations as the most influential news intermediaries, exerting influence over 'the whole ecology of [journalistic] production, distribution, and consumption'. As the *New Republic*'s former editor writes, 'tech companies dictate the patterns of work, their influence can affect the ethos of an entire profession' (Foer 2017: n.pag.). The international news industry is still contractually governed by what the International Federation of Journalists described as 'atypical work' (Walters et al. 2006: 6), meaning all kinds of freelance, casualized, informal and otherwise contingent labour arrangements. Journalists have to fight with their employers to maintain the rights they still have and do so in the context of declining trust and credibility in the eyes of audiences.

Behind the restructuring of power relations between publishers, journalists and audiences, there is a power struggle between opposing interests and wishes on a variety of issues (uses of [new] technologies, labour laws and even the definitions of what 'news' is, massive outsourcing, other forms of precarious labour, unionization among journalists, etc.) (Gregor 2000). In these power struggles, the weakest actors are the journalists. Media groups have the capital and own the means of production, so they have command over the news organizational process; audiences are fragmented and dispersed, but they have the purchasing power. In the end, journalists have only their labour force to sell and at an increasingly lower price (Deuze and Fortunati 2010).

Deuze and Fortunati (2010) propose to define today's journalists as immaterial labour workers. This category places journalists inside the large stratum of workers who must deal with abstract labour (Jenkins 2006), like academics, researchers, other media professionals and artists whose professional profiles, labour content and skills are reshaped by new media, digital culture and information and communications technology. While an increasing part of the working population is joining these professionals in doing immaterial labour (public servants, services workers and so on), it becomes a priority for post-Fordist production models – the flexible production process based on flexible machines or systems and an appropriately flexible workforce where its crucial hardware is micro-electronics-based information and communications technologies (Jessop 1992) – to break their power and reorganize all the sectors on a transnational scale as a huge, horizontal working-class sector (Deuze and Fortunati 2010). The impact of the economy on journalistic labour is therefore worth paying attention to, especially since recent developments in newsrooms continue to go in the direction of doing more with less – more content with less staff, more (and more varied) tasks in less time, more flexibility for less pay and so on (Deuze 2007; Cushion 2007; García Avilés et al. 2004).

Based on this argument, this research aims to illustrate the changing working conditions of journalists having a job in information websites in Greece and how they are linked with the quality of the produced content. Although the term 'quality' can be defined in numerous ways and can be measured from different perspectives, the supply-side approach, which is common among academic researchers, was selected to define the quality of the journalistic product. O'Donnell (2009) proposes that quality indicators might be best reclassified into three subsets: professional journalism skills (newsworthiness, research, writing, production and incisiveness); social/democratic priorities (impact, public benefit and ethics); and creative values (originality, innovation and creative flair) (Wilding et al. 2018).

The main research questions are:

RQ1. What is the situation in the digital media workplaces in the era of financial crisis, based on journalists' experiences?

RQ2. How and to what extent do journalists' working conditions affect the quality of the content they produce?

Purposeful sampling and thematic analysis

This qualitative descriptive research involves data gathered through eleven semi-structured, open-ended interviews with journalists working for digital media among the 605 websites that have joined the Online/Digital Media Register (emedia.media.gov.gr) of Greece provided they fulfil two criteria: (1) the content of the website they worked in is informational and (2) the digital media employ only professional journalists. Purposeful sampling was used, according to which participants were chosen according to pre-selected criteria about the research question. In total, five men and six women between 29 and 52 years old were interviewed. Ten out of eleven have previous experience in traditional media. Their total journalistic experience averaged 19 years, and ten out of eleven are insured with the Journalists' Unified Insurance and Healthcare Benefit Organization and are also members of the Journalists' Union of Athens Daily Newspapers (ESIEA). Seven of them hold a degree qualification relevant to journalism, and three of them hold degrees in other scientific fields, while one of them does not hold a university degree. Finally, seven of them are working at news feed positions, while four are chief editors.

For the analysis of the data, we adopted the method of thematic analysis, defined as 'the method for identifying, analysing, and reporting patterns (themes) within data' (Braun and Clarke 2006: 6). Interviews were conducted during August 2018 in Athens, Greece. During the analysis of the transcripts, three themes emerged:

1. Working conditions (employee/freelance, full-time/part-time, only occupation or not, salary, benefits, allowances, insurance, insured under journalistic capacity, working hours and days, number of employees, how many of them are journalists, workplace or remotely).
2. Produced content (original/copy-pasted/sponsored or branded, use of analytics, clickable articles).
3. Qualification requirements and tools (main skills, skills other than those required in traditional journalism, tools used).

'Under the counter' wages, copy-paste and the need for speed

Working conditions

All participants but one worked under private contracts and one in a complete undeclared, non-insured and untaxed status. Two of them received part of their wage in vouchers or 'under the counter'. The salary of those working in the newsroom (news feed/editor position) varied from €480–800 (net/per month), when, according to Eurostat, from 2012 to 2018, the national minimum gross wage in Greece was €683.8 per month. In the case of a print edition in the same media group, preparation of extra articles was included in that salary. For those who work as editors-in-chief, the salary varied from €950–1400 (net/per month).

All the participants were insured – under their capacity as journalists – except for the one who was working undeclared. Most of them had been insured under the capacity of a journalist since May 2018, when the regulatory framework changed, allowing the inclusion of digital media workers in the journalists' union and insurance body. Before that, they were insured as office employees or were paying for their insurance themselves. They worked six to nine hours per day, in shifts, and five days a week, plus in most of the cases one to two weekends per month, which were not paid extra. Regarding chief editors, their workday started early in the morning and stopped late at night, including 'more relaxed' weekends. The majority worked at a particular workplace and remotely on an exceptional basis. From the eleven different websites, most used to employ four to fifteen journalists and there were only two to three websites with more employees.

Many of this study's findings suggest attitudes to atypical work relationships as Walters et al. (2006) describe. In this context, digital media journalists in Greece can be characterized as atypical journalists, as they are entitled to fewer rights and benefits (lower pay, less secure environment, less access to insurance, less safe work practices) than their colleagues in the traditional media.

Type of produced content

Due to the small number of employees, all the participants said that they perform mostly a 'desktop job' by copy-pasting content from other media or news agencies and rewriting it for their news website in a percentage from 50 per cent to 85 per cent of the total number of posts published daily. Their sources are press releases, news agency material and content published by other, foreign or domestic media. The more the journalists who are working the lower the percentage of copy-paste is.

Regarding low-quality content, the newcomers, that is, those who have never worked in traditional (non-digital) media, represent a particular case.

'The majority of Greek websites, if they have no connection with a newspaper, radio or TV channel, work with no reporters or just one or two', one participant stated. That means that the majority of their staff, especially younger people who had never worked in a traditional media, doesn't know and can't understand the value of reporting, in respect to taking information or verifying it. This is the death of journalism.

(Participant MGM, LN: 84)

Most interviewees, especially those who were working in newsfeed posts, reported that they always take care to write something 'shareable' because the aim is to gain more 'clicks'. It is a daily work practice that conforms to clear directions provided by the employer/chief editor. Their work is described as producing content that will be shared and widely circulated according to Mosco's notion of the commodification of journalism, that is, a journalism production explicitly for its exchange value. 'I am a news seller. I try to find a way to sell my newsfeed to more people. In what I do now, some seminars on marketing are more helpful than my studies in journalism' (Participant AMF, LN: 75).

The ones who work in newsfeed positions said that what they do is non-stop posting, giving an industrialized picture of what their work looks like. Common to all of them was the lack of staff in the newsroom, stemming from the stance of the employers. They consider that more journalists would lead to content of higher quality. Although the internet and new technologies are here to facilitate and support the work of journalists, they are probably just the medium for communicating more and more content as quickly as possible, which leads to the loss of the substance of journalism.

Qualification requirements and tools

The main skill: The need for speed

According to all participants, speed is the most important skill in a digital newsroom. The participants have little downtime between tasks and are expected to multitask. The increased workload leaves no time for news analysis. The pressure for speed and clicks is so intense that sometimes they choose to publish first and to check later if any time is left. The skills someone needs to work in a digital newsroom are, besides speed, a computer and new technology literacy plus a good knowledge of the Greek language, something that is missing, as they noticed. Practically anyone with the above skills can do the work. So, as they stated, there is no need for journalists. 'The only difference an experienced journalist will make is that he can evaluate information faster' (Participant GTM, LN: 105). No surprise that the majority characterize themselves as news sellers, content producers and not journalists.

Existing academic research on the implications of digital technologies for the working conditions of journalists shows that the latter face increasing intensity of work as they are being forced to publish instantly and continuously; they are required to multitask and be multiskilled; they often feel stressed, exhausted and overworked; and that work is marked by temporal and functional flexibility, job insecurity and uncertainty (Deuze 2007; Paulussen 2012; Anderson 2013; Comor and Compton 2015). A lot of this work pressure is not inherent to digital technologies themselves, but rather flows from management and production strategies, which require media companies to produce massive amounts of content for a variety of platforms due to media concentration, declining revenue from print advertising, shrinking staff and competition, all stemming from for-profit logic of media production in the new capitalist environment and the conditions it sets (McChesney 2013; Daum and Scherer 2017).

Worrisome implications

Work intensification, a sometimes-drastic reduction in staff, dramatically worse conditions for those entering the job market and an increase in atypical employment relationships are just a few indicators of the perceived decline of the journalistic profession due to the conditions described in this study. These findings were reported in 2011 by the European Federation of Journalists (Bittner 2013). In 2018 in Greece, such indicators remain the main trends noticed and analysed in this research. Uncertainty, fear of unemployment, lack of working standards, high mobility, very low wages, the pressure to the point of exhaustion, multitasking, the speed at the expense of accuracy and reliability, which inevitably results in a journalistic product of poor quality, are the main features of the working landscape in digital media. Besides, burnout and stress are depicted in participants' statements, such as 'When I started to work in digital media, I used to start and finish my shift having heart pain. I was almost sick' (Participant PTM, LN: 123).

Surveys of the first generation of online journalists in Belgium and the Netherlands indicated that due to the small staff size in online newsrooms, web editors are compelled to perform a 'desktop job' that focuses on producing 'shovelware', taking content from other media and deploying or repurposing it for the news website (Deuze and Paulussen 2002). This is something that has been supported by many studies abroad (Quandt et al. 2006; Boczkowski 2009; Deuze and Paulussen 2002), and it is recorded in the participants' replies. All participants work under personal private contracts with low wages. They consider journalism as their main profession, although they do not consider what they do as journalism. The paradox here is that while they do not consider what they do as journalism in terms of the procedure they follow to produce content and the final quality of it, they really care about (1) the impact that what they publish has on their audiences and (2) the future of journalism.

Those who hold managerial positions seem to be less dissatisfied, although they are not paid much more by proportion. However, they enjoy more freedom in their working conditions and the content they create. Nonetheless, they feel exhausted as they work non-stop. All participants pointed out the need for more people in the newsrooms, a different organization of work, more focus on original reporting and better working conditions as major facts for having a better-quality result. Even though the participants, in their majority, said they do not take decisions based on analytics, they admitted that it is a very important factor of their work. 'We are Google's bitches. Although we do not decide what to publish, analytics decide the promotion of specific posts' (Participant AMF, LN: 67). Thus, most feel that their journalistic training and editorial judgment comes second to the information, after metrics (Dwyer and Martin 2017).

The apparent implications of changes in journalistic labour in the context of new capitalism on the quality of news (less accuracy, less diversity, less information) and the professionalism of journalists (risk of deskilling) are worrisome. This underlines the need for more research into working conditions and labour experiences of digital journalists, including the way they feel about themselves in the context of these working conditions; how they feel about the results of their work, if they experience professional fulfilment or not; how these working conditions affect their professional ethics; the social relations of labour in digital-first newsrooms; and the way journalists are responding. As Nicole Cohen (2018) points out, there are several worries that poor working conditions and the spread of precarious forms of work in journalism will limit the ability of people from diverse gender, class and racialized backgrounds to access work in journalism. Further, Iordanidou et al. (2020) suggest that in a working environment like this, censorship from the administration offices as well as self-censorship as a means of survival blooms.

Specifically, in Greece, the need for further research into the working conditions of journalists seems to be urgent because even now that an Online/ Digital Media Register exists, there is no clear picture of how many people are working on these websites and under what working conditions. Awareness of the damage caused to the journalistic profession and the subsequent reduction in content quality, because of the working conditions within which this content is produced, should be raised. Peer and collective pressure should be exerted by the journalists, along with the civil society, to claim quality jobs and, therefore, quality journalism.

REFERENCES

Altmeppen, K.-D. (2008), 'The structure of news production: The organizational approach to journalism research', in M. Löffelholz and D. Weaver (eds), *Global Journalism Research: Theories, Methods, Findings, Future*, Malden, MA: Blackwell, pp. 52–64.

Ananny, Mike and Crawford, Kate (2015), 'A liminal press: Situating news app designers within a field of networked news production', *Digital Journalism*, 3:2, pp. 192–208.

Anderson, C. W. (2013), *Rebuilding the News: Metropolitan Journalism in a Digital Age*, Philadelphia: Temple University Press.

Bittner, Andreas K. (2013), 'Managing change, innovation and trade unionism in the news industry', *European Federation of Journalists*, https://europeanjournalists.org/blog/2013/11/25/managing-change-in-journalism-innovation-and-trade-unions-in-the-news-industry/. Accessed 25 May 2021.

Boczkowski, P. J. (2009), 'Materiality and mimicry in the journalism field', in B. Zelizer (ed.), *The Changing Faces of Journalism: Tabloidization, Technology and Truthiness*, London: Routledge, pp. 56–67.

Braun, V. and Clarke, V. (2006), 'Using thematic analysis in psychology', *Qualitative Research in Psychology*, 3:2, pp. 77–101.

Braverman, Harry (1974), *Labour and Monopoly Capital*, New York: Monthly Review Press.

Cohen, N. S. (2018), 'At work in the digital newsroom', *Digital Journalism*, 7:5, pp. 571–91.

Comor, Edward and Compton, James (2015), 'Journalistic labour and technological fetishism', *Political Economy of Communication*, 3:2, pp. 74–87.

Cushion, S. (2007), 'Rich media, poor journalists: Journalists' salaries', *Journalism Practice*, 1:1, pp. 120–29.

Daum, Ev. and Scherer, J. (2017), 'Changing work routines and labour practices of sports journalists in the digital era: A case study of postmedia, media, culture and society', http://journals.sagepub.com/doi/abs/10.1177/0163443717714992. Accessed 25 May 2021.

Deuze, M. (2007), *Media Work*, Cambridge: Polity Press.

Deuze, M. (2009), 'Technology and the individual journalist', in B. Zelizer (ed.), *The Changing Faces of Journalism: Tabloidization, Technology and Truthiness*, London: Routledge, pp. 82–97.

Deuze, M. and Fortunati, L. (2010), 'Journalism without journalists', in G. Meikle and G. Redden (eds), *News Online: Transformations and Continuities*, Basingstoke: Palgrave Macmillan, pp. 164–77.

Deuze, M. and Paulussen, S. (2002), 'Online journalism in the Low Countries: Basic, occupational and professional characteristics of online journalists in Flanders and The Netherlands', *European Journal of Communication*, 17:2, pp. 237–45.

Dwyer, T. and Martin, F. (2017), 'Sharing news online', *Digital Journalism*, 5:8, pp. 1080–100.

Foer, F. (2017), 'When Silicon Valley took over journalism', *The Atlantic*, https://www.theatlantic.com/magazine/archive/2017/09/when-silicon-valley-took-overjournalism/534195/. Accessed 25 May 2021.

García Avilés, J. A, Bienvenido, L., Sanders, K. and Harrison, J. (2004), 'Journalists at digital television newsrooms in Britain and Spain: Workflow and multi-skilling in a competitive environment', *Journalism Studies*, 5:1, pp. 87–100.

Gregor, G. (2000), 'New technology, the labour process and employment relations in the provincial newspaper industry', *New Technology, Work and Employment*, 15:2, pp. 94–107.

Hardy, J. (2014), *Critical Political Economy of the Media*, London: Routledge, pp. 37–57.

Iordanidou, S., Takas, E., Vatikiotis, L. and García, P. (2020), 'Constructing silence: Processes of journalistic (self-)censorship during memoranda in Greece, Cyprus, and Spain', *Media and Communication*, 8:1, pp. 15–26.

Iosifidis, P. and Boucas, D. (2015), *Media Policy and Independent Journalism in Greece*, London: Open Society Foundations.

Jenkins, H. (2006), *Convergence Culture: Where Old and New Media Collide*, New York: New York University Press.

Jessop, B. (1992), 'Post-Fordism and flexible specialization: Contradictory complementary, commensurable, or simply different perspectives?', in H. Ernste and V. Meyer (eds), *Flexible Specialization and the New Regionalism*, London: Pinter, pp. 25–44.

Kline, Ronald R. (2015), *International Encyclopaedia of the Social & Behavioural Sciences*, Oxford: Elsevier Ltd.

McChesney, R. W. (2013), *Digital Disconnect: How Capitalism Is Turning the Internet against Democracy*, New York: The New Press.

O'Donnell, P. (2009), 'That's gold! Thinking about excellence in Australian journalism', *Australian Journalism Review*, 31:2, pp. 47–60.

Örnebring, H. (2010), 'Technology and journalism-as-labour: Historical perspectives', *Journalism*, 11:1, pp. 57–74.

Paulussen, S. (2012), 'Technology and the transformation of news work: Are labour conditions in (online) journalism changing?', in E. Siapera and A. Veglis (eds), *Handbook of Global Online Journalism*, Malden, MA: Wiley Blackwell, pp. 192–208.

Quandt, T., Löffelholz, M., Weaver, D. H., Hanitzsch, T. and Altmeppen, K.-D. (2006), 'American and German online journalists at the beginning of the 21st century', *Journalism Studies*, 7:2, pp. 171–86.

Rhomberg, M. (2012), 'Media convergence', in G. Ritzer (ed.), The *Wiley-Blackwell Encyclopedia of Globalization*, Chicester: Wiley-Blackwell.

Segal, D. (2015), 'Arianna Huffington's improbable, insatiable content machine', *New York Times Magazine*, http://www.nytimes.com/2015/07/05/magazine/arianna-huffingtons-improbable-insatiable-content-machine.html?_r=0. Accessed 25 May 2021.

Sennett, R. (1997), 'The new capitalism', *Social Research*, 64:2, pp. 161–80, http://www.jstor.org/stable/40971180. Accessed 25 May 2021.

Shade, C. (2015), 'Content creators of the world, unite!', *Pacific Standard*, http://www.psmag.com/books-and-culture/is-it-times-for-journalists-to-unionize. Accessed 25 May 2021.

Smyrnaios, N. (2015), 'Google and the algorithmic infomediation of news', *Media Fields*, 10, pp. 1–10.

Testa, J., Reinsberg, H., Misener, J. and Burton, S. A. (2014), 'Here's what female and male journalists actually make', BuzzFeed, https://www.buzzfeed.com/jtes/heres-what-female-and-male-journalists-actually-make. Accessed 25 May 2021.

Walters, E., Warren, C. and Dobbie, M. (2006), 'The changing nature of work: A global survey and case study of atypical work in the media industry', *International Federation of Journalists Supported by the International Labour Office*, https://www.ilo.org/sector/Resources/publications/WCMS_161547/lang--en/index.htm. Accessed 25 May 2021.

Wilding, D., Fray, P., Molitorisz, S. and McKewon, E. (2018), *The Impact of Digital Platforms on News and Journalistic Content*, Sydney: University of Technology Sydney, NSW.

Winseck, D. (2011), 'The political economies of media and the transformation of the global media industries', in D. Winseck and D. Yong Jin (eds), *The Political Economies of Media: The Transformation of Global Media Industries*, London: Bloomsbury, pp. 3–48.

6

Between a Rock and a Hard Place: Continued Struggle of Media and Journalism in Bulgaria's Media System

Lada Trifonova Price

Introduction and background

This chapter aims to show that the political and economic context is crucial to the current poor employment conditions for journalists in Bulgaria, one of the poorest member states of the European Union. With a GDP per capita at 50 per cent below the EU-28 average (Eurostat 2019; Antonov 2019), Bulgaria and its media are in financial dire straits. Difficult economic conditions have exacerbated the crisis in journalism, while journalists and editors have witnessed a consistent decline in press freedom in the past two decades. Bulgarian journalists and media workers have voiced their concerns about the difficult working conditions under which they exercise their profession on numerous occasions, stating that their concerns 'are not just a problem of the Bulgarian society, but of the entire European Union'. Journalists argue that the crisis engulfing journalism is a threat not only to Bulgarian society but to the EU as a whole (AEJ Bulgaria 2012). It is important to examine and understand the reasons for this state of affairs and to suggest some steps that can be taken to safeguard and enhance journalism in a country often classified as a 'flawed' democracy (Dobek-Ostrowska 2019: 112).

The annual Reporters Without Borders (RWB) Press Freedom Index places Bulgaria at 111th place (out of 180 monitored countries), demonstrating deterioration of media freedom indicators from previous years. Bulgaria's position on the list is lower than all other European states owing to a widespread corruption and collusion between media, politicians and local oligarchs (RWB 2020). Growing concentration of media ownership is a highly problematic issue for journalism as it threatens pluralism and media freedom (Wehofsits et al. 2018; IREX 2019).

Ownership is mostly used as a vehicle for fulfilling political, business and other agendas. A climate of fear and threats of violence against journalists is widespread to the extent that to be a journalist is now dangerous in Bulgaria (RWB 2019a). This affects how journalists do their jobs on a day-to-day basis and contributes to harsh employment conditions across the media sector.

Bulgaria was a staunch communist country up to 1989. During communism, the state-owned media were tightly controlled and censored; they were paramount in maintaining the power of the communist regimes throughout Eastern Europe. Used as an instrument for political purposes, rather than as a channel for communication and distribution of information, the communist media in Bulgaria were a vital instrument of control by the ruling Communist Party, namely used for propaganda of ideas, manipulation of citizens and maintenance of culture of fear of retribution experienced by political opponents of the regime (Sparks and Reading 1998; Gross 1999; Paletz and Jackubowizc 2003). The development of the media in Bulgaria since the start of democratization 30 years ago has been marked by numerous rapid changes. On the positive side, the immediate liberalization of the market created favourable conditions for expansion of the printed press, freed from the direct political censorship and the ideological restrictions of communism. The absence of strict regulation and the ease in starting a media outlet allowed for free speech, media pluralism and access to information to all citizens. Freedom of speech and expression was quickly enshrined in the new Bulgarian constitution, becoming an essential part of the democratic public sphere (Raycheva 2009). The press, keen to meet the new information demands of audiences, cherished its newly acquired functions as a watchdog for society and its increasing role in shaping public opinion. In the early years of democracy, the media played a central and pivotal role in establishing and representing the new power elites responsible for political governance (Znepolski 1997), quickly becoming an agent of public communication and the centre of power struggles where hostile and open wars between the elites were fought (Roudakova 2008; Dyczok 2009; Gaman-Golutvina 2009; Voltmer 2013). While the media market was undergoing a rapid transformation, scores of young journalists in Bulgaria were entering the profession and adopting new norms of value-free objective reporting (Foley 2006; Stewart 2013).

On the negative side, some of the major issues that currently plague the Bulgarian media landscape have their roots in the early 1990s. While the transition to democracy was peaceful as in other countries in the region, the former rulers converted their political capital into significant economic assets and social status without much difficulty (Steen and Ruus 2002). Continuity with the previous regime was exemplified by the desire of newly elected political and economic actors to control, own and influence the media for their own agendas. This is one of the main reasons why autonomous and independent press and broadcasters have failed to prosper. The new ruling elites perceived radio and television as very attractive channels of political communication deliberately inhibiting changes in this field, and 'fearing the loss of influence on the content of the reformed public media' (Dobek-Ostrowska 2019: 108). Whether public or private, most media have been subjected to continued political and economic pressure since the early days of transformation, especially those that are critical of the government in power. Journalists regularly experience interference with their work, which has led to widespread self-censorship (Centre for Media Pluralism and Media Freedom (CMPF) Media Pluralism Monitor [MPM], 2017; Trifonova Price 2018). News outlets often tailor coverage to suit the agendas of their owners (Freedom House 2019). Other problems include non-transparent media ownership and financing. The existing legal framework for disclosure of media ownership allows the actual owners of some media outlets to remain hidden to the public. While in theory there are sanctions for non-transparency, in practice, these have never been imposed on media outlets (Spassov 2019).

In 1990, there were 540 newspapers with total circulation of 1,098,632 copies, but by 2018, the number of newspapers had reduced to 239 (37 dailies) with a total circulation of 216,037 copies (Tsankova 2018; BNSI 2019). Like in many other countries Bulgarian daily newspaper circulation numbers have continued their steady decline. Severe competition and market constraints over the past two decades, including the fallout from the global financial crisis, from 2008 to 2013, have halved advertising income and brought many print media on the edge of collapse (Center for Study of Democracy [CSD] 2016; IREX 2014). As well as a sharp drop in circulation and significant decline in gross advertising budgets, newspapers have experienced a decline in trust (40 per cent in news overall) due largely to a dependence on funds from local oligarchs or foreign NGOs (Antonov 2019; Newman et al. 2020). In the early years of democratization, the media exerted considerable influence over public opinion and brought high polarization in Bulgarian society (Raycheva 2009). More recent years have also been defined by extreme polarization of the media and the return of control by political parties, which have their own TV channels (Antonov 2019). Yet, despite being in a difficult financial situation, print media still continue to wield substantial political clout in Bulgarian society just like they did in the early 1990s (CSD 2016). Similarly to Greece and Spain, licences to private broadcasters are often granted on the basis of strong friendship ties between businesses and ruling elites (Dobek-Ostrowska 2019). Several influential TV channels, such as the cable channel Evropa and the national Nova TV, are owned by people with close links to the government, ensuring positive coverage of policies and launching frequent attacks on government critics (Antonov 2019).

Democratic transformation in Bulgaria has been hampered by slow institutional and economic reforms and the lack of democratic culture with shared principles and values that guide their behaviour and attitude (Balčytienė 2015). A good example of low democratic culture is the deeply engrained culture of corruption in government, business and society, which has affected the development of the media landscape and journalism practice since the end of communism (Trifonova Price 2019b).

Corruption and media

Corruption is a serious impediment to economic reforms and democratization in any society, but it is particularly damaging to those often described as vulnerable or 'fragile', such as Bulgaria (Rupnik and Zielonka 2013). Despite the country becoming a member of the European Union (EU) more than a decade ago, anticorruption efforts have stalled. Bulgaria is ranked 77th out of 180 countries in the latest annual Transparency International Corruption Perceptions Index (TI CPI 2018), which rates countries by their level of public sector corruption. Bulgaria's position in the index has gradually deteriorated since 2007 when the country was ranked 64th on the list. Corruption actually worsened by 2010 from 2007 at the start of its EU membership. This is partly because once the accession criteria were met prior to membership, the Bulgarian government immediately scaled down its efforts to tackle corruption in society (Ganev 2013). Notable cases of large-scale embezzlement of EU funding forced the European Commission to temporarily stop practically all pre-accession funds directed to Bulgaria and to issue stern reports from Brussels (Andreev 2009; Ganev 2013). Since then, there has been very limited progress in the political corruption domain with rare convictions of corrupt high-ranking officials (Stoyanov et al. 2014; Wehofsits et al. 2018). Transparency International notes that 'persistent unaddressed problems including dirty money in politics, unregulated lobbying, a lack of uniform anti-corruption policies in public institutions, non-transparent appointments to key public offices and no clear ethics policy for the parliament' (Transparency International 2017: n.pag.) as some of the key concerns relating to corruption.

More than half of Bulgarian citizens believe that their government is not doing enough to combat corruption within its ranks (Pring 2016). The summer of 2020 has been defined by widespread protests against the government and the corrupt judiciary resulting in violent clashes between protesters and the police (Tsolova 2020). The media, along with civil society and the private sector, are usually seen as one of the pillars of a national integrity system, a framework that encompasses a variety of approaches to combating corruption worldwide (Pope 2000). However, there has long been doubt over the ability of the press and journalism to expose corruption, even in established liberal democracies (Curran and Park 2000; Petley 2004). If the media is plagued by corruption, it is unable to perform its role as a check on power. The situation in Bulgaria illustrates this well. Editorial corruption in Bulgaria is so widespread that some public relations agencies that are bidding for contracts with international companies have had to openly distance themselves from the common practice of having to pay journalists for news stories (Braun 2007; Trifonova Price 2019b).

One of the biggest problems that affects media content is the non-transparent and unregulated allocation of state advertising to certain media outlets in Bulgaria (see Antonov 2013; CSD 2016; IREX 2019). The practice has become more widespread since Bulgaria joined the EU because the money often comes from designated publicity funds from EU projects affecting the media's ability to act as a check on power on national and on regional level (Trifonova Price 2019b). Government control and censorship on the national and local level is exercised by allocating state advertising to media that are willing to provide pro-government coverage or avoid asking inconvenient questions: '[O]utlets are dependent on financial contributions from the state, often in the form of advertising, which can lead to demands for favorable coverage of the government' (Freedom House 2019: n.pag.). In practice this means that any topics that can potentially jeopardize the payments can be banned or blacklisted by the media owners and editors and that leads to widespread self-censorship among journalists (Trifonova Price 2018). A large proportion of regional media outlets relies on financing from the local government and political parties through contracts for information services and political advertising. Most owners and publishers are in direct contact with local political and council authorities (Tsankova 2018). It is common for politicians and journalists to maintain a close a relationship, which often leads to corruption and clientelism, as is the case in Bulgaria, Romania, Spain, Greece and other southern European countries (Dobek-Ostrowska 2019). Financial insecurity, inadequate contracts and low salaries are now the norm for many journalists in Bulgaria while trade union protection is essentially non-existent (MPM 2017). The average monthly wage for a reporter ranges from 1000 to 1500 Bulgarian Lev (BGN) (equivalent of €500 to 760), close to the national average (IREX 2019). This has not changed significantly since 2010 when the average monthly salary of a journalist was estimated to be less than 1,000 BGN (€500), which was slightly above the national average with journalists in regional outlets getting paid at the lower scale of the spectrum. (Štětka 2011). Many employers tend to pay reporters the minimum wage to save on statutory deductions and the rest of their salaries are handed to them 'in hand'. Continued closures of print media outlets and rising unemployment among journalists are accompanied by a lack of legal protection except for the state broadcasters (Štětka 2011: 15). Low pay and precarious job market conditions sometimes coerces reporters into corrupt or unethical practices that go against the principles of ethical journalism but can bring them a much-needed income. The continued uncertainty about the long-term economic survival of media outlets in a highly volatile political and economic environment is indicative of the impact of systemic corruption on journalistic culture, attitudes and behaviour (Trifonova Price 2019b). In a corrupt environment and weak judiciary, the state is either unable or unwilling to investigate and prosecute anyone who commits crimes against journalists, including harassment, verbal and physical abuse and intimidation. Observers have expressed concerns about the rise in crimes against journalists in Bulgaria, including violent attacks (IREX 2017).

Violence and self-censorship

One of the most recent and symptomatic cases is the murder of the TV presenter and journalist Viktoria Marinova from Ruse in 2018. Marinova had previously reported on fraud involving EU funding. Despite the authorities' insistence that the crime was not linked to Marinova's work, lingering doubts of a cover up of a botched investigation remained even after the quick arrest of a suspect (Mapping Media Freedom 2018; Freedom House 2019; RWB 2019a). The reporter's brutal assault and killing was condemned by numerous international organizations tasked with improving safety of journalists, such as Reporters Without Borders, Committee to Protect Journalists and OSCEE's Media Representative, and covered extensively by global media outlets. In 2018, another journalist, Hristo Geshov was attacked outside his home and two reporters were arrested and briefly detained while also investigating alleged fraud with EU funds (Freedom House 2019).

The Bulgarian national security agency and the police have been used to intimidate and harass journalists and critical media outlets through coercion to reveal sources, spying, threats, and blackmail (Trifonova Price 2014). In a recent example, the police summoned the journalist Assen Dimitrov, from the online news site *Blagoevgrad News* to issue a written warning after he covered a protest in the city of Blagoevgrad. The AJE Bulgaria stated that it is unacceptable for journalists to receive police warnings when they cover protests as they have a right to do so guaranteed by the Bulgarian Constitution and the Law for Radio and TV (AEJ Bulgaria 2018). There are numerous examples of physical and online abuse, arson of property, dismissal and verbal threats against reporters as well and legal harassment. Such types of intimidation and interference not only amount to censorship but also leads to widespread self-censorship among journalists, avoidance of certain topics and dulling of criticism (Blagov et al. 2014). During the protests of 2020, several journalists were verbally abused by protesters and beaten by the police despite identifying themselves as reporters. For example, the freelance journalist Dimitar Kenarov was detained while covering anti-government protests and beaten in police custody. Despite widespread condemnation, the investigation was unable to find those responsible for the assault of the journalist (RFI 2021). The AEJ–Bulgaria and other international organizations have strongly condemned the violence against journalists (AEJ 2020). The problem with violence against journalists and impunity is linked to the way Bulgarian media are owned and run and the environment of complex web of dependencies between owners, business, political and government actors.

Ownership and income

The majority, if not all, print and digital media in Bulgaria are unprofitable and depend on income from the owners' other business ventures (Antonova 2019). They do not aim to make a profit but operate with the sole purpose to 'trade influence while TV channels receive income from advertising and from cable network fees' (Antonova 2019: n.pag.). For the press, low incomes and online competition have further reduced readership and most foreign investors have left the market, a trend that started in 2010 when the German conglomerate Westdeutsche Allgemeine Zeitung (WAZ) sold its leading titles, citing formidable corruption and political dependencies as some of the main reasons for withdrawing (Trifonova Price 2014). Since then, the ownership of media outlets has largely transferred and concentrated in the hands of wealthy local businessmen, exposing journalists to political and economic pressure and threatening pluralism (Freedom House 2019). Risk of commercial and owners' influence over editorial content is high at 92 per cent. The concentration of media ownership in Bulgaria is also considered a high risk. Horizontal media ownership concentration is estimated to be as high as 96 per cent, and cross-media concentration of ownership and competition enforcement 88 per cent (MPM 2017).

Media legislation does not contain any specific measures to prevent a high degree of horizontal concentration of ownership in all media sectors. The general rules in the competition law do not include specific provisions for the media market, but the actual level of concentration is impossible to determine due to a lack of precise data (Spassov 2019). As already noted, due to considerable financial insecurity and small advertising market many news organizations rely on the state advertising, given in exchange for positive coverage of the government. This poses a strong barrier to media pluralism along with low media literacy (MPM 2017). The government's penchant for allocating EU funding to sympathetic media outlets has been likened to bribing whole media outlets to apply a soft touch approach when reporting on the government or to avoid certain topics and controversial news (Trifonova Price 2019b; RWB 2019a; Freedom House 2019). Judicial harassment of independent media has also increased. For example, in 2019, an investigative reporter from the business weekly *Capital*, owned by the independent publisher Economedia Rosen Bossev, was convicted of defamation and fined approximately €500 for expressing criticism of the former head of Bulgaria's Financial Supervision Commission (FSC) Stoyan Mavrodiev on a live TV broadcast in 2015 (RWB 2019b). While reflecting on the defamation case, which continued for four years, Bossev noted the negative impact on his professional and personal life, including the life of his family, and open intimidation from judicial police. The case has been submitted to the European Court of Human Rights because, according to the reporter, it is important that there are boundaries that should not be crossed when it comes to protecting freedom of speech and expression in Bulgaria (Bossev 2019).

Despite the continuous legal and financial pressure that the media has endured over the past two decades, before the pandemic in 2020 *Capital* and its publisher company Economedia had established a new model, which brought them some much-needed revenue. *Capital* is one of the few outlets in Bulgaria charging users for its online content and makes a small profit through organizing special events. The publisher invests in and focuses on quality content and journalism, which is then used for special editions on education, healthcare business, finance, property and others. The media takes these special editions further by organizing events and conferences, such as a conference that brings together the best experts in the field to talk about healthcare issues. The special editions and events were one of the biggest sources of income for the company. However, the emergency measures introduced by the government at the start of lockdown in Bulgaria ended most live events. While some are slowly returning, COVID-19 has exposed media in Europe, including those in Bulgaria, to considerable losses of advertising revenue and income from special events, drop in print circulation, redundancies, closure of news outlets and changes to journalistic routines (EJO 2020).

In the past decade the effects of digital technology on journalism in Bulgaria and Romania has manifested itself in three main areas: the new dynamics of news and information gathering, the changing professional practices and skills that are necessary to adapt in this digital environment and the changing status of traditional media.

(Trifonova-Price 2019a: 319)

The current media market in Bulgaria is also characterized by the dominant position of online media as a source of information. In 2018, 72.3 per cent of Bulgarian households have home internet access, while 71.5 per cent use broadband (BNSI 2018). Statistics show that the percentage of online sources of news, including social media, is relatively high (88 per cent) but only 7 per cent pay for news. Fifty-two per cent share news either by social media, message apps or email, while 41 percent comment on online news (Antonov 2019). Digital technology has improved access to news content and information and has created more opportunities for people to express their opinions on issues they care about (Antonova and Georgiev 2013). Nonetheless, most digital news media do not have an effective business model. In practice, online platforms can support only a very small team of journalists without specialist knowledge. They tend to copy content from traditional media organizations and news agencies compiling and aggregating information from different sources, which often amounts to a copy-paste exercise. For a large number of Bulgarian journalists, news gathering and production is influenced by social media, active audience participation in news content creation and use of user generated content (Slavtcheva-Petkova 2017). Digitalization has brought some positive changes in the Bulgarian media landscape and working practices, namely easier access to information, growing audience participation and gradual adaptation of journalists to new technological conditions. Worryingly, during the coronavirus pandemic in 2020, Bulgaria, just like many other countries, has seen a marked rise in disinformation and false news with very few policies and effective mechanisms to counteract this trend.

Conclusion

The observations on the Bulgarian media landscape show yet again that media organizations and journalists in fragile democracies without self-sustaining financial mechanisms are open for manipulation from state and corporate actors that can use them for personal gain and political agendas. This environment does nothing to improve employment conditions for Bulgarian journalists who are struggling with rising unemployment, low pay and are indeed in a very difficult social situation (Štětka 2011). Despite some gains, political and corporate interests prevent the majority of Bulgarian media and journalists to act as a check on power and in the public interest. The conflict between serving sponsors and serving society not only is affecting the quality of journalism but the way journalists do their jobs, feeding widespread self-censorship, and is inevitably lowering the trust in journalism. To regain credibility and confidence, Bulgarian media needs to fight for its independence and find sustainable mechanisms to prosper in its primary goal to serve the public and act as an agent of change. However, even in consolidated democracies such as the United States, there has been a rise in bias and political polarization, the quality of information media has significantly decreased and journalistic professionalism has deteriorated (Hallin and Mancini 2017). While this chapter has outlined difficult working conditions for journalists, exacerbated by the pandemic in 2020, that in many instances lead to poor and unethical journalism, it must be stressed that there are some media and journalists who are battling against the tide of political and economic pressures, investigating and exposing abuses of power despite the harsh everyday reality. In 2012, in response to the urgent concerns expressed by Bulgarian journalists and editors, Neelie Kroes, the EU Commissioner for Digital Economy and Society at the time, stated that without journalism there is no democracy and all countries in the EU should fight together for media freedom (Novinite 2012). Kroes vowed to make it a personal priority to drive improvement in the media market. Yet, despite this pledge and several others since then, nothing has changed for the better, and employment conditions for Bulgarian journalists continue to deteriorate. Despite the difficult conditions, there are some instances of innovative journalism practices in engaging with audiences eager for reliable, real-time news and information, including the introduction of new content and formats of journalism that have emerged during the COVID-19 health crisis. Further comparative research is needed to examine these not just in Bulgaria but across Eastern Europe. There is no straightforward solution to the problems analysed in this chapter, but it is imperative that the European Union stands up to its promises and begins to work together with Bulgarian journalists and media houses to protect their rights, safeguard media freedom and pluralism at state level. One solution to the crisis would be dedicated EU funding to independent media outlets on national and regional level, allowing them to end their dependency either on state advertising or sponsorship from media oligarchs. Those outlets are vital to the democratic public sphere in Bulgaria. Where there are signs of resilience and determination from journalists and newsrooms to serve their audiences, those should be actively encouraged and nurtured with EU funding, enabling them to grow and develop new business models.

REFERENCES

AEJ Bulgaria (2012), 'Open letter from Bulgarian journalists', http://new.aej-bulgaria.org/en/open-letter-from-bulgarian-journalists/. Accessed 15 November 2019.

AEJ Bulgaria (2018), 'Журналисти не бива да бъдат репресирани от полицията, ако отразяват протести' ('Journalists should be repressed by the police when covering protests'), http://www.aej-bulgaria.org/bul/p.php?post=10120&c=349&. Accessed 12 September 2019.

AEJ Bulgaria (2020), 'AEJ-Bulgaria condemns police violence against Bulgarian journalist', https://new.aej-bulgaria.org/en/aej-bulgaria-condemns-police-violence-against-bulgarian-journalist/. Accessed 3 September 2020.

Andreev, Svetlozar (2009), 'The unbearable lightness of membership: Bulgaria and Romania after the 2007 EU accession', *Communist and Post-Communist Studies*, 42, pp. 375–93.

Antonov, Stefan (2013), *The Age of the Oligarchs: How a Group of Political and Economic Magnates Have Taken Control of Bulgaria*, Oxford: University of Oxford, http://reutersinstitute.politics.ox.ac.uk/sites/default/files/The%20Age%20of%20Oligarchs.pdf. Accessed 21 July 2017.

Antonov, Stefan (2019), 'Reuters Digital News Report: Bulgaria', https://reutersinstitute.politics.ox.ac.uk/sites/default/files/2019-06/DNR_2019_FINAL_1.pdf. Accessed 12 September 2019.

Antonova, Vesislava and Georgiev, Andrian (2013), *Mapping Digital Media: Bulgaria*, Sofia: Open Society foundation, https://www.opensocietyfoundations.org/sites/default/files/mapping-digital-media-bulgaria-en-20130805.pdf. Accessed 12 September 2019.

Balčytienė, Auksė (2015), 'Institutions and cultures: An analytical framework for the study of democratisation and media transformations in Central and Eastern Europe', in B. Dobek-Ostrowska and M. Głowacki (eds), *Democracy and Media in Central and Eastern Europe 25 Years On*, Bern: Peter Lang, pp. 47–62.

Blagov, Krum, Orlin, Spassov, Spahr, Christian and Arndt, Marco (2014), *Influence on the Media: Owners, Politicians and Advertisers*, Sofia: Konrad-Adenauer-Stiftung, http://www.aej-bulgaria.org/wp-content/uploads/2014/11/KAS_BOOK.pdf. Accessed 12 September 2019.

Bossev, Rosen (2019), In-person interview with Rosen Bossev, senior court reporter from *Capital* newspaper conducted in Sofia, Bulgaria, 12 August.

Braun, Sandra (2007), 'The effects of the political environment on public relations in Bulgaria', *Journal of Public Relations Research*, 19:3, pp. 199–228.

Bulgarian National Statistical Institute (BSNI) (2018), 'Household who have internet access at home', http://www.nsi.bg/en/content/6099/households-who-have-internet-access-home. Accessed 12 September 2019.

Bulgarian National Statistical Institute (BSNI) (2019), Published periodical newspapers in Bulgaria (in Bulgarian), https://www.nsi.bg/bg/content/3596/издадени-вестници-по-периодичност. Accessed 12 September 2019.

Center for the Study of Democracy (CSD) (2016), 'Media (in)dependence in Bulgaria: Risks and Trends', Policy Brief no. 60, May, http://www.csd.bg/artShow.php?id=17658. Accessed 12 September 2019.

Centre for Media Pluralism and Media Freedom (CMPF) (2017), 'Media Pluralism Monitor results: Bulgaria', https://cadmus.eui.eu/bitstream/handle/1814/61132/2018_Bulgaria_EN.pdf?sequence=1&isAllowed=y. Accessed 12 September 2019.

Curran, James and Park, Myung-Jin (2000), 'Beyond globalization theory', in J. Curran and M. Park (eds), *De-Westernizing Media Studies*, Abingdon and New York: Routledge, pp. 3–18.

Dobek-Ostrowska, Boguslava (2019), *Polish Media System in a Comparative Perspective: Media in Politics, Politics in Media*, Peter Lang: Berlin.

Dyczok, Martha (2009), 'Introduction', in M. Dyczok and O. Gaman-Golutvina (eds), *Media, Democracy and Freedom: The Post-Communist Experience*, Bern: Peter Lang, pp. 9–16.

European Journalism Observatory (2020), 'The economic impact of Covid-19 on European media in 2020', https://en.ejo.ch/media-economics/the-economic-impact-of-covid-19-on-european-media-in-2020. Accessed 28 February 2021.

Eurostat (2019), 'GDP per capita, consumption per capita and price level indices', https://ec.europa.eu/eurostat/statistics-explained/index.php/GDP_per_capita,_consumption_per_capita_and_price_level_indices#Relative_volumes_of_GDP_per_capita. Accessed 12 September 2019.

Foley, Michael (2006), 'Promoting Values – as West meets East', *The International Journal of Communication Ethics*, 3:2&3, https://arrow.dit.ie/cgi/viewcontent.cgi?referer=&httpsredir=1&article=1042&context=aaschmedart. Accessed 12 September 2019.

Freedom House (2019), 'Freedom in the world: Bulgaria', https://freedomhouse.org/report/freedom-world/2019/bulgaria. Accessed 12 September 2019.

Gaman-Golutvina, Oxana (2009), 'Conclusions: Media and democracy in transformation design', in M. Dyczok and O. Gaman-Golutvina (eds), *Media, Democracy and Freedom: The Post-Communist Experience*, Bern: Peter Lang, pp. 231–42.

Ganev, Venelin (2013), 'Post-accession hooliganism: Democratic governance in Bulgaria and Romania after 2007', *East European Politics and Societies*, 23:1, pp. 26–44.

Gross, Peter (1999), 'Journalism education: Taking stock of the last 12 years', *The Global Network, Le Reseau Global*, 15/16, pp. 5–12.

Hallin, Daniel and Mancini, Paolo (2017), 'Ten years after comparing media systems: What have we learned?', *Political Communication*, 34:2, pp. 155–71.

IREX (2014), *Europe and Eurasia Media Sustainability Index: Bulgaria*, Washington DC: IREX, https://www.irex.org/sites/default/files/pdf/media-sustainability-index-europe-eurasia-2015-bulgaria.pdf. Accessed 12 September 2019.

IREX (2017), 'Media Sustainability Index: Bulgaria', https://www.irex.org/sites/default/files/pdf/media-sustainability-index-europe-eurasia-2017-bulgaria.pdf. Accessed 12 September 2019.

IREX (2019), 'Media Sustainability Index: Europe and Eurasia', https://www.irex.org/sites/default/files/pdf/media-sustainability-index-europe-eurasia-2019-full.pdf. Accessed 12 September 2019.

Mapping Media Freedom (2018), https://mappingmediafreedom.ushahidi.io/posts/22740. Accessed 12 September 2019.

Newman, Nic, Fletcher, Richard, Schulz, Anne, Andı, Simge and Kleis Nielsen, Rasmus (2020), 'Reuters Institute Digital News Report', https://reutersinstitute.politics.ox.ac.uk/sites/default/files/2020-06/DNR_2020_FINAL.pdf. Accessed 4 September 2020.

Novinite (2012), 'Neelie Kroes stands up for media freedom in Bulgaria', https://www.novinite.com/articles/140054/Neelie+Kroes+Stands+Up+for+Media+Freedom+in+Bulgaria. Accessed 17 November 2019.

Paletz, David and Jakubowicz, Karol (2003), *Business as Usual: Continuity and Change in East Central European Media*, Cresskill: Hampton Press.

Petley, Julian (2004), 'Fourth-rate estate', *Index on Censorship*, 2, pp. 33–68.

Pope, Jeremy (2000), *Confronting Corruption: The Elements of a National Integrity System*, Berlin: Transparency International.

Pring, Coralie (2016), 'Global corruption barometer. People and corruption: Europe and Asia 2016', Transparency International, https://www.transparency.org/whatwedo/publication/people_and_corruption_europe_and_central_asia_2016. Accessed 12 September 2019.

Raycheva, Lilia (2009), 'Mass media developments in Bulgaria', in A. Czepek, M. Hellwig and E. Nowak (eds), *Press Freedom and Pluralism in Europe: Concepts and Conditions*, Bristol: Intellect Publishing, pp. 165–76.

Reporters Without Borders (RWB) (2019a), 'Press Freedom Index: Bulgaria', https://rsf.org/en/bulgaria. Accessed 12 September 2019.

Reporters Without Borders (RWB) (2019b), 'Bulgarian reporter's defamation conviction sets dangerous precedent', https://rsf.org/en/news/bulgarian-reporters-defamation-conviction-sets-dangerous-precedent. Accessed 12 September 2019.

Reporters Without Borders (RWB) (2020), 'Press Freedom Index: Bulgaria', https://rsf.org/en/bulgaria. Accessed 3 September 2020.

RFI/RL (2021), 'Bulgaria condemned for refusal to probe journalist's violent arrest', https://www.rferl.org/a/bulgaria-condemned-journalist-dimitar-kenarov/31097935.html. Accessed 28 February 2021.

Roudakova, Natalia (2008), 'Media-political clientelism: Lessons from anthropology', *Media, Culture & Society*, 30, pp. 41–59.

Rupnik, Jacques and Zielonka, Jan (2013), 'The state of democracy 20 years on: Domestic and external factors', *East European Politics and Societies*, 27:1, pp. 3–27.

Slavtcheva-Petkova, Vera (2017), 'Journalists in Bulgaria. Country report', *Worlds of Journalism Study*, https://epub.ub.uni-muenchen.de/36881/7/Country_report_Bulgaria.pdf. Accessed 12 September 2019.

Sparks, C. and Reading, A. (1998), *Communism, Capitalism and the Mass Media*, London: Sage Publishing.

Spassov, Orlin (2019), 'Mapping media policy and journalism: Bulgaria', http://cmpf.eui.eu/mapping-media-policy-journalism/. Accessed 12 September 2019.

Steen, A. and Ruus, J. (2002), 'Change of regime – Continuity of Elites? The case of Estonia', *East European Politics & Societies*, 16, pp. 223–48.

Štětka, Václav (2011), 'Bulgaria: A country report for the ERC-funded project on media and democracy in Central and Eastern Europe', https://www.academia.edu/8568984/Bulgaria._A_country_report_for_the_ERC-funded_project_on_Media_and_Democracy_in_Central_and_Eastern_Europe. Accessed 17 November 2019.

Stewart, James (2013), 'A suitable cafe for transplant? The BBC and public service journalism in post-communist Romania', *Journalism Practice*, 7:3, pp. 329–44.

Stoyanov, Alxander, Stefanov, Ruslan and Velcheva, Boryana (2014), 'Background paper on Bulgaria. Bulgarian anti-corruption reforms: A lost decade?', http://www.againstcorrupt ion.eu/wp-content/uploads/2015/12/Bulgaria-Background-Report_final.pdf. Accessed 12 September 2019.

Transparency International (2017), '17 Commitments for a clean Bulgaria – Will politicians sign on?', https://www.transparency.org/news/feature/17_commitments_for_a_clean_bulgaria_ will_politicians_sign_on. Accessed 12 September 2019.

Transparency International (2018), 'Corruption Perceptions Index: Bulgaria' https://www.trans parency.org/cpi2018. Accessed 12 September 2019.

Trifonova-Price, Lada (2014), 'Media freedom under threat in Bulgaria', *British Journalism Review*, 23:3, pp. 50–54.

Trifonova-Price, Lada (2018), '"Bear in mind … and do not bite the hand that feeds you": Institutionalized self-censorship and its impact on journalistic practice in post-communist countries – The case of Bulgaria', in E. Freedman, R. Goodman and E. Steyn (eds), *Critical Perspectives on Journalistic Beliefs and Actions: Global Experiences*, Oxford: Routledge, pp. 211–21.

Trifonova-Price, Lada (2019a), 'Post-communist media and the impact of democratisation in Bulgaria and Romania', in E. Połońska and C. Beckett (eds), *Public Service Broadcasting and Media Systems in Troubled European Democracies*, London: Palgrave Macmillan, pp. 305–30.

Trifonova-Price, Lada (2019b), 'Media corruption and issues of journalistic and institutional integrity in post-communist countries: The case of Bulgaria', *Communist and Post-Communist Studies*, 52:1, pp. 71–79.

Tsankova, Svetla (2018), *Съвременна българска преса. Пазарни и качествени трансформации* (*Contemporary Bulgarian Press. Market and quality transformations*), Sofia: UNSS.

Tsolova, Tsvetelia (2020), 'Thousands protest against Bulgarian government, scuffle with police', Reuters, https://www.reuters.com/article/us-bulgaria-government/thousands-prot est-against-bulgarian-government-scuffle-with-police-idUSKBN25T1EA. Accessed 3 September 2020.

Voltmer, Katrin (2013), *The Media in Transitional Democracies*, Cambridge: Polity.

Wehofsits, Nora, Martino, Francesco and Vujovic, Oliver (2018), 'Bulgaria: Media ownership in a captured state. Report on the June 2018 joint Fact-Finding Mission', ECPMF, https:// www.ecpmf.eu/archive/files/ecpmf-ffm-bulgaria.pdf. Accessed 4 September 2020.

Znepolski, Ivan (1997), *Novata presa I prehodut. Trudnoto Konstituirane na Chetvartata Vlast* (*The New Press and Transition*), Sofia: Druzestvo Grazdanin.

PROPOSAL 4

'MEDIA OMBUDSMAN'

7

The Media Ombudsman Institution

Vasilis Sotiropoulos

Introduction

There is a widespread perception that media are going through a serious 'content' crisis.[1] The heterogeneity of journalistic sources and the deforming mirror of social media have fuelled discussions on ethics (Moyo 2016). Some basic rules of journalism are violated daily (Saoussen 2020); these are the principles that shape the ethics of the media and are sometimes embedded in codes of journalistic associations or media owner associations. Very often the courts themselves categorize these principles as 'the press ethics' (Bezanson 1999: 754–57). They include self-evident rules, such as the obligation to cross-check the accuracy of the news (Smyrnaios et al. 2017), the obligation to seek the opposing view, the duty of truth, respect for privacy and mourning, the presumption of innocence.[2] Journalistic ethics are challenged by the need to achieve speed, widen the audience, attract as many audiences as possible or even underground funding – the latter in more severe cases of expelled media and journalists. The problem with ethics in our time is that no one deals seriously with it, ethics are treated as trivial even by journalists who are concerned with the issue.

Ethics and enforcement

Violations of ethics are usually addressed with a sanctioning mechanism. Each journalistic association has a disciplinary board and, depending on the judgment of the board, a member who violates general principles is either punished with a disciplinary sanction (e.g., reprimand, dismissal, etc.) or acquitted. Usually, such decisions are also posted on the association's website so that there is some social implication for the offender. Another solution to ethical violations is law enforcement. In cases of spreading false or fake news, it is possible for a state attorney to initiate proceedings against the perpetrator or to have, for example, a radio station examined by a National Broadcasting Council or a Personal Data Protection Authority, depending on the infringement.

If private individuals are affected, they may even recourse to civil courts, seeking compensation for non-pecuniary damage. The problem with these traditional solutions, however, is that they only work afterward, suppressively. There is no preventive protection or supervision during the production and distribution of the 'message'. That is why traditional solutions are considered fragmented and inadequate for ensuring quality journalism since their aim is usually to secure union discipline and legitimacy rather than to produce meaningful content per se. The failure of the 'Press Complaints Commission' in the United Kingdom has been extensively highlighted by the top political leaders and institutional watchdogs as well as in the Leveson Inquiry Report.[3] All traditional models seem to be inadequate to address the ethical crisis in the media.

The subject matter: A media ombudsman

A more modern solution is to transplant the ombudsman institution into the media. The successful progress of the consumer's ombudsmen or local ombudspersons can give rise to the use of the same model at the specific sector of mass media. In Sweden, there is a Pressombudsman, overseeing press as an independent authority.[4] A similar service also exists in Ireland.[5] This is a centrally operating model.[6] Another model, self-regulating and decentralized, is the so-called 'public editor' (Harashima 2018: n.pag.) – a person who serves the media and is paid by them, while maintaining a degree of independence to gain the trust and respect of both journalists and citizens who engage with the media (readers/listeners/viewers, etc.).

This media ombudsman can be the personification of the rules of ethics: completely advisory either on their own (ex officio) or upon question or invitation, they can advise the journalistic team or individual journalist, editor, editor-in-chief, etc. on how to apply the principles of ethics. Also, when there are complaints from the public, it will be the ombudsman's objectivity and impartiality that will enable them to examine the complaints and decide whether or not the ethics have been complied with. In such a case, they may publicize the outcome of their investigation in the media itself, as a form of error recognition and as reparation.

It should be mentioned that the ombudsman solution is a completely different approach than the compliance executive that has been also proposed.[7] A compliance executive will always be considered an integrated part of the media outlet, without the glitter of the independence that crowns an ombudsman, even in theory.

Compliance is an obligation that you have to prove for yourself. Accountability refers to the practical mechanisms you enforce to yourself to ensure compliance. It should also be mentioned that the idea of a media ombudsman is not a very new one. The first journalist in the United States to suggest ombudsdmanship to regain trust was Ben H. Bagdikian in 1967 (Baydar n.d.), then an editor at the *Washington Post* subsequently. The first news ombudsman's post in the United States was created that year by the *Louisville Courier – Journal* in Kentucky. John Brown, who was the ombudsman at the *Edmonton Journal* (Canada), wrote a series of letters to his fellow ombudsmen in the late 1970s suggesting that an organization be established to share ideas and support each other.[8] In addition there was a big, bold and beautiful Organization of News Ombudsmen and Standard Editors (the 'ONO') established in the 1990s.

Accountability mechanism

The in-house ombudsman is already a reality in big media organisations. Persons of undoubted prestige and experience undertake to ensure that ethics are not only repressive (such as disciplinary boards, radio and television authorities and courts) but also preventive and, much more, for example, counselling and educational. The role of media ombudspersons is to shape a culture of respect for ethics rather than to denounce infringements in vain. A media outlet hiring a media ombudsman shows that it respects both its readers and its employees, adding yet another consultant to improve the quality of the content it produces. The media ombudsman is a person who offers added value to the operation of the media organisation itself, upgrades its relationship with the public and invests in enhancing its credibility (Dvorkin 2020). Ombudspersons in well-known international newspapers, such as the *Guardian*, have permanent columns in which they either develop ethical issues, answer questions and complaints from readers or comment on more general subjects concerning the principles of journalism. They are the new building block of an integrated accountability mechanism within the media organisation itself, as long as they adhere to the general principles governing good implementation by the institution.

However, there is still room for a central accountability media commission at the national level. The two forms of mechanism (ombudsman – commission) are not competitive, as has already been shown at the data protection field, where a national supervisory authority works together with the decentralized data protection officers. It is rather the 'proximity principle', namely the doctrine that the in-house ombudsman is better placed in order to deal with the targeted complaints that adds more value with the decentralized model (Getler 2017: n.pag.).

Scope

Stakeholders involved

The accountability mechanism that makes an advocate of the audience an integral part of it implies that the circle of those responsible is well defined. A law that would require, for example, the compulsory appointment of a media ombudsman, should specify which media organisations must appoint one.[9] This effort involves defining the circle of those media organisations that are primarily required to adhere to ethics. The answer to the question is not simple, as journalistic ethics by nature regulate journalistic activities of any kind, without specifying the media that must comply with it. It is about the scope of application and not businesses. But here we have to define the businesses themselves. And, as a result, we should exclude the ones that do not have to appoint an ombudsman.

It is certain that any multifaceted journalistic organization, regardless of the technical body integrating the news, would have to appoint an ombudsman. This includes any business in the field of television, print media and online information. The cycle is wide and does not seem to exclude any media category. One obvious exception, however, could be individual or very small media, such as blogs and personal websites. However, even in this case, a broader ombudsman for the media, one that does not solely serve such websites but has more media outlets under their supervision, could be provided for. In this way, no media would be excluded.

A question arises rapidly: To what extent is the application of an internal media ombudsman a realistic objective in an era where the number of permanent employees of media organizations is being constantly reduced. The answer is included in the question: The media ombudsman is a new work opportunity for journalists that already have a legal background. Furthermore, an experienced media ombudsman may have a very protecting function with the result of the extra-judicial resolution of disputes which could have led to lawsuits with enormous economic impact to the mere number of the other permanent employees. As the practical experience from the field of the data protection officers reality, the media ombudsman is a role that also can be outsourced (Donnely 2018).

Public and private media

The separation between public and private media is crucial in regard to legal provisions. Although journalistic ethics are common to the public and private sectors, there are some constitutional differences. Every public entity operates on the basis of the principle of legality, which means that the decision to operate an ombudsman must be integrated into a set of state rules of law, that is, legislation.

This was the example of the 'Auditor's Advocate' established by article 12 of Law 4173/2013 on the New Greek Internet Radio Television (NERIT):

Article 12 Mediator

1. The NERIT-SA Mediator is responsible for examining and expressing opinions on complaints and response requests on all the broadcasts and programmes of the Company.
2. The ombudsman shall be selected by the Board from a list of three candidates compiled by the Chief Executive Officer from reputable journalists, members of the NCRTV. The term of the ombudsman shall be three years and may be renewed for a maximum of one year. His compensation shall be determined by a joint decision of the Minister of Finance and the Minister responsible for Public Radio and Television in accordance with the relevant provisions in force.

However, this article was abolished by article 15 of Law 4324/2015.

In regard to private media, national legislation could also require the appointment of an ombudsman. The argument that this could be a form of state intervention in the operation of a private enterprise is certainly not negligible. Such an intervention would make the issue, by definition, self-regulatory. However, as the imposition of the definition of a Data Protection Officer (DPO) in private businesses has been acknowledged by the European legislator to be a legally legitimate intervention, the same could apply to media ombudspersons by analogy.

Even if there is no legislative intervention in the operation of the institution in the public or private sector, transparency is required in both cases. In the public sector, internal rules of procedure could regulate the functioning of the institution. In the private sector, a decision by the company's board of directors would be sufficient, and a possible amendment of the statute would also be an adequate institutional basis.

The selection process

The choice of the person that will embody the ombudsman is relevant to their qualifications. Opinion varies on whether a background in journalism or academia better prepares one for the media ombudsman's post (Baydar n.d.: 7). The issue of their qualifications, however, is directly related to the position they will have in the respective media organisation, as well as the tasks they will be called upon to perform. The procedure is more prestigious if it abides by a statutory decision regarding the general qualifications of the candidate. Journalist status may be desirable, with the problem of course being that they too would be subject to the journalistic ethics that they are required to persuade others to apply. However, this is not so much of a problem as it has already been addressed in the composition of the disciplinary boards of the authors' associations. Another solution would be, of course, to appoint an ombudsman or mediator of a different status.

Administrative status

Several parameters determine the position of the ombudsman within the journalistic organization they are called to serve. At the core of this position, the concept of independence needs to be found, that is, the moral prestige that emerges from it and the confidence of both the readers who will complain to the ombudsman and the journalists who serve in the media.

Management interlocutor

The media ombudsman must be called to all meetings (both at press meetings and at management meetings) to have a complete picture of the internal functioning of the media. Good knowledge of the internal operation of the instrument is not only necessary but a prerequisite for resolving disputes. The idea of having the independent ombudsman participate in management meetings was first adopted as a good practice by the Union of Data Protection Officers of the European Community institutions and subsequently formally established as a binding provision by the General Data Protection Regulation.[10]

Resources needed

To simply nominate a person as the ombudsman and to establish a set of internal rules does not suffice. What is required is effectiveness and this will only be ensured if the media administration provides the ombudsman with the necessary resources. This means initially setting up the administrative structure of an office and supporting the functioning of the institution with adequate staff. It also means the necessary salary. Finally, by analogy to GDPR provisions for DPOs, it also means the resources needed to maintain the ombudsman's expertise.[11]

Independence

Of course, the most crucial point, if the media ombudsman is to function properly, rests with their independence from the administration of the media they serve and the journalists who serve it. Independence is to a certain extent a matter for the ombudsman themselves: they of all people not only are to build trust relations with their colleagues but also with the public receiving the output of the media. For starters, it should be guaranteed that only the ombudsmen should edit ombudsmen's columns (Baydar n.d: 8). At the institutional level, independence is guaranteed by a ban on dismissal, equivalent to that of trade unionists. The dismissal of the ombudsman shall not be considered for reasons connected with the performance of their duties. However, the limitation of their term of office may also be a way to increase their independence: when one knows that they will serve in the media organisation on a contract with an expiry date, they will not easily compromise themselves, so they will be independent. But it not only is the term of their contract that could jeopardize the ombudsman's independence. Any negative change in the professional field can be considered a form of retaliation by the employer or the administration of the instrument. This means that sanctions and other adverse interference with the ombudsman's work, as established for the DPO, should be banned.[12]

Extroversion

The ombudsman not only is a diplomat who must communicate with the public but also with everyone in the media. They are the point of contact of the public with the media organisations. As in other segments of the market, there are customer service departments that receive requests and complaints, the ombudsman is the recipient of the feedback of the public and especially of negative statements on the part of media. This means that their name must be announced on the media website and must appear to have its place within the media organisation itself. An ombudsman's column in a newspaper, a five-minute radio or television station and their own microsite on the media website are forms of this extroversion. Of course, extroversion can include much more, such as organizing workshops and conferences, working with other ombudsmen as well as participating in ombudspersons' collective organizations. For example, the News Ombudsmen Organization holds an international conference every year.

Confidentiality

As much as the work of the ombudsman relates to transparency and openness, it is a given that trust is also built on respect for confidentiality. Not all complaints received by an ombudsman are disclosable. Although there are specific channels for reporting more serious and different corruption offenses, such as whistle-blower protection programmes, the ombudsman must respect the privacy and personal data of those who approach them. Breaching this confidentiality could not only result in the loss of confidence but also in legal penalties.

Tasks

The role of a media ombudsman is not very different from that of the other functions of an institution. Their job is to mediate when there is 'maladministration' or a breach of ethical rules. However, the nature of this mediation is not always bureaucratic and one-dimensional. There are several references for the different roles a news ombudsman has to play: the barking watchdog, the formal head of appeals, the anchor, the mediator, the representative of the audience, etc. (Mollerup n.d.). It seems the authors agree that a main form of a newspapers task is to write a weekly column in their newspaper or on the website discussing important complaints or comments sent by readers (Evers 2012).

Advising role

The basic attribute of a media ombudsman is knowledge of ethics and its practical application. As a source of knowledge for others and as a person constantly updated on good practices, they are inevitably a useful in-house consultant for journalists and other media workers. This role can be practiced completely informally, at the request of their colleagues in the media, as a legal adviser would do. That is why the ombudsman's extroversion will help journalists seek their advice on handling issues that they have to or are about to undertake. The counselling function is therefore preventive. Once the media ombudsman develops good relations with the media workers, they will have already made a very big step forward, one that can also help to avoid ethical violations.

Mediation mission

The core mission of every ombudsman is to receive complaints. A column of readers' letters always had a place in the press. At times, such letters highlighted omissions or illuminated readers' disagreements with media outlets. Hosting such letters was a democratic function of any media that sought dialogue with the reading public.

The ombudsman receives input from the media as well. They must therefore formulate a 'complaint box' to attract readers or other media to address them, citing their complaints. Consequently, shaping the conditions for receiving complaints is the first step of the mediation mission. An inaugural article is an ideal start. Along with announcing a phone line or email address or, ideally, formulating an online complaint form, where the complainant completes pre-set fields and is led step by step to submitting a complete and clear complaint to the ombudsman. Of course, before all these comes the obligation of the media organisation itself to inform the public about the existence of an ombudsman.

The second step to mediation is to establish the violation. Here the ombudsman has to investigate, first of all, whether the allegations actually hold. If the alleged problem has already taken place, the ombudsman must determine whether there is an ethical violation. This research may include interviews with the interested parties, research in literature, etc. The second stage of mediation ends with the decision that there is a violation of ethics – or not. If there is no violation, the mediation ends with an announcement to those concerned, and the case is considered closed.

But if there actually is an ethical violation, then the ombudsman should take action. In particular, they should propose a form of ethical 'rehabilitation'. In some cases, this can be done with a publication. For example, if it is found that the media outlet has reproduced fake news, then the ombudsman's intervention may move toward recommending that the truth be restored. A new publication with which the media outlet restores the truth, following the recommendation of the ombudsman, may be the appropriate restoration of ethics. The third stage of mediation is therefore the ombudsman's intervention aimed at such restoration. It is the most active stage of the mediation process.

The fourth and final stage is none other than the final outcome. Whatever the case, the ombudsman must inform the complainant of all the steps they have made and of the outcome of their intervention. If the media adheres to their recommendation, the fourth step is victorious. But if the media does not adhere, it is at this point that the ombudsman has the unpleasant role of separating their position and announcing what they have proposed and was ultimately rejected. Here they will confess of their failure, however, this will also prove their independence. It is also at this fourth stage when it can be announced that the complainant was ultimately not right and was found, for example, abusive or groundless.

Compliance monitoring

The ombudsman's broader mediation function may lead to different final outcomes. Their role is not only preventive (counselling) and firefighting (mediation) but also a general supervisory role for their ex-officio intervention when they find that something is wrong. The ombudsman must not only act when they are asked for advice or when they receive complaints but also when they notice violations. Their ex-officio intervention, when ethical violations are found, is also evidence of independence from the media itself. But it is also a potential pitfall in the ombudsman's attempt to build trust. Ex-officio investigations should not give the impression that the ombudsman is another internal auditor or prosecutor. Even when they discover ethics violations on their own, their mission as an ombudsman is to solve problems rather than create new ones. Therefore, the ombudsman will have to follow the mediation stages and, most notably, the third one, in which they propose solutions to restore ethics.

Conclusion

Clearly internal mediation is a tried and tested solution and a mechanism for effective application of journalistic ethics. The operating conditions vary slightly from public to private, but the general principles of transparency and accountability that are adhered to are central to the operation of any media organisation. The media ombudsman operates, on the one hand, as a sophisticated form of customer service for the media and, on the other, as an indispensable tool for preventing and finding practical solutions to remedy any ethical violations wherever they occur.

NOTES

1. See the Council of Europe's 'Guidelines on protecting freedom of expression and information in times of crisis' (Adopted by the Committee of Ministers on 26 September 2007 at the 1005th meeting of the Ministers' Deputies), and more recently, in the framework of the COVID-19 pandemic crisis, 'The impact of the sanitary crisis on freedom of expression and media freedom, Information Documents', SG/Inf(2020)19, 7 July 2020, http://www.coe.int.
2. See also International Federation of Journalists, Global Charter of Ethics for Journalists, https://www.ifj.org/who/rules-and-policy/global-charter-of-ethics-for-journalists.html (accessed 26 May 2021).
3. See also Lord Justice Leveson, *An Inquiry Into the Culture, Practices and Ethics of the Press*, Executive Summary, November 2012, p. 13, https://assets.publishing.service.gov.uk/government/uploads/system/uploads/attachment_data/file/229039/0779.pdf (accessed 26 May 2021).
4. Initially, Sweden decided in 1916 to establish a 'Swedish Press Council' to deal with the broad spectrum of complaints. The Council operated until 1969, when it was replaced by the Pressombudsman, 'as a response to increasing public dismay over unethical behaviour, particularly regarding violations of privacy, sensationalist reporting of crime and widespread character assassination of public figures'. See, for example, Baydar Y. (n.d.: 2), The ' "Lone Ranger" as the missionary of conscience: The role of the news ombudsman', https://bit.ly/3wu7mzi (accessed 26 May 2021).

5.   For further information, see also http://www.presscouncil.ie (accessed 26 May 2021).

6.   This was the suggestion for the United Kingdom, endorsed by the British and Irish Ombudsman Association. In a letter with the title 'The case for a media ombudsman' (27 March 2012) sent to the Leveson Inquiry Team, the Association proposed the establishment of a national media ombudsman service. See also https://bit.ly/3wAMG8S (accessed 26 May 2021).

7.   See also Lord Justice Leveson, *An Inquiry into the Culture, Practices and Ethics of the Press*, Executive Summary, November 2012, p. 37, https://bit.ly/3wthetc (accessed 26 May 2021).

8.   See also 'The history of ONO', https://www.newsombudsmen.org/the-history-of-ono/ (accessed 26 May 2021).

9.   This was the case with the EU General Regulation on Data Protection (the 'GDPR') which imposes for certain categories of controllers to appoint a 'data protection officer'.

10. 'The controller and the processor shall ensure that the data protection officer is involved, properly and in a timely manner, in all issues which relate to the protection of personal data.' Article 38 para. 1 to the GDPR.

11. 'The controller and processor shall support the data protection officer in performing the tasks referred to in Article 39 by providing resources necessary to carry out those tasks and access to personal data and processing operations, and to maintain his or her expert knowledge.' Article 38 para. 2 to the GDPR.

12. 'The controller and processor shall ensure that the data protection officer does not receive any instructions regarding the exercise of those tasks. He or she shall not be dismissed or penalised by the controller or the processor for performing his tasks. The data protection officer shall directly report to the highest management level of the controller or the processor.' Article 38 para. 3 to GDPR.

FURTHER READING

Ayeni, V. (1985), 'A typology of ombudsman institutions', *Occasional Paper*, 30, Edmonton Alta.: International Ombudsman Institute.

Baydar, Y. (n.d.), 'The "Lone Ranger" as the missionary of conscience: The role of the news ombudsman', UNESCO, http://www.unesco.org/new/fileadmin/MULTIMEDIA/HQ/CI/CI/pdf/Events/Journalism_Ethics_and_Self-regulation_in_Europe/background_papers/Yavuz%20Baydar%201.pdf. Accessed 24 May 2021.

Donnely, C. (2018), 'The DPO role and why you should consider outsourcing it', It Government, https://www.itgovernance.eu/blog/en/the-dpo-role-and-why-you-should-consider-outsourcing-it. Accessed 24 May 2021.

Dunne, S. (2017), 'Policing the press: The institutionalization of independent press regulation in a Liberal/North Atlantic media system', Ph.D. thesis, Dublin: Dublin City University, http://doras.dcu.ie/21957/1/Stephen_Dunne_PhD.pdf. Accessed 24 May 2021.

Dvorkin, J.A. (2016), 'Does an ombudsman do any good?', https://www.npr.org/sections/publi ceditor/2006/01/31/5180984/does-an-ombudsman-do-any-good?t=1572262500693. Accessed 24 May 2021.

Fielden, L. (2017), 'Regulating the press: A comparative study of international press councils', Reuter Institute, https://reutersinstitute.politics.ox.ac.uk/sites/default/files/2017-11/ Regulating%20the%20Press.pdf. Accessed 24 May 2021.

Foley, M. (2008), 'Finally: An ombudsman', Press Council and Code of Conduct for Ireland, https://arrow.dit.ie/cgi/viewcontent.cgi?article=1041&context=aaschmedart. Accessed 24 May 2021.

Palen, F. S. (1979), 'Media ombudsmen: A critical review', *Law & Society Review*, 13:3, pp. 79–850.

Salamone D. (2020), 'Does the mainstream media need to bring back the Ombudsman to restore credibility and trust?', University of Missouri, https://mospace.umsystem.edu/xmlui/ bitstream/handle/10355/79890/Salamone-analysis.pdf?sequence=2. Accessed 24 May 2021.

Zagoria, S. (1986), 'Press Ombudsmen', *Occasional Paper*, 34, Edmonton Alta: International Ombudsman Institute, n.pag.

REFERENCES

Bezanson, R. (1999), 'The developing law of editorial judgment', *Nebraska Law Review*, 78:4, pp. 754–57.

Dvorkin, J.A. (2020), 'The MODERN news ombudsman: A user's guide', https://www.newsom budsmen.org/wp-content/uploads/2020/02/ONO-HANDBOOK-REVISED-EDITION.pdf. Accessed 24 May 2021.

Evers, H. (2012), 'The news ombudsman: Lighting rod or watchdog?', Netherlands: Fontys University of Applied Sciences, https://cejc.ptks.pl/attachments/The-news-ombudsman-Lightn ing-rod-or-watchdog_2018-05-21_09-55-51.pdf. Accessed 24 May 2021.

Getler, M. (2017), 'Why media organisations need ombudsmen', European Journalism Observatory, https://en.ejo.ch/media-economics/why-news-organisations-need-ombudsmen. Accessed 24 May 2021.

Harashima Y. (2018), 'The grumpy scold in the house', ONO, https://www.newsombudsmen. org/the-grumpy-scold-in-the-house/?fbclid=IwAR1alPXipg5RczMB7n-snVSAJYVUhyCU 8KcJ7vOzFSuDuQKF04t8MccY7DE. Accessed 6 January 2022.

Mollerup, J. (n.d.), 'On public service broadcasting and ombudsmanship', http://www.unesco. org/new/fileadmin/MULTIMEDIA/HQ/CI/CI/pdf/Events/Journalism_Ethics_and_Self-regul ation_in_Europe/background_papers/Jacob%20Mollerup.pdf. Accessed 24 May 2021.

Moyo, L. (2016), 'Crossing taboo lines: Citizen journalism ethics in political crisis settings', https://link.springer.com/chapter/10.1057%2F9781137554505_3. Accessed 24 May 2021.

Saoussen B. C. (2020), 'Covid-19 exacerbates freedom of expression pressures in Middle East and North Africa', Ethical Journalism Network, https://ethicaljournalismnetwork.org/covid-19-exacerbates-freedom-of-expression-pressures-in-middle-east-and-north-africa?fbclid=IwAR3UCXQ4ZIO0FoaoyO8l90rLjSkb4PqlzyYIy5_nZnTPrQRZCz5sivk3-kM. Accessed 6 January 2022.

Smyrnaios, N., Chauvet. S, and Marty, E. (2017), 'The impact of CrossCheck on journalists & the audience', First Draft News, https://firstdraftnews.org/wp-content/uploads/2017/11/Crosscheck_rapport_EN_1129.pdf/. Accessed 24 May 2021.

PART III

JOURNALISM EDUCATION

PROPOSAL 5

TECHNOLOGY AND EDUCATION

8

Why Do We Need Trained Journalists? The Need for an Improved Training for Media Professionals Today and the Responsibility of Media Companies

Lida Tsene

Introduction

The field of media is facing a multifaceted crisis. More and more journalists are losing their jobs, while at the same time new digital skills become critical for traditional and experienced professionals as well as for younger ones (Gillmor 2010). This chapter aims to explore the reasons why it is absolutely necessary that journalists receive improved training by focusing on the skills they have to acquire and how media organisations can contribute. Media organizations every year score lower both on trust and on income as audiences ask for more transparency and pluralism in the process of gathering and disseminating information. According to a Gallup Poll from 2018, which measured confidence in major institutions in the United States, newspapers and television news were among the lowest, exceeded only by Congress. In addition, as Reuters Digital News Report for 2018 highlighted, over half (54 per cent) of the polled sample agree or strongly agree that they are concerned about what is real and fake on the internet. At the same time and according to the same source, 'most respondents believe that publishers (75 per cent) and platforms (71 per cent) have the biggest responsibility to fix problems of fake and unreliable news. This is because much of the news they complain about relates to biased or inaccurate news from the mainstream media rather than news that is completely made up or distributed by foreign powers' (Reuters 2018: 10).

In addition, established business models seem to fail due to the reduction of advertising budgets and the reluctance of citizens to pay for content they neither trust nor like (Newman et al. 2017). For example, 'measured by revenues, the newspaper industry in the United States has shrunk to 60 per cent of its size a decade ago' (Franklin 2014: 482). For the first time in their history, platforms such as Facebook are also facing a crisis, when it comes to news consumption. Users, according to Reuters Digital News Report (2018), prefer more personalized messaging applications (WhatsApp, Messenger, Viber) for sharing and commenting on the news, placing Facebook low in the list of credible media. In addition, fake news has invaded our reality, promoting numerous dubious stories, coming from traditional, digital and social media. At the same time, digital economy makes the boundaries of journalism fluid. In 2013, Arianna Huffington in an attempt to predict the future of journalism wrote, '[T]he future will definitely be a hybrid one, combining the best practices of traditional journalism – fairness, accuracy, storytelling, deep investigations – with the best tools available to the digital world – speed, transparency, and, above all, engagement' (Huffington 2013: n.pag.).

According to Chadwick (2017: 11), 'hybrid media systems are built upon the interaction between new and old media and all the related technologies, genres, behaviours and organizations'. Within this context, and to remain competitive and sustainable, professional journalism has to redefine constantly the list of necessary skills and knowledge and invest in a lifelong education and continuous and unproved training. However, media industries should realize that the most efficient and long-term investment does not involve equipment or technologies, but their personnel.

The need for ongoing journalism training

We live in an era where new media and social platforms bring changes to every aspect of human life. Whether we look in theoretical frameworks or practices, we see that the educational process is starting to move toward learning networks, collaborative learning, creativity, innovation, self-directed knowledge and a trend to adapt to the continuous changes in the environments in which learning is taking place (Sahlberg 2009). Education 2.0 is the current trend, deriving from more classical learning theories or communities of practice and heading to more modern theories,

> questioning the current educational models: (a) through the transformation of the teaching process (pedagogical aspect), (b) by placing new requirements in the administration of the teaching process (administrative aspect), (c) by involving new educational tools (technological aspect) that contribute to a more complete and without discrimination education for citizens.
>
> (Vagelatos, Foskolos, Komninos, 2010: 202)

Along with the new models, come new theories focusing on learner autonomy and connectivism. As stated by several researchers in the field of self-directed learning, learner autonomy is rather important (Kop and Fournier 2010), while web 3.0, 'an integrated Web experience where the machine will be able to understand and catalogue data in a manner similar to humans' (Rudman and Bruwer 2016: 137), is emerging. On the other hand, various social platforms create networks and advance peer to peer collaboration in the learning process too. According to Sein-Echaluce et al. (2019: 645) 'learning 2.0 supported by the Web 2.0 model is based on the idea that students are creators of resources that can be used by students and teachers'. In addition, learning does not take place in a single environment and educational routine changes frequently (Kop and Fournier 2010). In that context, educators and faculty members experiment and try to change the educational structures that have been the norm for centuries (Kop and Fournier 2010). As Poore (2014: 167) states,

> the role of the teacher in the Web 3.0 landscape must be understood as one of discernment – that is, the ability to judge and judge well on the part of both teacher *and* learner – for it is discernment that underlies the uniquely human ability to create meaning and thus make sense of the world.

Distance learning techniques and applications, e-learning, massive open online courses (MOOCs) and mobile learning are the growing trends in an era where knowledge is decentralized and distributed through different channels and where skills, and not degrees, are our access, not our assets.

Journalism today does require a mix of old and new skills, as technology evolves. Deuze (2006: 23) presented two journalism education models – a Western model and a blended model – that both provide 'practical skills training, on the one hand, and general contextual education and liberal arts courses, on the other hand'. At the same time, for more than a decade, research has shown a disconnection between the journalism skills learned in college and the needs of the workforce (Wenger et al. 2018). A 2013 Poynter News University study of journalism education found that just,

> 39 percent of [US] educators say journalism education keeps up with industry changes a little or not at all. News editors and staffers are even harsher, with 48 percent saying J-schools are not keeping up with changes in the field.
> (Poynter News University 2013: n.pag.)

According to research (Iordanidou and Tsene 2018), media professionals in Greece consider that new journalists are not efficiently groomed for what lies in the contemporary journalistic context. According to them, they are not exposed sufficiently to practical initiatives, or they lack a more theoretical background that will allow them to analyse and interpret information. Additionally, the need of professional journalists to cope with the new environment and face the crisis in their profession results in the need to develop lifelong learning programmes that will offer journalists new skills and capabilities, especially technological, multimedia and data skills. Auger et al. (2017) highlights the simultaneous conceptual and practical goals of a journalism curriculum, while Mensing and Ryfe (Poynter News University 2013) argue that the teaching hospital metaphor, a model of learning-by-doing that includes college students, professors and professionals working together under one ' "digital roof" for the benefit of a community' proffered by Newton (2013: n.pag.) and others, puts too much emphasis on production, turning journalism schools into 'production facilities staffed by industry professionals who have left an industry in deep distress'. The report on journalism education by Poynter News University (2013: n.pag.) suggests that reconnection with communities as participants rather than professionals,

> facilitation and moderation, experimenting with small entrepreneurial businesses, collaborating with computer scientists, artists, and urban planners might not produce coverage of many city council meetings (although it could) but it may help journalism programs contribute research and development that will be more valuable to the long-term future of journalism.

In an era where journalists seem unsatisfied with their basic education and where new needs arise in the context of digital economy, lifelong training appears to be a necessity.

The changing role of education: Journalism in the digital era and the need for new (old) skills

As the field of journalism is becoming more and more complex with different actors and different backgrounds co-producing the news, the definition and practice of journalism are becoming more complex as well.

> From CNN iReport contributors to reporters at the *New York Times*, all are capable of committing acts of journalism. Some do it better than others, some have more resources than others, and something is gained when reporting is done by stable organizations with money, logistics and legal services – but all are capable.
> (Peters and Tandoc 2013: 61–62)

However, Jeff Jarvis (2013: n.pag.) notes that 'there are not journalists, only the service of journalism'. At the same time, social media platforms and digital networks create a new media landscape. Audiences and various content producers can interact more, be connected, access multiple sources. In addition, a new culture is rising based on the virtues of collaboration, transparency and pluralism, opposing to the credibility and financial crisis of contemporary media organizations.

Within this framework, j-schools today are trying to keep up with all the new developments, balancing between theory and practice, to change the belief that journalists are not 'knowledge savvy'. Folkerts (2014: 289) maintains that

> a broader understanding is essential for journalism schools to survive in this new age. Journalism education has, to a great degree, ignored the larger contours of the digital age – the rise of an information society and the nature of convergence that goes beyond multi-platform applications and transition to mobile devices.

Which are the new (old) skills a journalist should acquire today? Jiang and Rafeeq (2019: 9) argue that 'several US studies of journalism job skills in 2012 and 2015 show that employers view social media and audience engagement, as well as web-posting, to be critical skills in newsrooms', while according to them, 'as newsrooms are redesigned to accommodate the demands of the digital media industry, new hires for journalism positions are "expected to have a basic knowledge of Google Fusion Tables, HTML, CSS, JavaScript and who knows what else. Some ability to use a more advanced programming language also appears as a requirement for some jobs"' (Vallance-Jones 2014: 19).

Although we are constantly talking about new skills in the media landscape, many surveys (Josephi 2019; Örnebring and Mellado 2018) prove that still, the most wanted skills by journalists are the most traditional, such as sourcing, verifying and communicating news,skills that ' set journalists apart from other information providers' (Josephi 2019: 685). According to Örnebring and Mellado's (2018: 458) cross-national comparative study in six European countries and in a sample of 2238 journalists, 'reporting skills are considered the most important everywhere, pointing to the overall cross-national dominance of the reporter ideal among journalists: being out in the field, talking to people, doing research, and working independently (alone)'. In addition, Patterson (2013) argues that even now, in our era, where we are discussing the new role of journalists, truth, transparency, verification of news, but mostly deep knowledge and understanding of contemporary society remain core values to media professionals. In the same vein, Iordanidou Tsene and Kyritsis' (2016) survey found that media professionals tend to think of journalists as professionals who have to be equipped with a vast knowledge-based background, stressing the opinion that skills are not enough and that despite the technological evolution, truth and fact-checking will always be important to the profession.

Why the improved training of every professional in the media is a necessity today and the role of media companies

One can argue that the need for trained journalists today not only is crucial for themselves but also for media companies and the media sector in general. And although, the list of answers to the question why we need trained journalists today is long, we will attempt to highlight the most important ones:

- Financial crisis stimulates competition. The more equipped you are today, the more chances you have to survive. The combination of journalistic research skills with more technical ones (editing, photojournalism etc.) allows for more flexibility.
- At the same time, the constant reduction of permanent personnel in media organizations creates new challenges. We are reliving the freelance era, and journalists seek new ways to offer their products and to fundraise.
- Technology changes the way we produce and consume news. Training for the new digital platforms but also for how they can be used for research and fact-checking is a necessity.
- As mentioned earlier, audiences keep doubting journalists and search for alternative means of information.
- Finally, audiences are becoming more demanding, asking for interesting stories presented with innovative storytelling techniques. The era of augmented reality and artificial intelligence is here.

The ongoing training of journalists is becoming crucial for them. Stephen Engelberg, ProPublica's editor-in-chief and co-CEO, has stated that 'we all know that the greatest need right now is people in the world of journalism who are not innumerate. And we know, when you train people in those fields, they will have jobs' (Lynch 2015: 27). Interaction between journalists, citizens, algorithms and computing machines makes the boundaries of journalism fluid, and within this fluidity, we are seeking the skills and factors that will allow journalism to survive. Knowledge could be one of those factors. In post-industrial journalism, Anderson et al. (2014: 50) remind us that,

> the journalist has not been replaced but displaced, moved higher up the editorial chain from the production of initial observations to a role that emphasizes

verification and interpretation, bringing sense to the streams of text, audio, photos and video produced by the public.

So, if journalists wish to remain competitive and relevant, they should move on from the role of content producer to the role of interpreter. That means nothing more than constant training and return to knowledge.

But what are the benefits for media companies? Why should they undertake the cost of retraining their staff? How could this investment contribute to the survival of quality journalism? In an era where the media are listed among the least trusted institutions (Edelman 2019), could well-trained journalists be part of the solution?

This question is related to a notion we come across so often, both as an academic term and as a demand from the audiences, but without a clear definition – quality journalism. 'Judgments of quality are often culture-specific or related to one's socio-economic background, level of education and so on' (Vehkoo 2010: 4). Going back to 1968, Merrill in Vehkoo (2010: 7) states that,

> a quality paper's popularity is not built on voyeurism, sensationalism, or prurience. It offers its readers facts (in a meaningful context), ideas, interpretation; in short, it presents a continuing education. It gives its reader the feeling that he is getting a synthesized look at the most significant happenings and thinking of the day.

After studying various criteria measuring quality journalism, Vehkoo (2010: 21) concludes that,

> my own view is, that much like good literature, good journalism tries to make sense of the chaotic world around us. It gives context and background to events. It interprets, analyses, and strives to give meaning to all the babbling that's going on. It looks beyond the obvious and behind the trickery, but also forward, to where we are being led by the ones who are in power.

Jeff Jarvis (2008: n.pag.) notes,

> I would add responsiveness as a mark of quality: Are we delivering to the public what it wants – and are we listening to find out what it wants? Do we open the means for our stories to be corrected and expanded? Do we have a way to hear the public's definition of quality? Collaboration, I'd say, is the highest form of responsiveness.

Bringing into the discussion the relationship between quality and money in the journalistic field, Lacy in Vehkoo (2010: 11) underlines 'ask any newspaper editor if money guarantees quality journalism, and the editor will likely deny it.

Yet, ask that same editor if money can help him or her improve the quality of news reporting and the answer will be "of course"'. The relationship between financing newsrooms and content quality is complex: 'Money is not sufficient for content quality, but for a news organization to produce high quality content consistently over time, sufficient financial support is crucial' (Lacy in Vehkoo 2010: 12). At the same time, as audiences become more demanding, media are trying to invent new ways for attracting and keeping them. Vehkoo (2010: 69) argues,

> [C]ontent must come before business models, for business reasons too. If you claim to offer high quality, then you need to invest in it. If you are thinking of charging for content, then you have to have the kind of content that people are willing to pay for.

Rosenstiel and Mitchell in Vehkoo (2010) attempted to identify whether good journalism is still good business. Their study pointed out 'that investing more in the newsroom (news hole, staffing, etc.) appears to have a more powerful association to growing revenues than investing in circulation and advertising departments' (Vehkoo 2010: 14).

Reuters has already developed multiple assets for training its journalists, from multimedia platforms to mobile journalism tools and from data journalism tools to interactive graphics apps (Ciobanu 2016). In a similar vein, the *New York Times* have initiated a course to teach their reporters data skills, which they then open-sourced to other media companies and journalists. Jane Barrett (Ciobanu 2016: n.pag.), global multimedia editor at *Reuters*, claims that 'changing people's mindsets and behaviours can be done by investing in skills and technology, and those two things should be done in tandem, like the pedals of a bicycle', as she stresses the need for media companies to undertake the effort and cost of educating their staff.

A rather interesting example of how well-trained journalists might lead to quality journalism is that of the BBC. BBC is a leading organization in media industry as

> more than half of people in the UK regard the BBC as their most trusted source of news, according to a survey commissioned by campaign group 38 Degrees, while half of respondents ranked it first as a trusted source of balanced and unbiased reporting.
>
> (Plunkett 2016: n.pag.)

The BBC in 2009 launched the BBC Academy with an aim to offer to its staff ongoing training in the fields of journalism, production, technology and leadership. With a combination of online and offline courses, access to various resources provides free training to the 7500 journalists working for the BBC and paid courses for collaborating journalists within the United Kingdom. As Mark Byford, Chair of the Academy Board, stated at the beginning of the initiative, 'The BBC is determined to support the wider UK media industry through difficult times and, by sharing valuable training resources like the College of Journalism, we can help to secure the best standards and learning in the world' (BBC 2009: n.pag.).

So, why should and how could media companies contribute to the training of their journalists? According to Reuters Institute for the study of Journalism, 'Media and technology trends and predictions' (Newman 2018) 36 per cent of the participants stated that the greatest obstacles in the success of media companies are not technological platforms and tools but internal hindrances such as their resistance to change and their inability to innovate. Investing in their staff's training could lead to an increase in productivity, creativity and innovation inside newsrooms. The Facebook Journalism Project highlights quality and innovation as core to its training scheme. As they state on their website,

> We work and invest in institutes dedicated to funding high-quality journalism and building sustainable futures for community-based news. We partner directly with news publishers and non-profit organizations to combat misinformation, promote news literacy, fund new initiatives, share best practices, and improve journalism on our platform.
>
> (facebookjournalismproject.com 2021: n.pag)

Since 2017, 13,000 journalists across 46 countries have been trained so far, while another 100,000 have enrolled into courses they created with Poynter Institute, proving an actual demand by journalists themselves to obtain more training. According to Poynter News University's report 'Constant training: New normal or missed opportunity?' (2014) almost nine out of ten journalists (i.e., 88 per cent) said they could absorb more training, especially training that is digitally focused. However, lack of time and lack of funds prevented them from obtaining the training they wanted. This is where media companies can contribute, by helping their staff to continually access more knowledge, covering expenses and allowing them time to participate in educational activities.

Conclusion

Vartan Gregorian, President of the Carnegie Corporation of New York, which recently funded an effort to improve journalism education, says, 'Journalism is "the quintessential knowledge profession"' and as such 'deserves the best educated and trained practitioners' (Mencher 2006: n.pag.). This statement summarizes the importance of educated journalists, especially in an era where the profession is being questioned and journalists are striving either to maintain their job or to find a new one. Media companies should realize that to stay competitive within a fast-changing market they have to invest in the production of quality content, engaging stories and impactful news items. According to a report by the Centre for International Media Assistance (2008: 36),

> [T]he reasoning is straightforward: better-trained journalists offer a direct path to transforming the overall media landscape. When professional expectations are raised, media professionals are more likely to strive to achieve better results. Quality reporting, editing and design can boost circulation and help develop a market-place better able to support independent media. Specialized training in investigative reporting can sharpen the media's role as public watchdog, helping developing nations battle stubborn problems of crime and corruption.

The ongoing training of their journalists might lead to such outcomes and create a new paradigm for newsrooms. But what kind of training do they need and what might be the impact of investing in lifelong learning? Knight Foundation's report *Digital Training Comes of Age* (2012: 3) argues, '[P]rofessional development has impact. Training helps journalists adopt new digital tools, create change in their organizations, or find new ways to be part of the news ecosystem'. Of course, understanding and handling digital platforms and multimedia tools is necessary. Is this enough, though? According to Franklin (2014), the transformation of journalism in this 'age of digital media' has not merely created new topics, themes and subjects for scholars to investigate and explore in order to complement the existing concerns of journalism studies. Rather, the considerable changes to all aspects of journalism have challenged journalism scholars to revisit in a fresh context and guise, perennial questions, such as, 'What is journalism?' and 'Who is a journalist?' As mentioned earlier, skills such as research, verification, understanding of contemporary society, critical thinking, ethics, as well as interdisciplinary knowledge remain rather important for journalists. The new model for today's journalist is close to what scholars (Mencher 2006; Patterson 2013) call knowledgeable reporter or knowledge-based journalist: a journalist that has a vast and interdisciplinary knowledge and is not only not only able to report news but also to fact-check, analyse and interpret them. To do that, training should mainly be focused on how a contemporary journalist should analyse and interpret news, act as a curator and a navigator for public opinion in the vast information landscape. Therefore, if media organizations are willing to undertake the cost, time and overall investment in equipping journalists with that knowledge background, maybe in a few years we will be able to talk about another revolution in the field of media: quality journalism.

REFERENCES

Anderson, C. W., Bell, E. and Shirky C. (2014), 'Post industrial journalism: Adapting to the present', *Tow Center for Digital Journalism*, New York: Columbia Journalism School, pp. 1–126.

Auger, G. A., Tanes-Ehle, Z. and Gee, C. (2017), 'A phenomenological study of student experiences in a multiplatform journalism course', *Journalism & Mass Communication Educator*, 72, pp. 212–27.

BBC (2009), 'Press Release: BBC opens up training to industry: Major new partnerships unveiled as BBC Academy launches', BBC, http://www.bbc.co.uk/pressoffice/pressreleases/stories/2009/12_december/14/academy.shtml. Accessed 15 September 2019.

Centre for International Media Assistance (2008), 'Empowering independent media', https://www.cima.ned.org/wp-content/uploads/2015/02/CIMA-Empowering_Independent_Media.pdf. Accessed 15 September 2019.

Chadwick, A. (2017), *The Hybrid Media System: Politics and Power*, Oxford: Oxford University Press.

Ciobanu, M. (2016), 'How Reuters trains its journalists to work with new technologies and collaborate in the newsroom', Journalism, https://www.journalism.co.uk/news/how-reuters-trains-its-journalists-to-work-with-new-technologies-and-collaborate-in-the-newsroom/s2/a694103/. Accessed 20 September 2019.

Deuze, M. (2006), 'Global journalism education: A conceptual approach', *Journalism Studies*, 7:1, pp. 19–34.

Edelman (2019), 'Edelman Trust Barometer 2019', https://www.edelman.com/trust-barometer. Accessed 20 September 2019.

Facebook Journalism Project (2021), facebookjournalismproject.com. Accessed 28 December 2019.

Folkerts, J. (2014), 'History of journalism education', *Journalism & Communication Monographs*, 16, pp. 227–99.

Franklin, B. (2014), 'The future of journalism', *Journalism Studies*, 15:5, pp. 481–99.

Gallup (2018), 'Americans' confidence in U.S. institutions, 2018', https://news.gallup.com/poll/236243/military-small-business-police-stir-confidence.aspx. Accessed 20 September 2019.

Gillmor, D. (2010), *Mediactive*, Sebastopol: Dan Gillmor.

Huffington, A. (2013), 'Bezos, Heraclitus and the hybrid future of journalism', *Huffington Post*, 14 August, https://www.huffpost.com/entry/future-of-journalism_b_3756207. Accessed 19 September 2019.

Iordanidou, S. and Tsene, L. (2018), 'Redefining journalism: Practicing and teaching journalism in Greece', unpublished research, Advanced Media Institute.

Iordanidou, S., Tsene, L. and Kyritsis, M. (2016), 'New learning skills for journalists in the digital era through open and e-learning platforms: The case of Greece and Cyprus', *Medias Numeriques & Communications Electronique*, 4th Intenational Conference Université du Havre, Actes du Colloque International, Université du Havre, 1–3 June, pp. 305–15.

Jarvis, J. (2008), 'Defining quality in journalism', Buzz Machine, https://buzzmachine.com/2008/04/27/defining-quality-in-journalism/. Accessed 25 September 2019.

Jarvis, J. (2013), 'There are no journalists', Buzz Machine, https://buzzmachine.com/2013/06/30/there-are-no-journalists-there-is-only-journalism/. Accessed 25 September 2019.

Jiang, S. and Rafeeq, A. (2019), 'Connecting the classroom with the newsroom in the digital age: An investigation of journalism education in the UAE, UK and USA', *Asia Pacific Media Educator*, 29:1, pp. 3–22.

Josephi, B. (2019), 'Which bedrock in a sea of change?', *Journalism*, 20:5, pp. 679–87.

Knight Foundation (2012), 'Digital training comes of an age', Knight Foundation, https://kf-site-production.s3.amazonaws.com/publications/pdfs/000/000/145/original/KFTrainingFieldReportWEB.pdf. Accessed 25 September 2019.

Kop, R. and Fournier, H. (2010), 'New dimensions to self-directed learning in an open networked learning environment', *International Journal of Self-Directed Learning*, 7:2, http://selfdirectedlearning.com/documents/Kop&Fournier2010.pdf. Accessed 16 September 2019.

Lynch, D. (2015), 'Above and beyond: Looking the future of journalism education', Knight Foundations, https://www.knightfoundation.org/media/uploads/publication_pdfs/KF-Above-and-Beyond-Report.pdf. Accessed 16 September 2019.

Mencher, M. (2006), 'Will the meaning of journalism survive?', *Nieman Reports*, https://niemanreports.org/articles/will-the-meaning-of-journalism-survive/. Accessed 15 September 2019.

Newman, N. (2018), 'Media and technology trends and predictions', Reuters Institute for the Study of Journalism, https://reutersinstitute.politics.ox.ac.uk/sites/default/files/2018-01/RISJ%20Trends%20and%20Predictions%202018%20NN.pdf. Accessed 25 September 2019.

Newman, N., Fletcher, R., Kalogeropoulos, A., Levy, D. A. L. and Nielsen, R. (2017), 'Digital news report', http://www.digitalnewsreport.org/survey/2017/. Accessed 25 September 2019.

Newman, N., Fletcher R., Kalogeropoulos, An., Levy D. A. L. and Nielsen, R. K. (2018), 'Digital news report', Reuters Institute for the Study of Journalism, http://media.digitalnewsreport.org/wp-content/uploads/2018/06/digital-news-report-2018.pdf?x89475. Accessed 25 September 2019.

Newton, E. (2013), 'Searchlights and sunglasses: Field notes from the digital age of journalism', Searchlights and Sunglasses, http://www.searchlightsandsunglasses.org. Accessed 15 September 2019.

Örnebring, H. and Mellado, C. (2018), 'Valued skills among journalists: An exploratory comparison of six European nations', *Journalism*, 19:4, pp. 445–63.

Patterson, T. (2013), 'Informing the news: The need for knowledge-based reporting', https://journalistsresource.org/tip-sheets/research/knowledge-based-reporting/. Accessed 25 September 2019.

Peters, J. and Tandoc, E. Jr. (2013), 'People who aren't really reporters at all, who gave no professional qualifications: Defining a journalist and deciding who may claim the privileges', *NYU Journal of Legislation and Public Policy Quorum* 34, pp. 34–63.

Plunkett, J. (2016), 'BBC "News most trusted source for more than half of people in the UK"', *The Guardian*, 10 March, https://www.theguardian.com/media/2016/mar/10/bbc-news-most-trusted-source-for-more-than-half-of-people-in-the-uk. Accessed 25 September 2019.

Poore, M. (2014), 'The next G Web: Discernment, meaning-making, and the implications of Web 3.0 for education', *Technology, Pedagogy and Education*, 23:2, pp. 167–80.

Poynter News University (2013), 'State of journalism education 2013', http://www.newsu.org/course_files/StateOfJournalismEducation2013.pdf. Accessed 8 September 2019.

Rudman, R. and Bruwer, R. (2016), 'Defining Web 3.0: Opportunities and challenges', *The Electronic Library*, 34:1, pp. 132–54.

Sahlberg, P. (2009), 'Creativity and innovation through lifelong learning', European Training Foundation, http://pasisahlberg.com/wp-content/uploads/2013/01/Creativity-and-innovation-in-LLL-2009.pdf. Accessed 5 September 2019.

Sein-Echaluce, M. L., Fidalgo-Blanco, Á. and Esteban-Escaño, J. (2019), 'Technological ecosystems and ontologies for an educational model based on Web 3.0', *Universal Access in the Information Society*, 18:3, pp. 645–58.

Shirky, C. (2008), 'What newspapers and journalism need now: Experimentation, not nostalgia', Britannica, http://www.britannica.com/blogs/2008/04/what-newspapers-and-journalism-need-now-experimentation-not-nostalgia/. Accessed 15 September 2019.

Vagelatos, A.T., Foskolos, F. K. and Komninos, T. P. (2010), 'Education 2.0: Bringing innovation to the classroom', Tripoli, Greece, 10–12 September, *14th Panhellenic Conference on Informatics*, pp. 201–04.

Vallance-Jones, F. (2014), 'Data journalism continues to gain popularity: There are more opportunities than ever to learn', *Media*, 16:2, pp. 19–20.

Vehkoo, J. (2010), 'What is quality journalism and how it can be saved', Reuters Institute for the Study of Journalism, https://reutersinstitute.politics.ox.ac.uk/sites/default/files/research/files/What%2520is%2520Quality%2520Journalism%2520and%2520how%2520can%2520it%2520be%2520saved%2527.pdf. Accessed 10 September 2019.

Wenger, D. H., Owens, L. C. and Cain, J. (2018), 'Help wanted: Realigning journalism education to meet the needs of top U.S. news companies', *Journalism & Mass Communication Educator*, 73:1, pp. 18–36.

9

Social Media:
Further Anxieties for
Media and Journalists?

Chrysi Dagoula

Introduction

The relationship between journalism and the internet has gone through various phases since the emergence of the World Wide Web in the early 1990s. Over the last decades, we have witnessed a transition from a diffused awkwardness to its full adaptation in journalistic practices, including different stages in between. A turning point though occurred around 2005, when this relationship entered a new phase, the so-called 'social media era'. This chapter approaches the incorporation of social media platforms into journalistic practices as a double-edged sword (Lee 2015), considering social media both as opportunity and as a challenge for journalism.[1] By focusing on arguably the most journalistic social media platform, Twitter, the chapter firstly frames the discussion and then it moves to an evaluation of previous research media actors' use of Twitter in the United Kingdom (as conducted by the author), by specifically looking into the adaptation of the platform by various media actors.

Focus: Twitter as a journalistic tool

What makes Twitter important for journalism is its journalistic potential – as Murthy highlights, 'Twitter has been prominently associated with journalism, both in terms of shifts in journalistic practice as well as its facilitating of citizen journalism'(Murthy 2013: 51). Contrary to other social networking sites (SNSs), Twitter is an open social networking space that enables every internet user to track breaking news on any occasion (Bruns 2012: 2). Profiles can be public, unlocked and accessible to anyone, either registered or non-registered users. When Twitter first emerged in 2006, it was characterized as the 'SMS of the Internet' or

> a short message service, a phone call, an e-mail and a blog: less cumbersome than keeping a blog, less exclusive than talking to one person on a phone, less formal than e-mail exchange and less elaborate than most SNSs.
>
> (van Dijck 2012: 3)

However, its user-centred philosophy along with the development of its conversational markers (replies, retweets) and hashtags changed the narrative very quickly. Farhi referred to the 'Twitter explosion' (2009), especially in relation to its journalistic potential; Bruno (2010) analysed the 'Twitter effect' with direct reference to 'the CNN effect'; Stross (2016) discussed Twitter as the 'first draft of the present' and even the 'first draft of journalism'. Besides, Twitter's CEO's words on its ninth birthday are quite revealing about this journalistic potential: 'Journalists were a big part of why we grew so quickly and still a big reason why people use Twitter: news. It's a natural fit. [...] We wouldn't be here without you' (2015 cited in Broersma and Graham 2016: 91).

Twitter through the prism of opportunities and challenges

By unpacking the related academic literature, it becomes evident that Twitter could be analysed through two distinct dimensions: (1) as offering opportunities, and (2) as posing challenges, both for (legacy) media organisations and for (professional) journalists as individuals.

Opportunities

Twitter can be viewed as 'accelerating the reach of McLuhan's global village' (Murthy 2013: 20), as much in terms of connectedness as in terms of awareness of the others in the 'village'. This perception highlights Twitter's capacity to facilitate news dissemination to wide audiences across the globe, an aspect that is particularly important for journalists aiming to substantially extend their readership. Confronting the conceptual limitations of this perception (from access restrictions to the corporate character of social networks as entities), Shah alternatively proposes the term 'global marketplace' (Shah 2008). This term underlines that news is a product and, within the Twitter's borders, should be treated as such. On that note, previous research on Twitter demonstrates that tweets coming from news organizations employ in their vast majority the 'Headline + Link' format with the sole purpose of guiding audiences to their respective websites, as a form of 'refined clickbait' (Dagoula 2017). What is more, Bernard suggests that Twitter fosters the existence of social capital and notes that 'as is true of for all forms of capital, the emphasis is not simply on the connections themselves, but rather the sum of potential power and opportunity facilitated by this set of relations' (Bernard 2016: 202). The narrative of the global marketplace highlights one more aspect that is very popular among journalists: personal branding. Various studies have discussed the marketization of the persona along with that of the journalistic product through social media platforms (Brems et al. 2016; Ottovordemgentschenfelde 2017). This is also manifested through the promotion of journalists' non-digital work, for example, by asking Twitter users to follow their work outside the platform as well (Dagoula 2017).

The benefits offered by Twitter are further emphasized when the medium is considered as an ambient news environment. According to Hermida (2010), this perception indicates that Twitter is an arena that always contains news and that it could also be perceived as an 'awareness system'. In this system, information on news is received in the periphery of users' attention and does not require their cognitive attention (Hermida 2010: 301). To understand this, Murthy offers a useful analogy to oxygen (news) and its significance for the physical ambient environment (Twitter) (Murthy 2013: 53). More importantly though, Twitter as an ambient news environment allows for a new form of journalism to flourish – that of ambient journalism. Hermida notes that ambient journalism 'conceptualizes journalism as a tele-mediated practice and experience driven by networked, always-on communication technologies and media systems of immediacy and instantaneity' (Hermida 2012: 311). In an ever-increasingly connected world, where social media platforms are more and more ingrained in people's everyday routines (Meijer and Kormelink 2014) and where incidental exposure to news is more and more likely to happen, media actors have the opportunity to expand their networks and to exploit opportunities related to social capital. Besides, one of the most crucial ways that Twitter affects journalism is that it offers to the audience the chance to be directly involved in journalistic practices, for example, in the processes of gathering, reporting and recommending the news (Hermida 2012). Therefore, the platform facilitates more collaborative journalistic practices either by inviting users to participate in the news production processes or by crowdsourcing – by using the 'wisdom of the crowds' to analyse large amounts of data or check materials (Murthy 2013: 55).

In a similar vein, a series of interviews with journalists working in the United Kingdom (Dagoula 2017) highlights their use of Twitter as a 'valuable newswire' which in terms of news gathering precedes other media forms, such as newspapers and their websites. By exploiting the platform's affordances, such as lists and news alerts, journalists have the opportunity to use Twitter primarily as a news source; however, they clarified also that sources are not exclusively the audience but also other journalists, especially when it comes to occasions that one cannot attend a certain event (Dagoula 2017: 179). Likewise, for journalists, Twitter is also crucial for asking questions, discovering experts when it comes to obscure topics or aggregate reactions (Dagoula 2017: 179). As Broersma and Graham put it, Twitter could be regarded as a pool of 'collective intelligence' (Broersma and Graham 2012: 404).

In addition, Broersma and Graham, through a meta-analysis of the related academic literature, developed 'a cross-national typology of seven dominant reporting practices and routines of political journalists on Twitter', which also includes the functions of monitoring, networking, engaging, sourcing, publishing, promoting and branding. As Broersma and Graham highlight in a previous work of theirs, Twitter has turned into 'an interesting and promising virtual biotope for reporters in search of news and information' (Broersma and Graham 2012: 403). In other words, journalists not only have the chance to promote themselves but also to exploit Twitter's affordances in a way that enhances their journalistic work. Moreover, Canter adds another function to the list: Twitter is also used as a tool that enables journalists to achieve greater transparency and accountability in their work (Canter 2015: 2).

Furthermore, it could be argued that on Twitter's streams one can find 'a constantly updated, live representation of the experiences, interests and opinions of users' (Hermida 2014: 360), or as Papacharissi adds, 'these are affective streams', where the news 'collaboratively constructed out of subjective experience, opinion, and emotion, all sustained by and sustaining ambient news environments' (Papacharissi 2015: 34). Even though this perception indicates that tweets can 'add flavour to a story because they convey personal impressions and experiences, or *couleur locale*' (Broersma and Graham 2016: 99), at the same time, it also underlines that within Twitter the short fragments of information come from a variety of formal and informal sources and include inputs from both professionals and non-professionals (Hermida 2012: 311), even though this can also bring some 'unwanted scrutiny' (Hermida 2018: 177).

Challenges

On the challenges front, and by placing this discussion into the information disorder era (Wardle and Derakhshan 2017) where misinformation and disinformation are also incorporated in this amalgam of news, it becomes evident that the amount of information as well as their filtering could become particularly challenging and time-consuming as much for Twitter users as for journalists (Mills et al. 2007). Adding to the scepticism, Crawford points to the aspect of 'following' and underlines that the selection of the people one follows on Twitter functions as a highly subjective filter that re-orders the news agenda (Crawford 2010: 116). Mills et al. (2007) add to the equation the spam tweets which are connected to certain accounts that attempt to increase traffic on their websites with the use of deceptive URLs and the extensive number of fake accounts. Furthermore, incidents of digital harassment heighten this argumentation. The issue is rather significant: Amnesty International analysed 228,000 tweets of 778 women politicians in the United Kingdom and found that women are harassed every 30 seconds. Twitter has published an anti-harassment list to block such actions, nevertheless the problem is not solved as yet (Eordogh 2019; Warzel 2016).

Scepticism is also reinforced when examining Twitter through its technological affordances. This dimension further emphasizes that Twitter is a 'third space' where 'journalists, sources, audiences and other stakeholders encounter each other', and this space has the potential to 'fundamentally affect and alter the power relations between the various participants in news and journalism' (Bruns and Nuernbergk 2019: 199). In this, 'a contested middle ground' (Hermida 2016), media actors need to balance the weight between institutional elites and diverse publics, especially when it comes to the use of the platform as a news source. The platform dimension also sheds light to technology companies themselves, which are putting effort to become central in the production, circulation and, most importantly, monetization of information, by developing data services and adopting a news direction. The latter brings into the spotlight the use of analytics that further showcases 'the growing interconnections between editorial and marketing imperatives' (Bruns 2018: 224), which could be considered as a severe challenge for journalists' everyday work.

Adaption: A long process

The dual framing of Twitter as a platform that can benefit but also hinder journalistic work (opportunities and challenges) is echoed in its adaptation by media organizations and journalists. Even though Twitter was embraced by media actors quite extensively (Farhi 2009), its use has altered and evolved in its short life span. At the beginning, the adoption of Twitter into journalistic practices 'has largely mirrored the path of earlier new media technologies such as blogging' (Hermida 2014: 362) – a process that Singer (2005) names 'normalization'. In her work, Singer examines how political journalistic bloggers attempted to fit blogging into their traditional professional norms and practices and found out that they considered this whole process as a migration to online interactive environments where 'the blog is being normalized as a component and, in some ways, an enhancement

of traditional journalistic norms and practices' (Singer 2005: 193). A similar analysis by Lasorsa, Lewis and Holton, who performed an extensive content analysis
on journalists' tweets (j-tweeters), demonstrated a two-way normalization of the
platform. As such, even though j-tweeters vary widely in the use of the platform,
they appear to be normalizing microblogs to fit into their norms and practices, but
they simultaneously appear to be adjusting these norms and practices to Twitter's
evolving ones (Lasorsa et al. 2012: 31).

When it comes to its adaptation, there are several factors that define how journalists adjust to new technologies. For instance, Gulyás' work (2013) shows that
this could be related to the media sector, the length of a journalist's professional
career as well as to the size of organization they are working for. Likewise, Hedman
and Djerf-Pierre identify three categories among journalists: the sceptical shunners
who are the journalists that avoid anything to do with social media and constitute
the minority; the pragmatic conformists who are journalists that use social media
regularly but are at the same time selective and judicious in their usage; and the
enthusiastic activists who 'fully lead a life online, being connected and twittering
and blogging continuously' – an approach that is common among younger journalists (Hedman and Djerf-Pierre 2013: 381). Similarly, Canter (2015: 2) suggests
that there are two distinct channels of communication evolving in social media: a
traditional function for news organizations and a social function for journalists.
When it comes to the social function, she further underlines that there are two gen-
eric types of journalists related to the use of the platform: those who solely promote
their platform by driving traffic to their company's website and those who expand
its use by sharing external material, collaborating with the public and engaging
with the audience. She also refers to the crossing of the 'historic line between the
professional and the personal' (Canter 2015: 3), pointing to the pressing question
of whether journalists should participate in the 'messy mixture of personal and
professional in social media' or if they should maintain their professional standards and use Twitter as simply another arena for publication (Rogstad 2014: 688).
The aforementioned factors and divisions indicate that the process of adaptation
is anything but univocal.

Therefore, it comes as no surprise that different media actors use the platform
differently and demonstrate different degrees of adaptation. For example, and despite the fact that Twitter 'has moved from small-scale experiment to core practice'
(Bruns 2018: 185), news organizations, either legacy or net-native, reveal a 'less
skillful' use (Engesser and Humprecht 2015: 519), where engagement with the
readers is still far from the norm (Hermida 2016; Dagoula 2017, 2020). In addition, journalists incorporate the platform into their practices, but they carry a
rather reserved attitude toward its networking possibilities. Therefore, they tend
to focus more on disseminating material and promoting their brand (or the self).

This shows minimum progress from previous studies that argued that Twitter's full potential as a community building and engagement tool has not been developed yet (Messner et al. 2011).

Pressures, anxiety, solutions

This 'opportunities versus challenges' framework seeks to capture the related academic literature on the use of Twitter as a journalistic tool. Reflecting on this framework, Hermida writes that 'social media is both a blessing and curse': on one hand, because 'it offers new ways to connect and engage with audiences in the spaces where they congregate [...] it offers the potential to tap into the core of loyal, dedicated readers and harness their enthusiasm to recommend and amplify a particular story'(2016: 87). On the other hand, because it has altered core journalistic routines, such as new agenda-setting processes, it 'undermine[s] mainstream media and allow[s] everyone to be their own news-editor' (Hermida 2016: 87).

Likewise, Hermida notes that social media 'is a space full of paradoxes. The news is everywhere and nowhere on social media [...] [N]ews can take place simultaneously outside of the logic of news institutions, yet is shaped and reshaped by the interplay with the institutional logic of the news' (Hermida 2016: 89). In such circumstances, these paradoxes can be particularly perplexing both for media organizations and for journalists. Studying the topic from a different angle, that of how media organizations guide their employees via official guidelines, Lee finds similar results: he underlines that legacy media outlets confront social media both as an opportunity and as a risk and adopts an attitude that is simultaneously promotion- and prevention-focused (Lee 2016: 107). He also found that the overall proportion of opportunity-framed instructions are less than a fifth of that of risk frames, although organizations like *The Guardian* encourage journalists to contribute by adding their voice and acknowledge these additions (Lee 2016: 120).

Lee's findings indirectly suggest a clash between the theoretical approaches to social media and their actual employment. This clash is also highlighted by previous empirical research on the ways in which various media actors use Twitter (Dagoula 2017). The research consisted of three distinct stages: (1) systematic analysis of the literature with regard to the opportunities/challenges frame; (2) extensive analysis of media and journalistic accounts on Twitter[2] so to understand their use of Twitter; and (3) interviews with journalists whose accounts have been analysed during the second stage of the research (Dagoula 2017). Having as an overall aim to understand how various actors incorporate Twitter in their work, the research found that legacy media accounts, in their majority, aim to enhance the dissemination of articles previously posted on their website and therefore attract audiences outside the platform. This strategy calls to mind the early years of the web, when media websites were dominated by the so-called 'shovelware', a term that refers to the print content recycled for the web (Deuze 1999: 374). As such, most of the media accounts function as pseudo-RSS feeds filled by parasitic content, whereas journalistic accounts prioritize the dissemination of journalistic pieces published elsewhere, thus promoting journalist's brand or product (Dagoula 2017). Furthermore, author's previous research in media actors' use of the platform underscores a very low degree of interaction with the audiences by both journalists and media accounts. Twitter's conversational markers (retweets, replies) and hashtags are not used for the purpose they are designed, that is, for enhancing the social interactions in the platform. In other words, the social aspect of Twitter is not exploited in full, and it is normalized to fit into the previous media strategies (Dagoula 2017: 212).

In addition, the results demonstrate that the gradual and slow adaptation to social media, along with the less skilful use by media outlets, have various possible explanations – for example, Hermida refers to 'a fundamental lack of new media literacy amongst some industry leaders' (cited in Bruns 2018: 179). In addition, one of the most important reasons is that social media platforms posed severe challenges to the journalistic market, adding to an already precarious situation. An indicative example is the dissemination of free content and the cultivation of the 'culture of free' that could be summed up in the reasoning that once people are accustomed to get[ting] something for free, it is difficult to get them [to] start paying again (Arrese 2016). Along with the new dynamics of new hybrid media space where social media platforms themselves have substantial economic and societal power, they have 'caused significant additional anxieties for an already highly anxious industry' (Bruns 2018: 177).

The process of seeking for explanations and solutions lead us to the discussion of the business side of contemporary journalism. As Hermida points out 'the potential immediate economic value [of social media] to media companies has been hotly debated' (Hermida 2016: 87). Media users make two very different kinds of investments in media content – this dual understanding is the key. First, we pay for content with attention and with time that we could have spent differently. This attention is then monetized by media organizations who are selling it to advertisers. Second, we pay for content with money, although the mix of time and money invested is important both for individual users and for media organizations (Kleis Nielsen 2019). Therefore, it could be argued that having a financial gain from the platforms might lead media organizations to pay closer attention to the benefits that these platforms could have for enhancing the journalistic profession in other ways as well. If social media are seen as 'another instance of allowing content to circulate freely without an opportunity to generate commercial returns from it' (Bruns 2018: 178), then their benefits could be potentially disregarded. That is not to say that the challenges will disappear overnight or that they are not important, rather it suggests that by trying to confront challenges such as the diffused abusive commentary, the focus should be on how social media platforms could be used as journalistic tools. In that sense, technology-related dilemmas are rather obsolete.

To conclude, social media platforms might pose a dilemma for media organizations and journalists on whether they want to get involved in this 'messy mixture'. However, such a dilemma could be considered anachronistic. More accurately, the dilemma now is to what extent journalists get involved with social media platforms. Thus, a solution might lie in a mindset shift. Even though 'a substantial number of journalists across diverse news organizations and national contexts have now developed their own social media presence' (Bruns 2018: 186), a structured approach at an institutional level could be proven much more effective. As Bruns points out, 'there is a need for a considerable formal institutional support' (Bruns 2018: 185). This support might be translated to formal training, the provision of opportunities to progress, the provision of resources that will allow the enhancement of journalists' social media literacy or the provision of thorough and well-curated guidelines. What matters at the end of the day is that there will be a 'coordinated effort to develop the social media skills of newsroom staff to a level where they are able to operate competently and effectively without constant oversight' (Bruns 2018: 185).

NOTES

1. This chapter focuses on professional journalism. This considers journalists as a professional group that shares a common code of professional values. It is a professional group that regards itself as having institutional standing manifest in and through codes of behaviour, ethical standards, self-regulation, editorial codes, codes of conduct, professional bodies and associations and so on.

2. Twitter research was conducted in a variety of accounts (from legacy media, net-native media and journalists) for a one-month period. The research concerned media actors from the United Kingdom. The criteria for choosing them were: the popularity of their websites and the popularity of their Twitter account, which is defined by the their number of followers. Likewise, the criteria for choosing specific journalists from each medium were their active presence on the website they work for (in the Politics section of each site), the popularity of their Twitter accounts defined by their number of followers and their active presence on Twitter, which is defined by the number of tweets they send.

REFERENCES

Arrese, Á. (2016), 'From gratis to paywalls: A brief history of a retro-innovation in the press's business', *Journalism Studies*, 17:8, pp. 1051–67.

Brems, C., Temmerman, M., Graham, T. and Broersma, M. (2016), 'Personal branding on Twitter', *Digital Journalism*, 5:4, pp. 443–59.

Broersma, M. and Graham, T. (2012), 'Social media as beat', *Journalism Practice*, 6:3, pp. 403–19.

Broersma, M. and Graham, T. (2016), 'Tipping the balance of power: Social media and the transformation of political journalism', in Ax. Bruns, G. Enli, El. Skogerbø, An. Olof Larsson and C. Christensen (eds.), *The Routledge Companion to Social Media and Politics*, New York: Routledge, pp. 89–103.

Bruno, N. (2010), 'Tweet first, verify later?', https://nicolabruno.files.wordpress.com/2011/05/tweet_first_verify_later2.pdf. Accessed 23 May 2019.

Bruns, Ax (2018), *Gatewatching and News Curation: Journalism, Social Media, and the Public Sphere*, New York: Peter Lang Publishing.

Bruns, Ax and Burgess, J. (2012), 'Researching news discussions on Twitter', *Journalism Studies*, 13:5&6, pp. 801–14.

Bruns, Ax and Nuernbergkt, C. (2019), 'Political journalists and their social media audiences: new power relations', *Media & Communication*, 7:1, pp. 198–212.

Canter, L. (2015), 'Personalised Tweeting', *Digital Journalism*, 3:6, pp. 1–20.

Costera Meijer, I. and Groot Kormelink, T. (2014), 'Checking, sharing, clicking and linking: Changing patterns of news use between 2004 and 2014', *Digital Journalism*, pp. 1–16.

Crawford, K. (2010), 'News to me: Twitter and the personal networking of news', in G. Meikle and G. Redden (eds), *News Online: Transformations and Continuinities*, New York: Palgrave Macmillan, pp. 115–30.

Dagoula, C. (2017), 'The ongoing structural transformations of the digital public sphere(s): The role of journalism', doctoral thesis, Sheffield: The University of Sheffield, http://etheses.whiterose.ac.uk/18499/. Accessed 26 May 2021.

Dagoula, C. (2020), *Mapping Greek Journalistic Twitter: A Theoretical and Empirical Approach*, Athens: Metamesonykties.

Deuze, M. (1999), 'Journalism and the web', *Gazette*, 61:5, pp. 373–90.

Engesser, S. and Humprecht, E. (2015), 'Frequency or skillfulness', *Journalism Studies*, 16:4, pp. 513–29.

Eordogh, F. (2019), 'Twitter's anti-harassment tools, reviewed', https://www.forbes.com/sites/fruzsinaeordogh/2019/03/11/twitters-anti-harassment-tools-reviewed/#7b4d520d1e13. Accessed 23 May 2019.

Farhi, P. (2009), 'The Twitter explosion', *American Journalism Review*, http://www.thepdfer.com/pdfs/Article.asp%3Fid=4756-12458.pdf. Accessed 27 November 2019.

Gulyás, A. (2013), 'The influence of professional variables on journalists' uses and views of social media', *Digital Journalism*, 1:2, pp. 270–85.

Hedman, U. and Djerf-Pierre, M. (2013), 'The social journalist', *Digital Journalism*, 1:3, pp. 368–85.

Hermida, A. (2010), 'Twittering the News', *Journalism Practice*, 4:3, pp. 297–308.

Hermida, A. (2014), 'Twitter as an ambient news network', in K. Weller, Ax. Bruns, J. Burgess, M. Mahrt and C. Puschmann (eds), *Twitter and Society*, New York: Peter Lang, pp. 359–72.

Hermida, A. (2016), 'Social media and the news', in T. Witschge, C. W. Anderson, D. Domingo and A. Hermida (eds), *The Sage Handbook of Digital Journalism*, London: SAGE publications, pp. 81–94.

Hermida, A. (2018), 'Social media and journalism', in A. Marwick (ed.), *The Sage Handbook of Social Media*, London: SAGE publications, pp. 497–511.

Kleis Nielsen, R. (2019), 'Economic contexts of journalism', in K. Wahl-Jorgensen and T. Hanitzsch (eds), *Handbook of Journalism Studies*, New York: Routledge.

Lasorsa, D. L., Lewis, S. C. and Holton, A. E. (2012), 'Normalizing Twitter: Journalism practice in an emerging communication space', *Journalism Studies*, 13:1, pp. 19–36.

Lee, J. (2015), 'The double-edged sword: The effects of journalists' social media activities on audience perceptions of journalists and their news products', *Journal of Computer-Mediated Communication*, 20:3, pp. 312–29.

Lee, J. (2016), 'Opportunity or risk? How news organizations frame social media in their guidelines for journalists', *The Communication Review*, 19:2, pp. 106–27.

Messner, M., Linke, M. and Eford, A. (2011), 'Shoveling Tweets: An analysis of the microblogging engagement of traditional news organizations', *International Symposium on Online Journalism*, Austin, TX, 1 April.

Mills, A., Chen, R., Lee, J. and Rao, H. R. (2007), 'Web 2.0 emergency applications: how useful can Twitter be for emergency response', *Journal of Information Privacy and Security*, 5:3, pp. 3–26.

Murthy, D. (2013), *Twitter*, Cambridge: Polity Press.

Papacharissi, Z. (2015), 'Towards new journalism(s): Affective news, hybridity, and liminal spaces', *Journalism Studies*, 16:1, pp. 27–40.

Rogstad, I. D. (2014), 'Political news journalists in social media', *Journalism Practice*, 8:6, pp. 688–703.

Shah, N. (2008), 'From global village to global marketplace: Metaphorical descriptions of the global Internet', *International Journal of Media and Cultural Politics*, 4:1, pp. 9–26.

Singer, J. B. (2005), 'The political j-blogger: "Normalizing" a new media form to fit old norms and practices', *Journalism*, 6:2, pp. 173–98.

Stross, R., (2016), 'Twitter has an old media problem: Here's a solution', *The New York Times*, https://www.nytimes.com/2016/10/27/opinion/twitter-has-an-old-media-problem-heres-a-solution.html?_r=1. Accessed 27 November 2019.

Twitter (2019), 'Twitter abusive behavior', https://help.twitter.com/en/rules-and-policies/abusive-behavior. Accessed 23 May 2019.

Wardle, C. and Derakhshan, H. (2017), 'Information disorder toward an interdisciplinary framework for research and policymaking', Council of Europe, https://rm.coe.int/information-disorder-toward-an-interdisciplinary-framework-for-researc/168076277c. Accessed 10 October 2020.

Warzel, C. (2016), '"A honeypot for assholes": Inside Twitter's 10-year failure to stop harassment', BuzzFeed News, https://www.buzzfeed.com/charliewarzel/a-honeypot-for-assholes-inside-twitters-10-year-failure-to-s?utm_term=.ix5obrW4L#.fgKwGXQPR. Accessed 27 November 2019.

van Dijck, J. (2012), 'Tracing Twitter: The rise of a microblogging platform', *International Journal of Media and Cultural Politics*, 7:3, pp. 333–48.

PROPOSAL 6

ACADEMIA AND PROFESSIONALS

10

Bridging the Gap between Journalists and Media Academics

Valia Kaimaki

Introduction

Bridging the gap between theory and practice is a problem described, documented and studied in relation to different scientific disciplines. It is not a problem inherent to journalism and media academics, however, in this case, the problem which has not been adequately researched. Even though it is valuable to look at the necessity of bridging the gap in general terms, it is essential to stress its urgency regarding journalism, especially in the post-truth era. As journalists, when proposing solutions, such as media literacy or fact-checking, to tackle the problem from a journalistic point of view, we almost always forget that academics could give a serious and strong helping hand. This is a fact that illustrates the problem and its solution at the same time. Therefore, in this chapter, we identify the gap, present a notorious example and document the necessity of bridging this gap.

The gap exists for everyone

Theoretical research in disciplines as different as educational studies, medicine, management accounting or personnel resource management is often criticized for not having an impact on practice. For example, Donald McIntyre (2005), examining the acknowledged gap between research and practice as a gap between two sharply contrasting kinds of knowledge in educational studies, suggests three possible ways of bridging it. In medicine, similar studies (Mallonee et al. 2007) are more pessimistic: their authors insist that research-to-practice gaps have always existed and progress in this subject has been slow. Among the factors they identify as being responsible for this situation are lapses in communication between researchers and practitioners, which is also true for journalism. They also evoke the uselessness of scientific publications in the field, which in some ways could be true in journalism. Other disciplines face similar problems: '[S]ystematic literature reviews that are common in engineering and medicine can bring together the academic knowledge that can contribute to solutions to the problem concerning management accounting' (Jansen 2018: 1486). Debra J. Cohen (2007) examines the difference between the academic study of personnel resource management and the practical performance of the same discipline in a real-life setting.

Unfortunately, there have been very few studies about journalism and the 'gap'. The University of Sheffield practitioner and academic Tony Harcup found evidence of a pervasive disconnect between research and teaching, between theory and practice (Harcup 2011). We are therefore discussing a subject that has only been treated in a different context, for example, in fields like media ethics where both theory and practice are collaborating in the case study model approach. And, even though journalism and media ethics share a great number of areas, the subject as such has not been analysed in depth in the relevant literature.

Before discussing any further the gap between theory and practice in journalism, it is essential to define media academia as a separate category from journalistic education or training. Media academia, in countries such as France and Greece, has been born mainly from sociology, whereas in other countries from arts or humanities. It has nothing to do with journalistic education, which is carried out mainly in separate 'schools' and very rarely inside academic institutions. Some of the latter have their own 'institutes', trying to keep the two separate. One of the main reasons is that education and/or training is considered vocational training and demands the educators/trainers to be journalists. In many occasions, however, the academic standards of journalists are not to the level required by academic institutions. Entering the general discussion about bridging the gap between vocational studies and academic education, as described by Raffe (2002), one – by no means the only but certainly the most useful for our argumentation – of the distinctive points between the two is the factor of research, namely, scientific, which increases the 'value' of the university, therefore its viability in a highly competitive academic market.

Things might have been quite different if journalism was considered also an 'art' and not only a 'science'. It could be considered an 'art' because it uses words, spoken or written, or video, which in many cases also have an artistic value. If we follow this train of thought, for example, we could argue that art academics don't gain value from the number of prestigious publications but from the value of the individuals they form. A great painter or a great film director add value to the school they graduated from, and they are more than welcome to teach as full-time professors at many schools. Art schools not only are composed of art critics but of artists as well. What is also important is the method of evaluation. Shouldn't journalists be asked to present excellent journalistic work instead of essays or papers? Even if this point of view needs more in-depth research, as it has not been adequately documented yet, we could refer to a recent study. In 2016, we presented a comparative study (Kaimaki and Roinioti 2016) at #RetreatConference2016 in Athens. Our aim was to prove that a journalistic paper can have the same value as a peer-reviewed paper. We studied two papers treating the propaganda techniques used by the American government to justify the war against Iraq in 2003. The first one was by Deepa Kumar, Associate Professor of media studies and Middle Eastern studies at Rutgers University (New Jersey), titled 'Media, war, and propaganda: Strategies of information management during the 2003 Iraq War' (Kumar 2006), and the other one was by Ignacio Ramonet, Director at the time of the prestigious French newspaper *Le Monde diplomatique*, titled 'Mensonges d'État' (Ramonet 2003). We divided the structural features of the above texts into two sections: (1) text structure and argumentation development and (2) linguistic elements. The first section revealed that both articles developed around three themes: (1) the state propaganda mechanism, (2) the media as a means of authorized propaganda and (3) the media as a means of state control. As far as linguistic elements are concerned, both articles shared common structural features, diverging only in individual components: Ramonet, for example, does not use passive voice, which is stereotypical in academic articles. Our conclusion was that quality journalism can meet academic standards. Of course, the next issue would be to determine quality articles, thus quality journalism, something which is not a desideratum in the arts, where one of the most (if not the most) important criterion is duration in time; journalism, however, is ephemeral by definition. Nonetheless, the definition of quality in journalism is still under discussion.

However, this point is worth noting, as one of the most comprehensive reports in the subject distinguishes journalists from academics. Academic researchers have examined quality journalism from both the demand and the supply side. The demand side emphasizes the interaction between content and the needs or wants of news consumers. The supply side tends to specify content characteristics that are associated with higher quality. Both approaches typically define quality journalism as a matter of degree. It is not a simple matter, like having or not having quality (Lacy and Rosenstiel 2015).

However, the definition of quality journalism by professionals 'has tended to take a product approach, usually listing elements of quality' (Lacy and Rosenstiel 2015: 20). One other excellent remark by these two authors is that most of the measures used in research projects tend to emphasize the individual consumer level and recourse to bundles of information from news outlets. Few of the studies examine quality from the community level. A few studies use source diversity but tend not to apply that beyond the outlet level (Lacy and Rosenstiel 2015). Of course, we would need to define community in specific terms, but this means that so far, the studies have not touched the most delicate subject of the definition of quality journalism for society (a broad notion of 'community'), and thus its impact on democracy that represents journalism's single reason for existence.

Bourdieu and a famous conflict

One of the most famous 'conflicts' between media and academics was the one evolving around Pierre Bourdieu (1930–2002), the twentieth century's renowned and well-respected French sociologist. Pierre Bourdieu's criticism of television was based on the analysis of the harmful effects of the advertising model at the political level. According to his analysis, privatizing television and funding it exclusively through advertising, instead of promoting the pluralism promised by its supporters, has resulted in the creation of a uniform market, where channels have the sole aim of maximization. However, by choosing the themes, content and types of programmes and population groups that need to make a profit, they are avoiding the interests of advertisers. This lies at the core of Bourdieu's famous small book *Sur la télévision* (Bourdieu 1996b), edited in early 1996.

The year of the publication is extremely important. In late 1995, Bourdieu took an open and active position in favour of strikers. At the time, a series of general strikes were organized in France, mostly in the public sector. The strikes received great popular support, despite paralysing the country's transportation infrastructure, along with a few other institutions. They occurred in the context of a larger social movement against the reform agenda led by Prime Minister Alain Juppé, and they constituted the largest social movement in France since May 1968. From then on, Bourdieu continued to intervene in favour of the unemployed or the illegal immigrants and against the liberal society that creates dozens of disinherited people or the 'neoliberal troika' of Blair, Jospin and Schroeder, as he called the European leaders of the United Kingdom, France and Germany at the time.

The harshest criticism to Bourdieu came from *Esprit* magazine (standing for the left liberals with Christian influences). He was accused of wanting to give lessons, increasingly 'confusing sociology with political engagement'. *Esprit* emphasized that at least the people of the magazine did not need any lessons from the 'dogmatic professor' (Bougnoux 1996: 183). Even if someone could argue that *Esprit* is not a 'real' media, but a journal by and for the intellectuals, there was still another conflict in France that involved Bourdieu. Invited at the famous *Arrêt sur images* (television programme on the 'La Cinquième', the Fifth, one of the public channels), Bourdieu – obviously mad at what he would later describe as a 'trap' – gave answers that did not do him credit, such as, '[I]t would take me two hours to answer' or 'Anyway, I didn't want to come here' (Bourdieu 1996a: 25).

The conflict did not stop there. In the April issue of the prestigious monthly review *Le Monde diplomatique*, Bourdieu wrote a full page that concluded: 'Television cannot criticize television [...] because it uses the same devices' (equality of speaking time, bonus to the one who speaks louder, debates which turn to box matches). 'My trust has been abused' (Bourdieu 1996a: 25), he complained. The following month, Daniel Schneidermann answered him angrily in the columns of the same monthly review: 'What is the essence of your reproaches? Not to have left you be the total master of the show? [...] you've had 20 minutes of talk time on 52 minutes, compared with 8 minutes for each of your two opponents' (Schneidermann 1996: 21).

This is one of the best (and most notorious) examples illustrating the tensions between academics and media. Of course, the particular conditions and persons have also played a major role. Nonetheless, journalism academics are often mocked by the media and stifled by universities. Likewise, journalists are also often looked down upon by academics. Beyond the surface, the intervention of Pierre Bourdieu can be linked to a more essential problem, that of the very existence of a critical analysis – about the media and in the media – that is not systematically condemned or 'at best condescendingly caricatured by a small elite troop of journalists and media intellectuals' (Dufour 2005: 445).

It is not our purpose to examine who was right and who was wrong. But the conflict did not promote the final goal, which was to inform the public of the strikes (and the reasons that led to them) from a journalistic point of view, as well as to examine whether the media did it well from an academic point of view. At the end, it did not help democracy. Underneath the tension, a political fight was connoted. One of the reasons it is so difficult to document the gap between theory and practice in journalism is because it has a strong affiliation with the society in which both parties evolve. And journalism is one of the most activist practices, but it cannot be an activist theory. Or maybe it can. And maybe it should.

When Bourdieu became political in his analysis, part of the media system rejected him, as if these particular journalists had become the guardians of objectivity. Usually, it is the other way round, and we could cite a multitude of examples of media taking sides in politics. It used to be a marginal phenomenon; it is becoming a more and more common one. As early as 1984, Hackett linked it to research. His essay (Hackett 1984) outlines emerging empirical, methodological and epistemological challenges to several key assumptions associated with conventional research on news bias. These assumptions are: (1) news can and ought to be objective, balanced and a reflection of social reality; (2) political attitudes of journalists or editorial decision-makers are a major determinant of news bias;

(3) bias in news content can be detected with existing reading methods; (4) the most important form of bias is partisanship.

The 'inside' context

Before we examine the social context in general, it is worth taking an insider's look at academics and journalists. Wendy Bacon describes well (Bacon 1999) the academic restrictions, focusing on five axes. The first is that universities are struggling to cope with government cutbacks. They are obliged to either look for areas of growth or defend existing teaching territory and jobs. At the same time private institutions are pitted against universities that are more actively seeking to meet market demand. To satisfy their own needs, major media employers want to influence the nature of that education, offering possibilities for growth, but on certain conditions. The pressure on universities to become more industry-focused reflects itself in (1) communication studies students who want more production courses and (2) production students who expect their universities to deliver on the promise of future jobs. Finally, inside the university, pressure to build research activities and funds means younger journalism educators are more likely to need a strong academic record on top of a professional one.

It is therefore clear that academics do not always have the choice or the means or even the time to focus on the subjects they would like to. They face multiple restrictions from the market, from their sponsors (usually the state, at least in Europe where most universities are public) and their clients (media). However, journalism in practice is facing three major challenges. The first one is the decline of old media and emergence of new ones. The death of printing has been predicted a while ago (Mims 2010). The fact that it is still artificially alive does not prove anything. Literature is exhaustive in this area, everything that can be said about the emergence of new technologies and the substitution of the press by the web, of the TV by streaming and more recently of the radio by podcasting, has been said already. And probably more papers are being written as we speak. To give a quick overview, we could mention publications such as Barthelemy et al. (2011) Papathanassopoulos (2001), Tefertiller (2018) and Cwynar (2015). In the early days, when we were trying to understand the transition, we would mostly study it from an economical point of view: What would be a viable model for the emerging news production? The fact that journalism would remain journalism was never questioned. If we divide journalism into three categories: news, analysis/reporting and editorials (opinions), 'only the first is in danger. The other two will be free to develop even further' (Kaimaki 1997: 45). At the time, we could not even imagine what would happen later: web pages copying each other, sensational titles, clickbait which 'has become a growing practice nowadays among the media outlets' (Md Main Uddin et al. 2018: 8216), misinformation. If we add the success of social media and the change of the reading mode (picking up what our friends post), journalism faces great challenges that touch the core of its essence.

The second one consists of the rising risks for the life of journalists, which according to the International Federation of Journalists have been increasing since 2017. Only in Europe and in Turkey 'seven journalists investigating corruption and abuse of public money scams have been found dead, most of them murdered in ways that bring to mind organized crime' (Katsoura 2019: n.pag.). More and more regions of the world have become 'reportorial black holes, because it is so dangerous for reporters to get in there' (Rajan 2019: n.pag.).

The third, and maybe the most important one, is the lack of a viable economic model for the future. To ensure both economic sustainability and independent, quality media coverage, three factors are crucial: (1) the overall economic environment and media-market structure, (2) sources of revenue for media organizations, and (3) media organizations' resources and structures. These correspond to the macro-, mid-, and micro-levels (DW Akademie 2015). But we still have no answers. We do have some successful examples, but no real roadmap. The one thing everyone agrees on is that '[i]f journalism is going to survive, readers will have to pay for it' (Barnett 2019: n.pag.). Nevertheless, for the time being, they seem unwilling. And one of the main reasons is lack of trust in the media.

The social context

Of the many factors that shape our social lives, there is one which touches journalism in a life-changing way: the emergence of populism. We will once again remember Pierre Bourdieu, who had excellent reasons to remark, during his conflict with the media, that precariousness in media employment could result in the reinforcement of conformism and the marginalization of the disagreeing voices. The situation worsens in times of crisis: In Europe, the new working environment that has emerged as a result of the economic crisis has given rise to the replacement of experienced and well-paid professionals with younger trainees, which caused deficiencies in the defense of the labour code and the journalism code itself, leading to professional 'poverty' (Iordanidou et al. 2020).

Coming from a completely different approach, the same was predicted by Herman and Chomsky (1988). In their book, the writers claim that the media agenda is set by a handful of media companies with access to the general public, who raise a huge barrier to keep smaller, independent voices out of public dialogue. Their business model is based on large advertising campaigns and not on the publication of articles, which they consider controversial or unpleasant. From their part, journalists rely on their cooperation with 'high-level' sources, a symbiotic relationship that prevents the press from publishing anything that may be contrary to the views of those sources. The result is a false national consensus that ignores facts, opinions and ideas (Kaimaki 2017). In the United States, it is called 'consensus'; in France it is called 'pensée unique'. Whatever name is used, it will slowly 'kill' the press, which is gradually losing its credibility.

Across all countries, the average level of trust in the news in general is down by two percentage points, to 42 per cent. Less than half of the people (49 per cent) agree that they trust the news media they themselves use. Confidence levels in France have fallen to just 24 per cent (-11) in the last year, as the media were attacked for their coverage of the Yellow Vests movement. Trust in the news found following a search (33 per cent) and in the social media remains stable but extremely low (23 per cent) (Newman 2019: 10).

Even though a decline in confidence had already been observed since the 1990s, populism has given it the final push, conveying to the readers/audience one simple message: '[T]he media is lying to you'. And because of the consensus or pensée unique, people have believed it. When President Trump first spoke of 'fake news', he did it to criticize mainstream media. And it worked: 'The rise of strongmen leaders around the world, from President Trump to Prime Minister Modi, has created a new climate of intolerance toward journalists, many of whom are now facing constant hostility' (Rajan 2019: n.pag.).

The urgency of a bridge

An article by Academic Anonymous (academics and journalists who wish to remain anonymous) in the *Guardian* explains the problem from a different point of view, as if someone, who is caught in the middle of the conflict between media and academics, is trying to do both. He explains that 'journalists tend to mock academia, while relying on it for the training that industry no longer provides' (Academic 2015: n.pag.). However, the message from universities is confusing: 'They advertise practitioner posts with an expectation that applicants will undertake research, but then they advertise separate research-only posts which push hybrids like myself away from practice' (Academic 2015: n.pag.). Here is someone who tries to exist in both worlds but finds it very difficult. And yet democracy needs both in more urgent ways that are evident on the surface, where one finds misinformation, mistrust and danger. Underneath, there are even more dangerous situations for our democracy, such as concentration of media in a few hands, be them public or private.

It is thus evident that both journalists and academics need to work closely with each other. As mentioned by Barkho (2017), Vin Ray is perhaps the most important reference in the subject 'Journalists and scholars: A short manifesto' puts forward three propositions to 'bridge the chasm between the two camps'. The first step is the requirement for a journalism research forum that connects media organizations with research scholars. The second is a call for journalists to use academic research as a form of source material. This could be achieved through a webbased journalism research database that allows them to easily access at least the abstracts. The third suggestion is for scholars to become better at disseminating their work – through blogs and social media.

In a set of interviews, we put these propositions to the test by presenting them to a group of both parties. The results were inconclusive. For example, some academics could not see any interest in social media dissemination while others preferred a specific channel (i.e., the institution's social media accounts) to do so. Nonetheless they all insisted in a more structured and/or institutional forms of the above propositions in the form of an institute, for example, that could 'co-host' their work. However, this needs to be further researched and formulated.

It is apparent that journalists' work would have benefited by an enhancement of their understanding and conceptualisation of the world they live in, and by the invention of more viable economic models. For these, they would need academics, and, before dismissing their work, they should think twice of the damage in the long run. Additionally, academics' work could be advanced by a better understanding of the challenges that journalists face, as well as of a better understanding of how the world of media functions in reality.

REFERENCES

Academic Anonymous (2015), 'Journalism academics: Mocked by the media and stifled by universities', *The Guardian*, 7 May, https://www.theguardian.com/higher-education-netw ork/2015/may/07/journalism-academics-mocked-by-the-media-and-stifled-by-universities Accessed 3 October 2019.

Bacon, Wendy (1999), 'What is a journalist in a university?', *Media International Australia Incorporating Culture and Policy*, 90:1, pp. 79–90.

Barkho, Leon (2017), 'Introduction: Theory is not enough: How to convert media and journalism studies into relevant, useful and practical research', in L. Barkho (ed.), *Towards a Praxis-Based Media and Journalism Research*, Intellect: Bristol, pp. 1–12.

Barnett, David (2019), 'If journalism is going to survive, readers are going to have to pay for it', *The Independent*, https://www.independent.co.uk/news/media/death-digital-printing-new spapers-information-new-york-times-a8769626.html. Accessed on 28 September 2019.

Barthelemy, Samantha, Bethell, Matthew, Christiansen, Tim, Jarsvall, Adrienne and Koinis, Katerina (2011), 'The future of print media', *Microsoft Word – World Newsmedia Innovations Study – Capstone Workshop*, New York, Spring.

Bougnoux, Daniel (1996), *Pierre Bourdieu, sociologue boudeur*, Paris: Esprit Presse, https://esprit.presse.fr/article/bougnoux-daniel/pierre-bourdieu-sociologue-boudeur-10560. Accessed 28 October 2021.

Bourdieu, Pierre (1996a), 'Analyse d'un passage à l'antenne', *Le Monde diplomatique*, Avril, p. 25.

Bourdieu, Pierre (1996b), *Sur la télévision*, Paris: Raisons d'agir.

Cohen, Debra J. (2007), 'The very separate worlds of academic and practitioner publications in human resource management: Reasons for the divide and concrete solutions for bridging the gap', *Academy of Management Journal*, 50:5, pp. 1013–19.

Cwynar, Christopher (2015), 'More than a "VCR for Radio": The CBC, the Radio 3 Podcast, and the uses of an emerging medium', *Journal of Radio & Audio Media*, 22:2, pp. 190–99.

Dufour, Lucas (2005), 'Roger Chartier, Patrick Champagne, Pierre Bourdieu & les médias', *Questions de communication*, Paris: Éd. L'Harmattan/INA, coll., Les médias en actes, pp. 445–47.

DW Akademie (2015), 'The long term: Sustainable media, viable media | DW', dw.com, https://www.dw.com/en/the-long-term-sustainable-media-viable-media/a-18670796. Accessed 20 October 2019.

Hackett, Robert A. (1984), 'Decline of a paradigm? Bias and objectivity in news media studies', *Critical Studies in Mass Communication*, 1:3, pp. 229–59.

Harcup, Tony (2011), 'Hackademics at the Chalkface', *Journalism Practice*, 5:1, pp. 34–50.

Herman, Edward S. and Chomsky, Noam (1988), *Manufacturing Consent*, New York: Pantheon Books.

Iordanidou, Sofia, Vatikiotis, Leonidas, Suarez, P. G. and Takas, Emmanuel (2020), 'Constructing silence: Processes of journalistic (self) censorship during memoranda in Greece, Cyprus and Spain', in K. Skare Orgeret and W. Tayeebwa (eds), *Rethinking Safety of Journalists: Media and Communication*, https://www.cogitatiopress.com/mediaandcommunication/article/view/2634. Accessed 12 October 2020.

Jansen, E. Pieter (2018), 'Bridging the gap between theory and practice in management accounting', *Accounting, Auditing & Accountability Journal*, 31:5, pp. 1486–509.

Kaimaki, Valia (1997), *Αμφίδρομη επικοινωνία έντυπων ΜΜΕ και internet (Bidirectional communication between printed mass media and the internet)*, Athens: Papasotiriou.

Kaimaki, Valia (2017), 'Fak (the) News: Η βιομηχανία των ειδήσεων την εποχή της μετανεωτερικότητας' 'Fak the news: News industry in the era of post-modernism', *Daily H Αυγή*, Απρίλιος, http://www.avgi.gr/article/10965/8074026/e-biomechania-ton-eideseon-ten-epoche-tes-metaneoterikotetas. Accessed 28 September 2019.

Kaimaki, Valia and Roinioti, Elina (2016), 'Δημοσιογραφική Έρευνα ή Ακαδημαϊκή Μελέτη; Πόσο Απέχουν, Πόσο Συγκλίνουν' 'Journalistic research or academic study? How far away they stand, how much they converge', in *Athensretreat2016 Conference*, https://bit.ly/33uHxAY. Accessed 10 October 2019, Athens, Greece, 23–25 September.

Katsoura, Archontia (2019), 'Ένα επάγγελμα εκ προοιμίου επικίνδυνο [Μέρος Β']' 'A dangerous profession by default', *Daily Η Εφημερίδα των Συντακτών*, https://www.efsyn.gr/kosmos/ 184245_ena-epaggelma-ek-prooimioy-epikindyno-meros-b. Accessed 20 September 2019.

Kumar, Deepa (2006), 'Media, war, and propaganda: Strategies of information management during the 2003 Iraq War', *Communication and Critical/Cultural Studies*, 3:1, pp. 48–69.

Lacy, Stephen and Rosenstiel Tom (2015), 'Defining and measuring quality journalism', research report, Rutgers School of Communication and Information, http://mpii.rutgers.edu/wp-cont ent/uploads/sites/129/2015/04/Defining-and-Measuring-Quality-Journalism.pdf. Accessed 24 September 2019.

Mallonee, S., Fowler, Carolyn and Istre, Gregory R. (2007), 'Bridging the gap between research and practice: A continuing challenge', Research Gate, https://www.researchgate.net/publ ication/6630234_Bridging_the_gap_between_research_and_practice_A_continuing_challe nge. Accessed 19 September 2019.

McIntyre, Donald (2005), 'Bridging the gap between research and practice', *Cambridge Journal of Education*, 35:3, pp. 357–82.

Md Main Uddin, Rony, Naeemul, Hassan and Yousuf, Mohammad (2018), 'BaitBuster: A clickbait identification framework', *AITopics,* https://aitopics.org/doc/conferences:5A4A4 6D3/. Accessed 2 October 2019.

Mims, Christopher (2010), 'Predicting the death of print', *MIT Technology Review*, https:// www.technologyreview.com/s/420329/predicting-the-death-of-print. Accessed 27 September 2019.

Newman, Nic, Fletcher, Richard, Kalogeropoulos, Antonis and Nielsen, Rasmus Kleis (2019), 'Reuters Institute digital news report 2019', Reuters Institute for the Study of Journalism. https://reutersinstitute.politics.ox.ac.uk/sites/default/files/inline-files/DNR_2019_FINAL. pdf. Accessed 29 September 2019.

Papathanassopoulos, Stelios (2001), 'The decline of newspapers: The case of the Greek press', *Journalism Studies*, 2:1, pp. 109–23.

Raffe, David (2002), 'Bringing academic education and vocational training closer together', *ESRC Research Project on The Introduction of a Unified System*, Edinburgh: Centre for Educational Sociology, University of Edinburgh, pp. 49–65.

Rajan, Amol (2019), 'The new threats to journalism', BBC News, https://www.bbc.com/news/ entertainment-arts-48945604. Accessed 26 September 2019.

Ramonet, Ignacio (2003), 'Mensonges d'État', *Le Monde diplomatique*, https://institutions. mondediplo.com/2003/07/RAMONET/10193. Accessed 1 October 2019.

Schneidermann, Daniel (1996), 'Réponse à Pierre Bourdieu', *Le Monde diplomatique*, https://www.monde-diplomatique.fr/1996/05/SCHNEIDERMANN/5483. Accessed 28 October 2021.

Tefertiller, Alec (2018), 'Media substitution in cable cord-cutting: The adoption of web-streaming television', *Journal of Broadcasting & Electronic Media*, 62:3, pp. 390–407.

11

Opportunities and Challenges for Academic Engagement in the Multi-Stakeholder Agenda to Safeguard Journalists

Sara Torsner

Introduction

Collaboration between academics and non-academics to achieve 'the co-production of knowledge' to 'simultaneously yield greater academic insight and public
benefit' (Campbell and Vanderhoven 2016: 11) for the purpose of addressing complex societal challenges is a matter of ongoing debate. The nature of the engagement of 'academic research with the wider world' (Campbell and Vanderhoven
2016: 12) and the imperative to 'demonstrate the usefulness of [research] findings'
lies at the very centre of such debate.

As such, to enhance practical knowledge of a societal problem, like attacks on
the safety of journalists, combining various analytical perspectives for the purpose
of understanding how societal circumstances endanger free and independent journalism, seems like a good, if not obvious, idea. Indeed, without this pooling of perspectives and resources, it would be difficult to achieve an adequate understanding
of environments that are hostile to journalism. Contributing to these discussions
on research impact, this chapter capitalizes on a collaborative research project
on how to strengthen information about attacks against the safety of journalists
to give an example of how research quality and impact can be achieved through
processes of knowledge exchange between academic and non-academic actors.

Using work undertaken at the Centre for the Freedom of the Media (CFOM),[1]
University of Sheffield, which focuses on strengthening the monitoring of and systematic information gathering on instances of violations of the safety of journalist

practitioners,[2] the chapter uses the UN Action Plan on the Safety of Journalists and the Issue of Impunity (UN Action Plan) (UN 2012) as an example of an international standard setting framework. This framework is important for academic engagement as it establishes the need to address problems of safety violations against journalists through multi-stakeholder involvement by academia, civil society organizations, media professionals and institutions and UN agencies. Two themes are taken up. First, understanding what the academic contribution and value is to multi-stakeholder processes of policy development. Second, what is the significance of multi-stakeholder engagement and exchange for the purpose of ensuring the relevance of an academic contribution to policy agendas. This chapter concludes with a set of observations on how to build mutually beneficial relationships between academic and non-academic stakeholders in ways that facilitate the building of an empirical evidence base which can serve to establish a comprehensive understanding of safety threats to journalists by tackling current knowledge gaps.

Understanding the academic contribution to the agenda to safeguard journalism: Current challenges

In recognition of increased aggressions and attacks facing journalists who pursue their profession of reporting matters of public concern, international human rights law and normative standard setting frameworks, such as the UN Action Plan on the safety of journalists (UN 2012), firmly establish the desirability and necessity to safeguard journalistic practice and journalists.[3] For instance, general comment No. 34 on Article 19 of the International Covenant on Civil and Political Rights states that '[a] free, uncensored and unhindered press or other media is essential in any society to ensure freedom of opinion and expression and the enjoyment of other Covenant rights. It constitutes one of the cornerstones of a democratic society' (HRC 2011: para 13). From this legalistic human rights perspective, the issue of concern thus becomes how risk to journalists can be mitigated and redressed through the force of law by holding perpetrators of crimes against journalists to account and ensuring that states and other actors uphold their obligations under international law to ensure that human rights are upheld.

This legal reasoning for safeguarding journalists forms a critical rationale of justification when it comes to efforts to develop policies that safeguard (1) the practice of free and independent journalism and (2) the rights of journalists, the net effect of which is to raise the alarm when such rights are infringed. In this way, the issue of threats to the safety of journalist practitioners can be framed as a policy problem in need of solutions generated via a public response (Marier

2017).[4] Such a public response however depends on input from various sources of influence to ensure that political will exists and is translated into efficient measures to address safety problems.

The UN Action Plan emphasizes that since 'the issue of the safety of journalists is much too complex and complicated to be able to be resolved by any single actor' (UNESCO 2015a: 34), a multi-stakeholder and holistic approach is needed. The hope is that such an approach will make it possible to 'build coalitions, mobilize resources, and enhance impact, as well as combine or harmonise efforts in contexts where there is potential for enhanced impact through concerted efforts' (UNESCO 2015b: 35). Essentially, this kind of multi-stakeholder view acknowledges 'that all stakeholders have relevant experience, knowledge and information that ultimately will inform and improve the quality of the decision-making process as well as any actions that [may] result' (Dodds and Benson 2010: 1). In practice this not only requires coordination within the UN system and among its agencies but also collaboration with other international and regional organizations, governments and state institutions, courts, the judiciary and law enforcement as well as civil society organizations, professional associations, media houses and journalists themselves. Academia is expressly mentioned as one of these stakeholders and is understood to 'contribute to creation of safer working conditions for all who practice journalism' (UNESCO 2015b: 1) by developing research-driven understandings of the complex nature of safety problems.

Developing an approach to understanding possibilities for academic engagement with policy problems, Paris argues that academic research can play a key role when it comes to framing the policy problem itself and thus ' " order the world" for practitioners' (Paris 2011: 60). From this perspective, policy problems 'are not given by nature' but 'reflect stated and unstated assumptions about the nature and scope of the problem and why it warrants attention' (Paris 2011: 60). According to Paris, the framing and definition of a problem is key when it comes to 'open up certain kinds of policy responses, while foreclosing others' (Paris 2011: 60), but even more fundamentally, it matters when it comes to establishing an empirical evidence base on which effective policy measures and responses can be formulated and implemented.

For Paris, this understanding of the academic contribution to policy agendas reflects a 'broader view of relevance' that goes beyond making 'specific recommendations that practitioners can directly implement' (Paris 2011: 61) to mitigate a specific policy problem. Indeed, Paris sees academic research as potentially contributing to the process of framing policy issues in three ways: '(1) by identifying and characterizing the policy problem itself; (2) by constructing causal narratives to account for the problem; and (3) by conceptualizing frameworks for responding to the problem' (Paris 2011: 61).

Monitoring instances of violations against the safety of journalists is understood to be an integral part of the UN's work to safeguard journalism. Such monitoring is carried out through various mechanisms within the UN system: through reports outlining progress and regress with regards to trends in press and media freedom,[5] as well as country level statistics accounting for various types of attacks on journalists.[6] Recently, the Sustainable Development Goals (SDG) Agenda with indicator 16.10.1 proposed an important monitoring programme for the global recording of the 'number of verified cases of killing, enforced disappearance, torture, arbitrary detention, kidnapping and other harmful acts committed against journalists [...] on an annual basis' (UN 2019a; 2019b). In parallel with these UN-led initiatives, crucial monitoring efforts are also conducted by civil society organizations that gather statistics.[7]

From a legal, advocacy or policy perspective, the monitoring of violations against journalists may be described as serving vital objectives, such as functioning as a tool to hold perpetrators to account, possibilities to track progress and regress over time, as well as supporting the development of effective policy measures to reduce existing problems. For instance, the SDG agenda can be described as having been developed in a political context where indicators have been agreed upon through negotiations and compromise between nation states. As such, SDG indicators are crucial as a tool reflecting political commitment to address the issues outlined.

Considering the potential contribution of academic research to such processes of monitoring safety violations, academic engagement starts with a yet more underlying and fundamental concern, namely the need to accurately capture what is going on and to understand problems of safety violations as they occur in the real world. This is arguably also the rationale and intention behind current monitoring efforts. However, whereas gathering statistics, for instance, on how many journalists are killed or imprisoned on a yearly basis, is valuable information that can be used to identify a problem and to pressurize a state to address this problem; what needs to be understood, from an academic perspective, are the reasons behind such violations. Indeed, how can we 'understand the nature, dynamics and consequences of threats (some of which culminate in killings) and [...] shifting trends in journalism safety' (Torsner 2017: 131)? What is needed is a shift from attempting to record *that* safety violations occur and in *what way they occur* to uncovering *how* and *why* these violations occur.

Such an approach has been adopted by CFOM. In a project on 'strengthening the systematic gathering of information on violations of the safety of journalist practitioners',[8] existing international, regional and local data sets that gather statistical information on violations against journalists were assessed for their utility in aiding a comprehensive understanding of the features of environments that are hostile to journalists and how they emerge. Thus, for example, data sets were assessed to see if they could be used to specify the circumstances under which attacks on journalists escalate and become more violent. Or why certain types of aggressions (like imprisonment) happen in certain countries but not others? What these kinds of 'how and why' questions do is look for 'stated and unstated assumptions' (Paris 2011: 60) and bring these assumptions to light in a manner useful to policymakers.

Problematically, after having carried out a systematic analysis of datasets recording violations against journalists, we found that the current empirical data does not in many cases lend itself to these somewhat more complex 'how and why' queries. The reasons being: (1) a lack of data on a range of different types of violations with existing data being overly focused on killings of journalists; (2) a lack of conceptual consistency, with definitions of different categories of violations being underdeveloped or not specified as well as differing across data sets; (3) a lack of sophisticated and disaggregated categorization and sub-categorization of violations and contextual information; and (4) a lack of methodological transparency with regards to how information is recorded and categorized.[9] Other forms of academic scrutiny of such empirical outputs derived from monitoring and measuring safety violations or, more broadly, the state of press freedom reveal a related and equally fundamental problem. Namely and as expressed by Burgess (2010: 8):

> In the world of media freedom advocacy and in government policy circles, the conceptual explication of media freedom has taken a back seat to problems of measurement [...] Never mind the obvious point that it is hard to measure something if you do not know exactly what it is.

Despite such measurement challenges, the statistics and reports produced by the UN and civil society organizations are primary sources of information for academic researchers seeking to engage with safety problems.[10]

While being oriented toward the same end goal – the safeguarding of journalism through effective monitoring – the domains of law, policy, advocacy and academic research ultimately approach this issue from their distinct perspectives. Although it is our experience that what academia 'actually does' is not widely understood among non-academic actors. The reasons for this are of course likely to be diverse and potentially related to the failure of the academic community to effectively communicate how they work and what their contribution to policy agendas actually is. Nevertheless, the complementary functions of these various domains are often highlighted as essential for the purpose of addressing social problems. This is the case not least in the ambitious and commendable aim of the UN Action Plan to bring a diverse range of actors together to collectively and in collaboration work to address problems of safety. However, in practice, the incorporation of academic insight and research into the agenda to safeguard journalism is not something that happens automatically and without effort. The United Nations Educational, Scientific and Cultural Organization (UNESCO), which is tasked to carry out the overall coordination of the UN Action Plan, has carried out a range of initiatives to increase academic engagement with issues of safety. These include, for instance, the launching of a Research Agenda on the Safety of Journalists in 2015 and the arranging of a yearly academic conference on the safety of journalists held in conjunction with UNESCO's World Press Freedom Day celebrations.[11]

These initiatives have served in important ways to encourage academics to focus research efforts on issues of safety and work toward addressing the fact that 'unlike the issues of journalism and freedom of expression, journalists' safety has not been a very popular topic of academic research. It has rarely been discussed as a specific research question' (UNESCO 2015b: 1). Building on and expanding the knowledge base in this way is undeniably important; however, to integrate academic research into the wider safety agenda and to ensure that the academic production of knowledge does not simply occur in a silo and disconnect from the policy context within which it exists, academic research arguably needs platforms for exchange and avenues for engagement with relevant non-academic stakeholders. As acknowledged in the 2017 report on UNESCO's multi-stakeholder consultation on strengthening the UN Action Plan on the safety of journalists,

> [t]here appears to be a gap between policy-makers, NGOs, media and the academy that is linked to their different priorities and agendas. A lesson learnt by academics is that there appears to be a lack of knowledge and attendant misconception among these actors of what academic research entails, what it does, how it works and importantly its direct relevance to current problems/issues. There is also an apparent lack of clarity among academics/researchers of how other actors conceive of the role of research and the academy.
>
> (UNESCO 2017: 37)

This mutual lack of understanding of respective roles and contributions arguably stand in the way of developing synergies between academia and stakeholders as well as the 'translation of academic research into something that is practicable, relevant and applicable' (UNESCO 2017: 37). From the point of view of academia, such a disconnect with the needs and priorities of policy and advocacy agendas is likely to make it more difficult for academic research to have real world relevance and be impactful. For policy and advocacy initiatives, however, incorporating research-derived knowledge would allow proposals and actions to be firmly supported by a reliable evidence base. This would serve to strengthen claims and opportunities to propose effective measures that address safety problems.

Pointing to the benefits of exchange between academia and non-academic stakeholders, Harrison writes that

> [w]hile work within disciplinary boundaries of course produces highly valued specialist knowledge, many contemporary complex problems we face require greater research capacity which comes from both depth and breadth of knowledge as well as new methodological innovations, alongside input from those who have practical knowledge and experience.
>
> (Harrison 2017: 109)

The issue now is the ways in which this can be achieved. One such way has been the development of collaborative research partnerships, and another has been the establishment of a CFOM research network, Journalism Safety Research Network (JSRN), which serves to support these aims as a platform of knowledge exchange.[12]

Possibilities for the collaborative co-production of knowledge through platforms of exchange between academic and non-academic actors

What the previous discussion shows is the need to link research aims with an effort to achieve both comprehensive and systematic data collection, and this requires engaging in this process of multi-stakeholder dialogue. Ideally such dialogue produces collaborative partnerships that have genuine value.

Participating in technical meetings on indicator 16.10.1 arranged by UNESCO made it possible for us to share our research with a range of stakeholders and to consider how to produce synergies between research and practical monitoring needs. Ultimately, this led to the identification of a collaborative partner in the Dutch press freedom organization Free Press Unlimited (FPU).[13] We started our research collaboration in 2018 and have since engaged in iterative processes of exchange where our proposals for methodological development have been tested against the practical expertise and utility-driven research needs of FPU. The partnership with FPU has been essential to 'frame, inform and drive forward the outcomes of research' (Fenby-Hulse et al. 2019: xiii) and ultimately to ensure the 'real-world' relevance of the research undertaken.

Through this process, we have also been able to mobilize interdisciplinary research expertise and capacity from the departments of journalism studies and computer science at the University of Sheffield to ensure that we can develop sophisticated methodologies to redress identified knowledge gaps. To this end, we have continued to link our research priorities within the project to the wider SDG agenda and indicator 16.10.1, while focusing specifically on the issue of how to build the monitoring capacity of nationally based civil society organizations that collect information on violations from their immediate local environment as a priority of FPU.

As shown in research carried out by the International Federation Expression Exchange (IFEX 2011: 20–22), local data collection often faces challenges as it involves having to gather data in the field from volatile and often conflict-ridden societies. Furthermore, institutionalized local mechanisms for data collection that could facilitate the systematic collection of data on abuses may be under development or completely absent in many contexts (both conflict and non-conflict) (Pöyhtäri 2016: 177; UNESCO 2015c: 14–17).[14] In addition, locally collected data is 'rarely compiled into a common repository of data that can be used for structural cross-country comparison or the domestic analysis of trends and cases to prioritise for judicial investigation' (Torsner 2017: 130).

The extensive global outreach of FPU's activities, for instance, when it comes to supporting local monitoring initiatives, has proved to be important for us as a way of connecting with local organizations and enabled the distribution of a survey to start mapping in a systematic way what monitoring is going on within various national contexts. While the process of identifying exactly which research outputs will be of most use to support local monitoring of the 16.10.1 indicators in local contexts is ongoing, and will continue through iterative dialogue, the collaborative multi-stakeholder approach has allowed us to begin identifying potential research outputs and design prototype tools. We hope these will serve to address various research and monitoring needs by eventually being developed into a toolkit that aims to facilitate processes of generating, categorizing and systematizing quality data on a range of various types of safety violations against journalists that are also tailored to the distinct needs of the diverse range of monitoring organizations.

Opportunities for academic contributions to the multi-stakeholder agenda to safeguard journalism: A proposal

Derived from this discussion, the following observations are made to building mutually beneficial relationships between academic and non-academic stakeholders. Central to achieving such collaboration is the formulation and communication of what the academic contribution and value is to multi-stakeholder processes of policy development. From our experience, communicating how to understand the 'real world' relevance of academic research is key to establishing trust when undertaking processes of collaborative research. This could, for instance, mean explaining in concrete terms how highly specialized academic expertise can concretely be applied to a specific problem, or how theoretical and conceptual frameworks can facilitate the systematic scrutiny and understanding of an issue.

For the purpose of the research project on monitoring safety threats, the identification of a wider line of inquiry within which data improvement must occur has been central to developing our academic approach. This has meant introducing a narrative of risk to journalism as multidimensional and in need of holistic assessment to comprehensively understand various types of risk to journalistic practice. This process is essentially about establishing an evidence base that can be used to describe the nature and dynamics of the problems of a wide range of types of risk to journalism. This requires not only tracking the incidence and nature of violations themselves (their manifestation), which is the focus of current approaches to gather data, but also their causes and consequences.[15] While our broader research interest thus concerns the holistic assessment and understanding of violations that incorporates these three dimensions of risk (causes, manifestations and consequences), we are also able to hone in on specific aspects of this more overarching narrative in order to focus on the methodological improvement of the fundamental dimension of manifestations of violations against journalists, which is of immediate interest to monitoring efforts such as SDG 16.10.1. At the same time, it enables us to carry out this research within a conceptual framework that allows us to contribute with input not only by identifying ways to facilitate the generation of more empirical data of the same kind that already exists but also importantly to develop methodologies to improve existing data so that it captures the contextual complexity necessary to understand problems of safety in a more comprehensive way. Consequently, our engagement with the issue of safety problems is, on the one hand, to support monitoring initiatives, such as the one introduced by the SDG agenda through the creation of knowledge that can be used to achieve formulated monitoring goals. On the other hand, an essential contribution of academic research is also to engage with such initiatives, not by simply accepting the delineated measurement framework but to challenge it and explore how it can be strengthened or complemented for the purpose of building a reliable and comprehensive evidence base that allows for the best possible understanding of the issue of safety threats. In our experience, discussions with partners and stakeholders around this latter point constitute a critical opportunity for exchange and discussion on how to collaboratively translate such research findings into practical use.

Engaging with the multi-stakeholder policy processes concerning the agenda to safeguard journalism is certainly something we as academics have found worthwhile. Interestingly, it has not only strengthened collaboration with non-academic actors has but also opened possibilities for collaboration across disciplinary academic boundaries. We have found that to contribute effectively to the international efforts to safeguard journalists, it has also been necessary to mobilize academic expertise from various disciplines. Whereas research at the Department of Journalism Studies at the University of Sheffield has served to formulate the research problem and refine our understanding of current knowledge gaps, bringing in competence from the fields of linguistics and computer science has made it possible to begin to adapt and develop methods and technical tools within those fields to be applied to the specific problem of monitoring safety threats. An interdisciplinary approach of this kind has opened exciting opportunities for research synergies and development. Work that has recently been further strengthened by the development of the JSRN, which functions as a knowledge-network mobilizing cross-disciplinary academic and professional expertise to build research capacity and enable the sharing of knowledge on issues of journalism safety.

This kind of partnership shows that there are numerous benefits of engaging with and working to develop various platforms of exchange between academics. Benefits that cover research capacity, data gathering, enhancing the evidential basis of research, engagement with 'the wider world', increasing the potential to influence policy and with that impact in driving change, increasing the representative range of stakeholders through various levels of engagement. Finally, partnerships aid the development of concrete collaborative research projects whereby they can join or lead participation in local and international forums for dialogue, thereby co-producing deeper knowledge – in our case, as described in this chapter, deeper knowledge and understanding of journalism safety.

NOTES

1. CFOM is also the home of the UNESCO Chair on Media Freedom, Journalism Safety, and the Issue of Impunity which is held by Professor Jackie Harrison. Established in 2018, the Chair acts as a 'bridgehead between academia and policy through the production of high quality research, information, documentation and teaching within the Sustainable Development Goals agenda'. See: http://www.cfom.org.uk/about/unesco-chair-on-media-freedom-journalism-safety-and-the-issue-of-impunity/ (accessed 26 May 2021).

2. See, for example, http://www.cfom.org.uk/2019/07/18/cfom-and-unesco-arrange-journalism-safety-research-network-panel-on-the-monitoring-of-sdg-indicator-16-10-1-at-iamcr-in-madrid/ (accessed 26 May 2021).

3. See, for instance, work undertaken in this regard by UNESCO (https://en.unesco.org/themes/safety-journalists), OSCE (https://www.osce.org/representative-on-freedom-of-media/106283) and COE (https://www.coe.int/en/web/media-freedom). See also UNESCO's general website: https://en.unesco.org/un-plan-action-safety-journalists and Article 19 (2017) (accessed 26 May 2021).

4. Keyword: Policy problem.
5. See, for instance, UNESCO's reports on world trends in freedom of expression and media development, https://en.unesco.org/world-media-trends (accessed 26 May 2021).
6. See UNESCO's Observatory of killed journalists, https://unesdoc.unesco.org/ark:/48223/pf0000246014 (accessed 26 May 2021).
7. See, for instance, the Committee to Protect Journalists (https://cpj.org/), the International News Safety Institute (https://newssafety.org/home/), the International Federation of Journalists (https://www.ifj.org/), the International Press Institute (https://ipi.media/), Reporters Without Borders (https://rsf.org/) (accessed 26 May 2021).
8. The research team consists of Jackie Harrison, Diana Maynard and Sara Torsner. See also, Torsner (2019) on the discussion of the need for a holistic approach to comprehensively understand risk to journalism through three dimensions of risk including its causes, manifestations and consequences.
9. For a more in-depth analysis of this, see Torsner (2019).
10. See Torsner (2017) for a more in-depth discussion on these limitations.
11. See, for example, http://www.cfom.org.uk/our-networks/journalism-safety-research-network-new/world-press-freedom-day-journalism-safety-research-conferences/ (accessed 26 May 2021).
12. The JSRN brings together academic and non-academic actors that engage in research on issues of journalism safety. Established in 2017 during the UNESCO World Press Freedom Day celebrations in Helsinki, Finland, the JSRN currently has around 180 members from around the world. See http://www.cfom.org.uk/our-networks/journalism-safety-research-network-new/ (accessed 26 May 2021).
13. See https://www.freepressunlimited.org/en (accessed 26 May 2021).
14. See UNESCO's initiatives to progress data collection on threats within various national contexts through the application of JSI assessments. JSI assessments have for instance been carried out in Guatemala, Kenya, Nepal and Pakistan. https://en.unesco.org/themes/safety-of-journalists/journalists-safety-indicators (accessed 26 May 2021).
15. See Torsner (2019).

REFERENCES

Burgess, J. (2010), 'Evaluating the evaluators: Media freedom indexes and what they measure', Monitoring and Evaluation, https://repository.upenn.edu/cgi/viewcontent.cgi?article=1001&context=cgcs_monitoringandeval_videos. Accessed 24 May 2021.

Campbell, H. and Vanderhoven, D. (2016), *Knowledge That Matters: Realising the Potential of Co-Production*, United Kingdom: N8/ESRC Research Programme, Economic Social Research Council.

Dodds, F. and Benson E. (2010), 'Multi-stakeholder Dialogue Toolkit Johannesburg: Civicus', Civicus, http://www.civicus.org/images/PGX_D_Multistakeholder%20Dialogue.pdf. Accessed 24 May 2021.

Fenby-Hulse, K., Heywood, Em. and Walker, K. (2019), *Research Impact and the Early Career Researcher: Lived Experiences, New Perspectives*, London: Routledge.

Harrison, J. (2017), 'Setting a new research agenda: The establishment of a journalism safety research network', in U. Carlsson and R. Pöyhtäri (eds), *The Assault on Journalism: Building Knowledge to Protect Freedom of Expression*, Göteborg: Nordicom, http://www.unesco.se/wp-content/uploads/2017/04/The-Assault-on-Journalism.pdf. Accessed 24 May 2021.

HRC (2011), 'General comment no. 34: Article 19, Freedoms of opinion and expression', https://www.undocs.org/CCPR/C/GC/34. Accessed 24 May 2021.

IFEX (2011), 'Journalists killed methodology research project', https://ifex.org/images/campaigns/2012/01/04/journalistskilledresearchfinaldec2011.pdf. Accessed 24 May 2021.

Marier, P. (2017), *Oxford Research Encyclopedia of Politics*, https://oxfordre.com/politics. Accessed 24 May 2021.

Paris, R. (2011), 'Ordering the world: Academic research and policymaking on fragile states', *International Studies Review*, 13:1, pp. 58–71.

Pöyhtäri, R. (2016), 'The (un)safe practice of journalism: An analysis based on UNESCO's Journalists' Safety Indicators assessments', in U. Carlsson (ed.), *Freedom of Expression and Media in Transition: Studies and Reflections in the Digital Age*, Gothenburg: Nordicom, pp. 175–82.

Torsner, S. (2017), 'Measuring journalism safety. Methodological challenges', in U. Carlsson and R. Pöyhtäri (eds), *The Assault on Journalism. Building Knowledge to Protect Freedom of Expression*, Gothenburg: Nordicom, http://www.unesco.se/wp-content/uploads/2017/04/The-Assault-on-Journalism.pdf. Accessed 24 May 2021.

Torsner, S. (2019), 'Profiling the civil diminishment of journalism: How to understand the causes, manifestations and consequences of risk to journalism', doctoral thesis, Sheffield: The University of Sheffield.

UN (2012), 'UN Plan of Action on the Safety of Journalists and the issue of impunity', https://en.unesco.org/sites/default/files/un-plan-on-safety-journalists_en.pdf. Accessed 24 May 2021.

UN (2019a), 'SDG Global Indicator Platform. 16.10.1 killing, kidnapping, enforced disappearance, arbitrary detention and torture of journalists, associated media personnel, trade unionists and human rights advocates', https://sdg.tracking-progress.org/indicator/16-10-1-killing-kidnapping-enforced-disappearance-arbitrary-detention-and-torture-of-journalists-associated-media-personnel-trade-unionists-and-human-rights-advocates-previous-12-months/. Accessed 24 May 2021.

UN (2019b), 'Guidance for reporting on SDG 16', https://www.sdg16hub.org/system/files/2019-05/SDG%2016%20Reporting%20Guidance%20Final.pdf. Accessed 24 May 2021.

UNESCO (2015a), *UN Plan of Action on the Safety of Journalists and the Issue of Impunity. Implementation Review Report for the Period 2013–2014*, https://en.unesco.org/system/files/reviewreportunplan_of_action_on_safety_of_journalist_fin.pdf. Accessed 24 May 2021.

UNESCO (2015b), *Towards a Research Agenda on the Safety of Journalists*, http://www.unesco. org/new/fileadmin/MULTIMEDIA/HQ/CI/CI/images/Themes/Freedom_of_expression/safety _of_journalists/Draft_Research_Agenda_Safety_of_Journalists_06_2015.pdf. Accessed 24 May 2021.

UNESCO (2015c), *Applying UNESCO's Journalists' Safety Indicators (JSIs): A Practical Guide-book to Assist Researchers*, https://unesdoc.unesco.org/ark:/48223/pf0000260894. Accessed 24 May 2021.

UNESCO (2017), *Stakeholder Consultation on Strengthening the Implementation of the UN Plan of Action on the Safety of Journalists and the Issue of Impunity*, https://en.unesco. org/sites/default/files/report_-_multi-stakeholder_consultation.pdf. Accessed 24 May 2021.

PROPOSAL 7

MEDIA LITERACY

12

Accessing, Evaluating and Engaging with News: The Value of a User-Centric Approach for Rethinking Media Literacy

Joëlle Swart

Introduction

Educational institutions are increasingly paying attention to media literacy. Concerns around misinformation, privacy and filter bubbles (Pariser 2011) have sparked a variety of programmes, tailored toward turning young people into critical, mindful and active news users who can confidently navigate the media-saturated society they live in (Mihailidis 2012). These curricula are based on the premise that by training students to become more critical toward the information they receive and the technologies they use, they become less susceptible to the potential dangers that media pose, such as fake news or privacy invasions (Bulger and Davison 2018; Lewandowsky et al. 2017). However, recent work has shown that such media literacy interventions might also backfire (boyd 2017). First, schools have struggled to find the delicate balance between promoting healthy scepticism and turning youth into cynical citizens who come to distrust any source of information (Mihailidis 2018; Vraga and Tully 2019). Second, studies show that a high awareness of the importance of privacy online may translate into passive media users who no longer dare to engage publicly with news at all, especially if it concerns sensitive topics (Marwick and boyd 2014; Thorson 2014). Finally, the current focus of media literacy initiatives on the evaluation of content, while undoubtedly important, means the way platforms and algorithms may impact such information remains largely neglected. This is reflected in people's varying levels of algorithmic awareness (Fletcher and Kleis Nielsen 2019; Powers 2017). Such findings challenge current approaches to media education, raising the question of how media literacy could be facilitated in a way that *empowers* users to access, analyse, evaluate and engage with news and media (Hobbs 2011; Maksl et al. 2015; Mihailidis 2018).

This chapter explores these questions by departing from the practices and experiences of media users themselves. What skills, competences and knowledge do *they* perceive as helpful to build up an understanding of the public world? How and under what circumstances does media literacy become useful? What is the actual impact of media literacy – and reversely, what are the problematic consequences of being media illiterate – for people in everyday life? This chapter shows how such an emic approach to media literacy helps to create more nuanced and layered understandings of how to foster people's abilities to use media in a thoughtful, deliberate manner.

Its research draws upon a series of semi-structured, in-depth interviews I conducted in the first half of 2019 with 36 Dutch young people (between 16 and 22 years old) about their social media use and media literacy, focusing on students in lower vocational education (MBO) in particular. This is both the lowest and most common level of tertiary education in the Dutch education system. Despite previous work that shows level of education is one of the strongest predictors of young people's level of news and media literacy (Kleemans and Eggink 2016), most media literacy research still remains focused at college or university students. This study addresses this underrepresented group. Its sample included young people of different gender, ages and ethnicity, recruited via their teachers at schools in three different regions in The Netherlands, who were enrolled in a mix of programmes (from automotive engineering to personal healthcare to administrative assistance) and in different phases of their studies (first-, second- and third-year students). Students from journalism-related programmes were excluded from the sample. Prior to the interview, students were asked to sign an informed consent form; for underage participants, parents were asked to give permission and sign the form in advance. The interviews discussed four major themes: young people's (1) everyday media habits (2) use of social media (3) (social) media literacy and (4) their civic engagement on social media platforms. Students did not receive a reward for participation but could participate in the research as a substitute activity during class. Inductive, thematic analysis (Corbin and Strauss 2015) was used to analyse the interview data (see Swart 2021 for a full description of the study's methodology).

Based on its findings, this chapter discusses the value of taking a user-centric approach to studying media literacy, in relation to three issues in particular. First, it explores the topic of trustworthiness of news content on social media and how to help young media users to critically evaluate (mis)information in these spaces. Second, the chapter delves into the issue of teaching students how to engage with news while simultaneously managing their privacy online, at a time when their digital news consumption is continuously subject to surveillance. Finally, it explores how an emic approach may expand our understandings of how to enable young people to follow their news interests in an increasingly algorithmically tailored news environment.

Evaluating news and discerning misinformation

Recent debates about 'fake news' and fears around young people's vulnerability to misinformation have resulted in a rise of media literacy initiatives. The underlying argument for these programmes is that the ability to recognize accurate, credible and reliable news is vital to people's practices of informed citizenship and to democracy more generally. Klurfeld and Schneider (2014) argue that citizens' ability to discern quality journalism is crucial to its survival. This applies to both its economic endurance and to journalism's symbolic role as a primary sense-making institution in society, whose relevance depends on users' collective attention to its content (Hartley 1996; Swart 2018). Distinguishing news, however, requires an ever-increasing level of skills. People need to make sense of a variety of sources that are not necessarily produced by professional journalists. Moreover, the mixture of different information genres in social media feeds raises questions about what 'news' or 'journalism' actually is (Edgerly 2017). Given this complexity, it is unsurprising that much research on media literacy highlights the importance of training critical thinking skills for encouraging media literacy (e.g., Kahne and Bowyer 2017; Vraga and Tully 2019).

However, as has been widely noted (boyd 2017; Broersma 2018; Mihailidis 2018), the focus on possible deficits of news media that comes with the scrutiny of critically evaluating news content can have the unintended side-effect of fostering distrust for *all* media. The interviews reflect such scepticism by default. In particular, young people who had grown up in households where news was not (or only sporadically) consumed or discussed were cynical about classic notions of objectivity. Unlike their classmates, when I asked what they thought was news, they did not refer to any classical news values (Harcup and O'Neill 2016), such as the story's public magnitude, the timeliness of the issue or its contribution to wider public debate. For them, anything that was novel and recent could potentially be news. Because they automatically equated such classifications of 'newness' with judgments about reliability and credibility (see Edgerly and Vraga 2020), this made trusting news or media problematic. When the boundaries of what counts as reliable information are not clearly delineated, for example, Lisa[1] (18) argued this also implies exactly the opposite: that any content you come across may be inaccurate or even a deliberate attempt to mislead you.

In general, confirming earlier findings (Craft et al. 2016), these young people knew little about how news is produced, who makes editorial decisions in reporting, or the economics behind news production, even when they came from news-rich backgrounds. Although most interviewees had a good overview of the national media landscape and could name major news brands, they rarely referred to political leanings of media organizations or whether such a source might be sponsored and influenced by commercial logics. This was exemplary of students' broader lack of knowledge about news production and about processes of framing, bias and gatekeeping. Without such a frame of reference to rely upon, even with a toolkit of potential ways to verify and cross-check information up your sleeve, it is easy to become cynical about journalism as a whole.

Moreover, the findings suggest that the problem lies not so much with young people not being aware of any verification strategies they can use but with the perceived *usefulness* and practicality of these strategies (see also Vraga et al. 2021). Regardless of their level of media education, most could list at least one strategy for validating information, such as cross-checking with another source or looking up the author of a piece or the organization that had published the story. Also, students' awareness that content might be misinformation was high. With platform rather than source functioning as the major cue for reliability (cf. Sterrett et al. 2019), they were particularly hesitant to trust news on Facebook, which had a notoriously bad reputation among young people for presenting fabricated stories. In practice, however, such verification strategies were seldomly employed. They were considered cumbersome, time-consuming and difficult to align with students' everyday news routines. Students' most common practice of consuming news was scrolling, that is, navigating through their social media news feeds continuously. Users were already hesitant to break this flow to click on a story to read it in full, confirming previous findings (Groot Kormelink and Costera Meijer 2019), let alone to seek confirmation from other news sources. Taking everything with a grain of salt, therefore, was considered a far less laborious alternative. Less cynical students solved the issue of judging the trustworthiness of news stories by relying on a variety of shortcuts. For instance, Sanne (18) used the news brand as a cue for reliability, whereas Daan (21) checked the comments below a news story to verify it. While such tactics were perceived as imperfect rough estimations, rather than full assessments of trustworthiness, they were simultaneously experienced as far more practical in everyday life. Therefore, they were also applied more frequently. Thus, equipping students with a broad set of authentication strategies and tactics, while indicating strengths and pitfalls, might help to counter young people's lack of agency regarding misinformation.

Engaging with news and managing privacy

Second, we turn to the value of a user-centric perspective for understanding youth's privacy practices. Students of programmes where media education was part of the curriculum (typically embedded in broader 'Citizenship' courses) described the importance of managing privacy online as one of the most prominent focal points of these programmes. A frequently used exercise, for instance, was having students google their own names to give them insight into the digital traces of their online behaviour. The interviewees also mentioned how privacy management was being emphasized by their parents, in stories by peers and in the mass media, for example, in the popular MTV show *Catfish*. These messages tended to stress users' individual responsibility for shaping their online visibility and image.

However, as Hargittai and Marwick (2016) note, '[T]he ability of individuals to control the spread of their personal information is compromised by both technological and social violations of privacy' (3572). Youth don't see privacy online as personally constructed, but as networked (De Wolf 2020; Marwick and boyd 2014). This is reflected in their experiences of media education. On the individual level, these educational programmes might seem highly effective. Most interviewees could reflect in detail on what information they shared on which social media platform, what results searching for their name in Google would yield and showed in-depth knowledge of social media's privacy settings. However, students simultaneously experienced privacy as, at least partially, out of their control. The interviews showcase a sense of what De Wolf (2020) has been labelled as 'networked defeatism', that is, a perceived lack of individual control over one's privacy on social media. Some students, therefore, in addition to personal privacy management, had social safeguards in place, such as having an agreement with their friends to always ask for permission prior to uploading group pictures. As previous work has suggested (Choi et al. 2018), the application of such tactics was motivated by a sense of fatalism, as for instance Romy (20) explains:

> I've closed off my Insta, but I'm easy with accepting people. On Facebook there's what school I go to, what school I went to before, where I work, in which city I live, just my street isn't on there. You know what it is? If you're a bit Big Brother, if you want to, you'll find out anyway. It's very difficult to close everything off.

Reflecting social norms expressed by parents, popular media and educators, students were much more concerned about social privacy (i.e., hiding information from people they know) than with risks of institutional surveillance (cf. Sujon 2018). Remarkably, only two students mentioned the topic of digital surveillance and the harvesting of personal data by commercial companies, giving the

Cambridge Analytica scandal as an example. With the context collapse on many social media platforms jeopardizing users' ability to restrict information to particular subgroups (Marwick and boyd 2014), youth were much more concerned with what information family members, classmates and employers could view. Young people's perceptions of these privacy risks were strongly gendered: while girls often referred to the peril of sharing nude pictures and being 'exposed', boys were more likely to mention how drunk photos could lead to missed employment opportunities.

Young people deal with their lack of control over who can see what they post in various ways, employing both individual and intrapersonal privacy management tactics (De Wolf 2020). Romy (20) operated a complex system of multiple social media accounts and even SIM cards. Where she was mainly 'lurking' while using accounts under her own name, she frequently engaged in online debates with the accounts she had registered under a pseudonym. Pablo (18) likewise used a fake name to comment on YouTube videos about public issues, but simultaneously noted that others considered such behaviour 'odd' and risky. For most young people, however, their need for online privacy indeed meant they would rarely post or even share content, especially in relation to news and politics (Thorson 2014).

The challenge for media educators, thus, is to promote mindful media use that acknowledges the permanence of content that is posted while still encouraging youth to craft their own story and shape their online image. For example, Ashley (17), an avid photographer, experienced the current emphasis of her peers and school on individual privacy management as very restrictive. She told how her desire to express herself creatively through pictures on Instagram would often prompt negative responses by her classmates who were concerned about the digital traces she left. One possible way forward, suggested by youth themselves and supported by earlier research (e.g., Hobbs et al. 2013), could be to offer more best practices of how social media technologies can be employed in a beneficial manner. For example, young people expressed they would like to learn how they employ social media to keep up to date on personal interests, engage with public issues they find important, or to present themselves to future employers. Such empowering examples may help to make youth aware of, as Tim (18) put it, 'not just its bad features, but also its functional side'.

Accessing news and personalizing news environments

Finally, we explore how an emic approach can give more insight into people's experiences of and practices around the algorithmic selection of news. While most media education programmes pay limited attention to the topic of 'algorithmic literacy' (D'Ignazio and Bhargava 2015; Head et al. 2020), the increased use of personalized platforms for news suggests that users' ability to understand and intervene in algorithmic selection is becoming increasingly important. Like most young people (Newman et al. 2020), the interviewees strongly depended on algorithmically tailored news, with Facebook, YouTube and news widgets on their smartphones (like Apple News and Google News) featuring as the most prominent sources in their media diets. This represents a major shift in how users come to encounter news. Much audience research has conceptualized people's news use as either directed practices, influenced by users' individual characteristics and needs – in line with uses and gratifications theory (Katz et al. 1973) – or as heavily shaped by the context of people's daily habits and routines (e.g., Couldry et al. 2016). For the interviewees, however, the selection of news they consumed was usually neither purposeful nor a ritual but predominantly driven by algorithmic recommendations. Convinced that the news they needed to know would find them when it was really important (for similar folk theories, see Toff and Kleis Nielsen 2018), most participants were very passive in their search for news. While a few checked a news app on their smartphone or watched the TV news along with their parents, most of them strongly relied on social media highlighting stories that were relevant for them. Moreover, actively tailoring these platforms to their personal interests by liking specific news brands or setting up filters was rare. News, for the interviewees, was something that would simply 'come along', making the consumption of a news story fortuitous.

Given young people's dependence on algorithms for news, one might expect them to develop algorithmic imaginaries (Bucher 2017) folk theories (DeVito et al. 2017) about these mechanisms. In some cases, however, youth did not realize that the content they encountered was personalized. Youth's algorithmic awareness (or the lack of it) varied considerably between platforms. The fact that Facebook would not simply display posts of the friends and pages they followed chronologically was relatively well-known, although some interviewees were still under the impression that they would see all content their friends had posted if they would only scroll down far enough (cf. Powers 2017; Eslami et al. 2015). Similarly, many were familiar with YouTube's mechanism of prolonging users' attention via its Suggested Videos feature. For example, Mariam (20) complained how YouTube's algorithm tended to consider her interests too narrow and would show her videos that she considered too similar to each other, if she did not intervene actively with the content selection herself. However, most interviewees were unaware of algorithmic curation on other platforms they used, in particular with regard to Instagram, Twitter and Snapchat. Likewise, students had difficulty to describe what news was shown by Apple News and Google News on their smartphones' home screens, or even who supplied the content of these widgets, despite checking them daily. After they had updated their operating system one day, they explained, such news was 'simply there'. Some had noticed that particular news brands did show up often, but in general, they did not question how such content was selected.

The findings above are indicative of a broader lack of insight into what algorithms are and do (cf. Eslami et al. 2015; Head et al. 2020). Even when interviewees they were aware that the news they consumed on a particular platform was personalized, they tended to imagine these algorithms as neutral gatekeepers. Some theorized such mechanisms were fed by what content they clicked and viewed; most interviewees, however, contrary to previous findings (cf. Monzer et al. 2020), were unaware how their own online behaviour and supplied user data shaped the content displayed on their timelines. Algorithmic selection was also rarely connected to broader societal issues like fragmentation.

Given the interviewees' gaps in algorithmic literacy, it is unsurprising that hardly any young people in the sample tried to actively engage with or intervene in the algorithmic personalization of news. One of these exceptions was Daan (21), who deliberately followed a variety of political parties on Twitter to ensure he would get a multifaceted view on public issues. This is an example of how users might try to reverse-engineer algorithms and influence news selection (see Rader and Gray 2015). The interview data suggest that young people like Daan, with higher levels of algorithmic literacy, who might feel more empowered to tailor their social media feeds to their personal interests, could be more likely to apply such knowledge to challenge algorithms' decisions (for instance with the aim to create more diverse news feeds) and might have more satisfactory experiences using news on social media. More work from a user-centric perspective could provide insight into the impact of algorithmic literacy on users' practices and experiences around personalized news.

Conclusion

Changing practices of news use force us to rethink what skills, competences and knowledge are necessary for users to confidently and critically navigate the current media landscape. This chapter has considered these questions from the perspective of young people themselves, advocating for a user-centric approach to media literacy. It has shown how starting from the perspective of media users themselves can offer further direction to media educators how to guide students regarding the complexities of contemporary media use. Consequently, it proposes three suggestions on how to align media literacy programmes more closely to young people's everyday news practices and experiences.

First, while current approaches appeared successful in equipping students with a variety of news verification strategies and tactics, interviewees generally had little insight into the broader context of media production, media effects and the political, economic and societal role of journalism (see also Craft et al. 2016). Providing young people with such a broader frame of reference could not only help them to discern misinformation and judge the accuracy and trustworthiness of news more effectively but might also be beneficial to decrease cynicism as a potential by-effect of media education (boyd 2017), preventing young people from tuning out from news. Such higher level literacy is difficult to attain autodidactically or through peers, leaving a key role for media educators.

Second, the interviews show the importance of going beyond merely teaching knowledge and skills and giving concrete illustrations of how such media literacy can successfully be applied in practice, considering young people's everyday contexts of media use and the social norms and dynamics these might be subject to. One clear example is public engagement around news, a civic expectation that young people perceived as contradictory with standards around privacy management that promote cautionary, passive online behaviour. A more empowering approach here, aligning with the contemporary role of media in young people's everyday life, might be to focus on how youth can actually employ digital technologies for purposes of 'personal branding' (Peters 1997), show examples of how and when they might employ more open (public timelines) and relatively closed (chat apps, private groups) platforms for different purposes and help them take ownership over the way they present themselves online.

Third, the interviews show the value of a user-centric approach to algorithmic selection for understanding the growing role of algorithms in shaping young people's news use. It highlights the necessity of not only focusing on media content but also on facilitating students' knowledge of the contexts in which such information is consumed. The gaps found in young people's algorithmic literacy, for instance, are concerning given their heavy dependence on algorithmically tailored news sources. As Powers (2017) has argued, without basic insight into what algorithms are and do, it becomes difficult to assess the balance and the completeness of one's news feeds or to engage in tactics to intervene in such selections.

Overall, the chapter argues that if we aim to equip young people with the necessary tools to use media critically, mindfully and effectively, this requires rethinking media literacy from the perspective of the practices and experiences of users themselves. After all, facilitating people's skills, competences and knowledge around media only matters if these are actually applied in practice. The user-centric approach proposed in this study offers a way forward regarding how media literacy might be studied in a way that highlights its usefulness and impact in everyday life and how scholars may generate insights into how to empower citizens to navigate today's complex media landscape.

Acknowledgements

I would like to thank Laurence Guérin, Paulo Moekotte and Daan van Riet for their valuable feedback during the set-up of the research project and their help with recruiting participants. I would also like to express my gratitude to the teachers participating in the project (in alphabetical order): Anneloes Haagsman, Edwin Bollema, Elske Mooijman, Houda Al Abouti, Ingeborg Kertesz, Kübra Gögen, Lidy Winters, Marc Visscher, Marit Montsanto, Monique Greefhorst, Menno de Waal, Michel Dalen and Natasha Meijer.

NOTE

1. All participants are mentioned by pseudonyms to protect their privacy.

REFERENCES

boyd, danah (2017), 'Did media literacy backfire?', *Journal of Applied Youth Studies*, 1:4, pp. 83–89.

Broersma, Marcel (2018), 'Epilogue: Situating journalism in the digital: A plea for studying news flows, users, and materiality', in S. Eldridge and B. Franklin (eds), *The Routledge Handbook of Developments in Digital Journalism Studies*, Routledge, pp. 515–26.

Bucher, Taina (2017), 'The algorithmic imaginary: Exploring the ordinary effects of Facebook algorithms', *Information, Communication & Society*, 20:1, pp. 30–44.

Bulger, Monica and Davison, Patrick (2018), 'The promises, challenges, and futures of media literacy', Data & Society Research Institute, https://digital.fundacionceibal.edu.uy/jspui/bitstream/123456789/227/1/DataAndSociety_Media_Literacy_2018.pdf. Accessed 3 October 2019.

Choi, Hanbyul, Park, Jongwha and Jung, Yoonhyuk (2018), 'The role of privacy fatigue in online privacy behavior', *Computers in Human Behavior*, 81, pp. 42–51.

Corbin, Juliet and Strauss, Anselm (2015), *Basics of Qualitative Research: Techniques and Procedures for Developing Grounded Theory*, Thousand Oaks: Sage.

Couldry, Nick, Livingstone, Sonia and Markham, Tim (2010), *Media Consumption and Public Engagement: Beyond The Presumption Of Attention*, Basingstoke: Palgrave Macmillan.

Craft, Stephanie, Ashley, Seth and Maksl, Adam (2016), 'Elements of news literacy: A focus group study of how teenagers define news and why they consume it', *Electronic News*, 10:3, pp. 143–60.

DeVito, Michael, Gergle, Darren and Birnholtz, Jeremy (2017), 'Algorithms ruin everything: # RIPTwitter, folk theories, and resistance to algorithmic change in social media', in *Proceedings of the 2017 CHI Conference on Human Factors in Computing Systems*, Denver, 6–11 May, Denver: ACM, pp. 3163–74.

De Wolf, Ralf (2020), 'Contextualizing how teens manage personal and interpersonal privacy on social media', *New Media & Society*, 22:6, pp. 1058–75.

D'Ignazio, Catherine and Bhargava, Rahul (2015), 'Approaches to big data literacy', in *Proceedings of the Bloomberg Data for Good Exchange Conference*, New York, 28 September.

Edgerly, Stephanie (2017), 'Making sense and drawing lines: Young adults and the mixing of news and entertainment', *Journalism Studies*, 18:8, pp. 1052–69.

Edgerly, Stephanie and Vraga, Emily (2020), 'That's not news: Audience perceptions of "newsness" and why it matters', *Mass Communication & Society*, 23:5, pp. 730–54.

Eslami, Motahhare, Rickman, Aimee, Vaccaro, Kristen, Aleyasen, Amirhossein, Vuong, Andy, Karahalios, Kyratso George, Hamilton, Kevin and Sandvig Christian (2015), '"I always assumed I wasn't really that close to [her]": Reasoning about invisible algorithms in news feeds', in *Proceedings of the 33rd Annual CHI Conference on Human Factors in Computing Systems*, Seoul, Korea, 18–23 April, pp. 153–62.

Fletcher, Richard and Kleis Nielsen, Rasmus (2019), 'Generalised scepticism: How people navigate news on social media', *Information, Communication & Society*, 22:12, pp. 1751–69.

Groot Kormelink, Tim and Costera Meijer, Irene (2019), 'Material and sensory dimensions of everyday news use', *Media, Culture & Society*, 41:5, pp. 637–53.

Harcup, Tony and O'Neill, Deirdre (2016), 'What is news? Galtung and Ruge revisited (again)', *Journalism Studies*, 18:12, pp. 1470–88.

Hargittai, Eszter and Marwick, Alice (2016), '"What can I really do?" Explaining the privacy paradox with online apathy', *International Journal of Communication*, 10, pp. 3737–57.

Hartley, John (1996), *Popular Reality: Journalism, Modernity, Popular Culture*, London: Arnold.

Head, Alison, Fister, Barbara and MacMillan, Margy (2020), 'Information literacy in the age of algorithms: Student experiences with news and information, and the need for change', Project Information Literacy, https://files.eric.ed.gov/fulltext/ED605109.pdf. Accessed 25 May 2020.

Hobbs, Renee, (2011), 'The state of media literacy: A response to Potter', *Journal of Broadcasting & Electronic Media*, 55:3, pp. 419–30.

Hobbs, Renee, Donnelly, Katie, Friesem, Jonathan and Moen, Mary (2013), 'Learning to engage: How positive attitudes about the news, media literacy and video production contribute to adolescent civic engagement', *Educational Media International*, 50:4, pp. 231–46.

Kahne, Joseph and Bowyer, Benjamin (2017), 'Educating for democracy in a partisan age: Confronting the challenges of motivated reasoning and misinformation', *American Educational Research Journal*, 54:1, pp. 3–34.

Katz, Elihu, Blumler, Jay and Gurevitch, Michael (1973), 'Uses and gratifications research', *The Public Opinion Quarterly*, 37:4, pp. 509–23.

Kleemans, Mariska and Eggink, Gonnie, (2016), 'Understanding news: The impact of media literacy education on teenagers' news literacy', *Journalism Education*, 5:1, pp. 74–88.

Klurfeld, James and Schneider, Howard (2014), 'News literacy: Teaching the internet generation to make reliable information choices', Brookings Institution Research Paper, https://www.brookings.edu/wp-content/uploads/2016/07/Klurfeld-Schneider_News-Literacy_June-2014.pdf. Accessed 3 October 2019.

Lewandowsky, Stephan, Ecker, Ullrich and Cook, John (2017), 'Beyond misinformation: Understanding and coping with the "post-truth" era', *Journal of Applied Research in Memory and Cognition*, 6:4, pp. 353–69.

Maksl, Adam, Ashley, Seth and Craft, Stephanie (2015), 'Measuring news media literacy', *Journal of Media Literacy Education*, 6:3, pp. 29–45.

Marwick, Alice and boyd, danah (2014), 'Networked privacy: How teenagers negotiate context in social media', *New Media & Society*, 16:7, pp. 1051–67.

Mihailidis, Paul (2012), *News Literacy: Global Perspectives for the Newsroom and the Classroom*, New York: Peter Lang.

Mihailidis, Paul (2018), 'Civic media literacies: re-Imagining engagement for civic intentionality', *Learning, Media and Technology*, 43:2, pp. 152–64.

Monzer, Cristina, Moeller, Judith, Helberger, Natali and Eskens, Sarah (2020), 'User perspectives on the news personalisation process: Agency, trust and utility as building blocks', *Digital Journalism*, 8:9, pp. 1142–62.

Newman, Nic, Fletcher, Richard, Schulz, Anne, Andi, Smige and Kleis Nielsen, Rasmus (2020), 'Reuters Institute Digital News Report 2020', Reuters Institute for the Study of Journalism, https://reutersinstitute.politics.ox.ac.uk/sites/default/files/2020-06/DNR_2020_FINAL.pdf. Accessed 2 July 2020.

Pariser, Eli (2011), *The Filter Bubble: What the Internet Is Hiding from You*, London: Penguin.

Peters, Tom (1997), 'The brand called you', *Fast Company Magazine*, https://www.fastcompany.com/28905/brand-called-you. Accessed 3 October 2019.

Powers, Elia (2017), 'My news feed is filtered? Awareness of news personalization among college students', *Digital Journalism*, 5:10, pp. 1315–35.

Rader, Emilee and Gray, Rebecca (2015), 'Understanding user beliefs about algorithmic curation in the Facebook news feed', in *Proceedings of the 33rd Annual ACM Conference on Human Factors in Computing Systems*, Seoul, Korea, 18–23 April, Seoul, Korea: CHI, pp. 173–82.

Sujon, Zoetanya (2018), 'The triumph of social privacy: Understanding the privacy logics of sharing behaviors across social media', *International Journal of Communication*, 12, pp. 3751–71.

Sterrett, David, Malato, Dan, Benz, Jennifer, Kantor, Liz, Tompson, Trevor, Rosenstiel, Tom, Sonderman, Jeff and Loker, Kevin (2019), 'Who shared it? Deciding what news to trust on social media', *Digital Journalism*, 7:6, pp. 783–801.

Swart, Joëlle (2018), 'Haven't you heard? The connective role of news and journalism in everyday life', Ph.D. thesis, Groningen, The Netherlands: University of Groningen.

Swart, Joëlle (2021), 'Tactics of news literacy. How young people access, evaluate, and engage with news on social media', *New Media & Society*, online-first, pp. 1–17.

Thorson, Kjerstin (2014), 'Facing an uncertain reception: Young citizens and political interaction on Facebook', *Information, Communication & Society*, 17:2, pp. 203–16.

Toff, Benjamin and Kleis Nielsen, Rasmus (2018), '"I just Google it": Folk theories of distributed discovery', *Journal of Communication*, 68:3, pp. 636–57.

Vraga, Emily and Tully, Melissa (2019), 'News literacy, social media behaviors, and skepticism toward information on social media', *Information, Communication & Society*, 24:2, pp. 150–66.

Vraga, Emily, Tully, Melissa, Maksl, Adam, Craft, Stephanie and Ashley, Seth (2021), 'Theorizing news literacy behaviors', *Communication Theory*, 031:1, pp. 1–21.

13

Media Literacy Meets the Twenty-First-Century Challenges

Sofia Papadimitriou and Lina P. Valsamidou

Introduction

The emergence of digital media has changed the way and the intensity with which young people live, communicate, work, learn and relax. However, young people take risks when they are online and might be subjected to manipulation or be misinformed, even though it is often assumed that every young person uses digital media in a competent way or will gradually learn to do so (EMELS 2018). As such, providing young people with a key set of competences is important for their education and work prospects, as well as personal well-being. In that sense, digital and social media are powerful tools not only to help people develop better media and information literacy (MIL) skills (UNESCO 2014) but also to raise awareness about the importance of MIL to all levels of society.

Notably, digital and social media not only are part of students' daily life in a wide range of activities within the school context but also outside of it. Within the framework of educational activities, they offer opportunities for discovery, participation and creative production. For example, when participating in media literacy activities, students work in original learning environments, benefit from teamwork, creativity and social interaction. The incorporation of media in teaching along with the creation of new content by teachers and students brings changes in modern education and puts emphasis on critical and active approaches and on collaborative effort (Iordanidou and Papadimitriou 2017).

This chapter illustrates the potential of media literacy to be part of modern education, especially in the digital era. As part of various educational activities, media literacy enables young people to connect with others and actively participate in a mediatized society in a more efficient manner. This potential is exemplified by recent media literacy initiatives and good practices of using media in the contemporary school that emphasize the pedagogical use of media platforms within the classroom. As such the chapter firstly discusses the Media and Information Literacy: Critical-thinking, Creativity, Literacy, Intercultural, Citizenship, Knowledge and Sustainability (MIL CLICKS) by the Global Alliance for Partnerships on Media and Information Literacy (UNESCO-GAPMIL). It then moves to EMELS (European Media Literacy Standard for Youth Workers), and lastly, it focuses on the MIL/Peer projects Media and Information Literacy Platform for Exchanging Educational Resources). These initiatives act at a European level and aim to enhance and promote media literacy to young people. Good practices from Greece and Cyprus are also discussed, by highlighting specific cases that implement critical thinking of media in classrooms and that aim to empower students to be informed and active citizens. Their positive outcome acts as the sound motivation of teachers to apply, modify and adapt such methods in their teaching frameworks.

What is media literacy?

Media literacy concerns 'the ability to access, evaluate, assess and communicate' a variety of media messages, drawing attention to the skills of critical analysis and synthesis with the use of audiovisual texts, tools and technologies (Aufderheide and Firestone 1993: 8, in Hobbs 2007: 59). In addition, media literacy 'urges people to think and act critically, to communicate effectively and to be active citizens' (Mihailidis 2018: 376). Furthermore, media literacy is 'the ability to access, understand and create forms of communication within a variety of contexts' (Buckingham 2007: 14), where *access* includes the skills and abilities that are required to discover media content by means of using the available technologies and the related software; *understanding* includes the ability to decode or interpret media content, the knowledge of production processes, and the ability to criticize media, whereas *creation* includes the ability to use the media to construct and communicate messages, either for reasons of self-expression or for influencing and interacting with others. In a broader sense, literacy includes *analysis, evaluation* and *critical thinking*, as it is realized through various forms of social practice and presupposes the existence of a *metalanguage*, that is, certain methods of describing the nature and structure of a specific form of communication and the way that these contexts affect human experience and practices. Media literacy, therefore, may be seen as a form of *critical* literacy that presupposes analysis, evaluation and critical reflection, while also entailing the acquisition of a 'metalanguage'. Additionally, it includes a broader understanding of the social, economic and institutional context of communication, as well as the way that these affect human experience and practices (Luke 2000 in Buckingham 2008: 89).

Therefore, it is crucial for media literacy initiatives to emphasize the development of critical thinking skills of individuals (Iordanidou 2018; Samaras and Iordanidou 2017), starting from childhood (Iordanidou et al. 2020; Valsamidou 2019; 2017). In this respect, critical media literacy analyses relationships between media and audiences, information and power, and more specifically,

> it involves cultivating skills in analysing media codes and conventions, abilities to criticize stereotypes, dominant values, and ideologies, and competencies to interpret the multiple meanings and messages generated by media texts. Media literacy helps people to discriminate and evaluate Media content, to critically dissect media forms, to investigate media effects and uses, to use media intelligently, and to construct alternative media.
>
> (Kellner and Share 2007: 4)

Five key questions and competences

A set of key questions has been developed by the media literacy community to assess one's media literacy skills. These questions are the cornerstone of media literacy education (CML n.d.) and include:

- Who created this message?
- Which creative techniques are used to attract my attention?
- How might different people interpret this message?
- Which lifestyles, values and points of view are represented – or missing?
- Why is this message being sent?

Similarly, there are five key competences for media and digital literacy (Hobbs 2010) that citizens, adults and also children, must possess. These are (1) access, (2) analysis and evaluation, (3) creation, (4) reflection and (5) action, and they 'work together in a spiral of empowerment, supporting people's active participation [...] through the processes of both consuming and creating messages' (Hobbs 2010: 18). More specifically, access concerns finding and using media and technology tools skillfully and sharing appropriate and relevant information with others. Analysis and evaluation relate to comprehending messages and using critical thinking to analyse the quality, credibility and point of view of a message (Iordanidou 2018). Creation refers to composing or generating content using creativity and confidence in self-expression, with awareness of purpose, audience and composition techniques. Reflection involves applying social responsibility and ethical principles to one's own identity and lived experience, communication

189

behavior and conduct. Lastly, action is about working individually and collaboratively to share knowledge and solve problems in the family, the workplace and the community and participating as a member of a community at local, regional, national and international levels (Hobbs 2010).

Media Literacy Initiatives

Three sound initiatives to enhance and support MIL that are discussed in this section are:

- Media and Information Literacy: Critical-thinking, Creativity, Literacy, Intercultural, Citizenship, Knowledge and Sustainability) (MIL CLICKS) by the Global Alliance for Partnerships on Media and Information Literacy (UNESCO-GAPMIL).
- European Media Literacy Standard for Youth Workers (EMELS).
- Media and Information Literacy Platform for Exchanging Educational Resources (MIL/Peer projects).

The MIL CLICKS framework (MIL CLICKS n.d.) takes a collaborative approach between GAPMIL, current and future partner organizations and other MIL community actors (GAPMIL n.d.). In addition to MIL competences training and awareness raising, MIL CLICKS strives to increase the likelihood of media reporting on MIL to introduce a new public policy promoting MIL and to augment the number of partner organizations that are part of the movement for online literacy. The MIL CLICKS initiative targets policymakers, MIL experts, teachers without MIL expertise, development agencies, private sector organizations and the general public.

The need for the development of a common reference framework in the field of youth work that highlights what it means to be digitally savvy in an increasingly digitized world led to the emergence of the initiative EMELS (n.d.). EMELS is a tool to improve young people's media literacy skills and helps to raise the quality of youth work and training in the field of media education. It works on different settings, such as youth-led organizations, organizations for youth, informal groups or youth services and public authorities. EMELS is co-funded by the *Erasmus+* Program of the European Union as a strategic partnership project. EMELS Standard describes media literacy as a process of preparing individuals for competent, safe and creative use and understanding of digital media. The standard identifies five areas of digital competence:

1. Information and data (how to search for information effectively and critically approach it).

2. Media creation and communication (how media can be used for self-expression and to create meaning, in terms of both technical skills and creative process).
3. Resistance and empowerment (how to stay safe using the media, protect our rights and use media to impact a wider community).
4. Understanding media usage of children and young people (what we need to know about media and young people and where to find this information).
5. Training skills and development (how to run media education activities and develop further).

These five areas are developed into sixteen competences, followed by practical examples of knowledge, skills and attitudes. The competences are also complemented by best practices and training resources, namely materials that are used by educators all over Europe to improve young people's media literacy skills and to guide and inspire educators/teachers. Lastly, MIL/Peer is a tool developed by Evens Foundation and Modern Poland Foundation to prepare, translate and publish educational resources (MIL/Peer n.d.a). It aims to increase the number and quality of media literacy projects in Europe by encouraging international cooperation among media literacy organizations and by supporting them in applying for European funds.

The MIL/Peer provides support with regards to fundraising and international cooperation, and it offers tools for sharing educational materials. In addition, it allows organizations to collaboratively work on joint projects. MIL/Peer is a free-licensed software, and many of the published materials are also available under open licenses, which means one can use them, change and publish adapted versions free of charge. Good practices from Greece and Cyprus that are discussed in the following section have been evaluated and highlighted in the MIL/Peer project.

Good practices of media literacy

In the following section, we focus on good practices of using media in the contemporary school that emphasize the development of critical skills. In particular, these practices include a variety of concrete methods that raise awareness among students and allow them to familiarize themselves with the concepts of persuasion, propaganda, hate speech, fake news, disinformation and misinformation.

These good practices of using media have been implemented in schools in various frameworks and have been selected due to their (Papadimitriou and Sofos 2019; Costa et al. 2017) positive evaluation by educational communities, awards in competitions and sustainability for numerous years. All of them can be transferred within the educational contexts in which they have been implemented (e.g., curricula, supporting complementary non-formal learning activities) or can be extended to different educational contexts (e.g., in curricula of other countries). The MIL/Peer project includes a special section with finished and upcoming good practices-resources (MIL/Peer n.d.a) which are freely available for teachers to implement, modify and adapt into their teaching practices.

European School Radio: Fighting hate speech (Greece)

The European School Radio (ESR)[1] is a web radio with audio productions from hundreds of school radio groups all over Greece, Cyprus and some other European countries (MIL/Peer n.d.d.d). Thousands of pupils, encouraged and supported by their teachers, produce a fully scheduled weekly radio programme in a variety of shows, spots, music and speech broadcasts. Through team activities, pupils develop cooperative and communication skills, cultivate critical thinking, approaching critically and consciously media content (MIL/Peer n.d.d.d; Valsamidou 2018). In addition, the ESR organizes an annual Radio School Festival, contests, events and projects with the participation of thousands of students and teachers.

During 2018–19, the radio contest 'Make-it-heard' was held with the topic: 'Our voice is a shield against hate speech' (ESR 2019) and was oriented to all schools of Primary and Secondary Education in Greece and Cyprus. The event, that was co-organized by the ESR, the Educational Radiotelevision[2] of the Ministry of Education in Greece and the Pedagogical Institute of Cyprus aimed to raise awareness on the topic of hate speech, as aggressive rhetoric is nowadays adopted toward anything foreign or anything which is different from our perceptions, often resulting in aggressive behaviour and the propagation of hatred (Iordanidou et al. 2018). Hate rhetoric occurs in the form of written or oral speech, images, symbols, electronic or other games, intended to express or propagate a message of violence. Particularly in the online world and social media, criticism easily dominates over the effort to understand the opposite position.

The contest focused on stimulating students' creativity, developing their emotional world and cultivating critical thinking, respect, courtesy and acceptance. Through 120 radio messages and 100 songs, students raised their voice against hate speech, and they also:

- communicated their personal experience of aggressive rhetoric or hate speech,
- recognized and rejected aggressive rhetoric,
- understood the limits between freedom of speech and hate speech,
- initiated a rhetoric of acceptance and respect in an experiential and enjoyable way,
- understood the value of sharing and collaborating through the creation of radio and music-based discourse.

Analysing the media critically (Greece)

The student action 'VideoMuseums: Our Opinion and Written Critics Competition' aimed at the creation of short documentaries by groups of students who engage with ideas from their environment, neighborhood and culture and decide what is worth saving in forthcoming years. This action, a follow-up to the Hellenic Student Competition 'Short Film VideoMuseums' of 2014, was recognized by the Institute for Media Research and Media Education as one of the twelve best projects for audiovisual education in Europe (Karpos n.d.)

In the framework of the project, eleven awarded videos of the contest were selected and screened in a film festival organized by schools. The action aimed at motivating students to participate in a creative discussion for issues they are interested in, develop a clear argumentation and express their views while developing audiovisual literacy skills. Moreover, it promoted a series of characteristics that a cinema film viewer should have, such as:

- the concept of the wide distribution of films and the common experience of connecting different people,
- the critical attitude of each viewer, expressed through the award of symbolic public distinctions,
- the development of critical reasoning and the formulation of arguments arising from the attempt to justify the choices of each group of viewers and the publication of their choices on an online platform.

Media Education Month (Cyprus)

The practice Media Education Month (MIL/Peer n.d.c) includes twelve lesson plans for pupils 9–12 years old and has been implemented in a primary school in Cyprus in the framework of a Master's thesis at the School of Communications and New Journalism of the Open University of Cyprus. The project, which is available on the section of finished resources of the MIL/Peer project, was also awarded by the Evens Foundation's MIL/Peer competition in 2015. These comprehensive lesson plans are based on proposed methods that emerge through the literature review (Buckingham 2003; Masterman 2001; UNESCO 2011) and have been developed especially for promoting media literacy critical skills. They provide an in-depth and detailed understanding of the media system through the study of media education key concepts. Briefly, students learn about the constructed nature of media products, develop their ability to analyse and criticize media, engage in creative media production and systematically (self) reflect on the significance of mass media and modern civilization in general.

The practice aims to help students acquire skills to access, analyse, evaluate and create media. According to the learning outcomes of the practice, students are able to:

- explore the influence of media on their daily lives,
- engage in the critical inquiry of media,
- identify hidden media messages,
- interpret messages presented through various media forms,
- discuss the effect of media on culture,
- create, analyse and evaluate media content.

The *'Media Education Month'* consists of twelve optional escalating activities, namely: A1. Investigating students' media use and attitudes; A2–A3. Investigating media audiences; A4. Media deprivation experience; A5. Case study: Students' favorite TV programme; A6. Photojournalism (visual literacy); A7–A10. Critical analysis of advertisements/news headlines/newspaper articles/ television news; A11. media vocabulary; and A12. Self-reflection and final questionnaire.

During the project, students are encouraged to work in groups and to discuss, analyse and categorize various aspects of media and their content. For example, for activities A6, A7, A8, A9, A10, students focus on the critical analysis of advertisements, news headlines, newspaper articles and television news, and they collaborate to identify and classify media content according to its importance. In doing so, they deliberate on topics, images, protagonists, vocabulary, stereotypes and conventions, obvious purposes and implicit messages, as well as journalists' and the experts' arguments. For instance, students put the advertisements in the middle of the triangle and analyse them according to the 'media triangle methodology' (Baker n.d.). As Hobbs (2010) has highlighted, being critical is not criticizing everything but asking hard questions. Finally, all activities of critical approach are combined with a production stage so students become active creators of media content, which includes advertisements, video recordings, articles, printed or digital newspaper/magazine covers, TV news clips and word-clouds.

CAT – Cyprus Artefact Treasure in Action

The Cyprus Artefact Treasure in action-CAT is a media education project intended for Greek and Turkish Cypriot communities, as well as international communities of the island, focusing on Cypriot archaeological artefacts (Costa et al. 2017). The CAT project enables cross-curricular communication and promotes peace by implementing media education through the lens of archaeological heritage. Children and adults have the opportunity to interact and create different media products, to illustrate and to bring their common culture to life and to build long-lasting friendships and sincere dialogue between communities. The CAT project (MIL/Peer n.d.b; Costa et al. 2017) promotes strategies for conflict resolution, intercultural dialogue and respect for human rights and works with media on the common cultural heritage of both parts of Cyprus. Target groups consisted of twenty children; 10–11 years old. There were two different groups and ten teachers in a conflict or post-conflict zone. The joint work and discussions about archaeological objects sparked a dialogue between communities and thus initiated the establishment of long-lasting and sustainable links among participants.

For purposes of self-expression, young people used media to participate throughout the project: they discussed their culture and history of their country in mixed groups; they planned a story, they realized the story in a stop motion video; and in the end, they presented their videos. The CAT project was implemented for two years (2010–12) and built on three levels which established and emphasized media education competences of citizenship, cross-cultural communication and conflict resolution (Andriopoulou et al. 2014).

Conclusion

The initiatives MIL CLICKS by UNESCO-GAPMIL at an international level and the European funded projects EMELS and MIL/Peer that were presented in this chapter showcase that media literacy is a key necessity of the digital era. Indeed, the necessity and importance of media literacy has been underlined by both the European Commission (2009) and UNESCO (2011). The European Commission urges member states of the European Union to include media literacy in the curricula of compulsory education. Likewise, UNESCO stresses the importance of media and information literacy, emphasizing that it is now a fundamental human right.

Focusing on the use of media in the contemporary school and in modern education, this chapter highlights that, especially in Greece and Cyprus, this is still at an early stage, and only a few teachers are aware of methods on how to integrate media literacy practices into their classrooms. Nevertheless, today there is a wealth of available open media resources and good practices, which can be retrieved and accessed to support rich learning environments responding to students' expectations (Iordanidou et al. 2018). Therefore, teachers can use media in accordance to reinforce pedagogical methods within the classroom and/or in online learning environments. Learning based on media presupposes that teachers can encourage, guide and support their students and engage them in open and student-centered forms of learning.

The variety of good practices presented in this chapter highlights the importance of a critical reading of media content regardless of its source or its broadcast channel or platform. Concrete methods have been successfully implemented in schools in both Greece and Cyprus, allowing students to be part of a fully mediatized world and to obtain media literacy skills for the purpose of acquiring active citizenship, engaging in cross-cultural communication, applying non-aggressive rhetoric and understanding conflict resolution. However, it is crucial that good learning practices and initiatives that rely on media need to be implemented into school education. In addition, educational policies should focus on the professional development of teachers in primary and secondary education enabling them to further promote media literacy.

NOTES

1. See also http://www.europeanschoolradio.eu/. Accessed 26 May 2021.
2. See also www.edutv.gr. Accessed 26 May 2021.

REFERENCES

Andriopoulou, Irene, Papadimitriou, Sofia and Kourti, Evangelia (2014), 'Media and Information Literacy Policies in Greece (2013)', Paris: ANR TRANSLIT and COST Transforming Audiences/Transforming Societies, http://ppemi.ens-cachan.fr/data/media/colloque140528/rapports/GREECE_2014.pdf. Accessed 30 August 2019.

Aufderheide, Patricia and Firestone, Charles (1993), *Media Literacy: National Leadership Conference: Report*, Washington, D.C.: Aspen Institute.

Baker, Frank (n.d.), 'Media Literacy Clearing House', The Media Triangle Methodology, http://www.frankwbaker.com/Mediatriangle.htm. Accessed 30 August 2019.

Buckingham, David (2003), *Media Education: Literacy, Learning and Contemporary Culture*, Cambridge: Polity Press.

Buckingham, David (2007), 'Digital media literacies: Re-examining media education in the internet age', in Stelios Papathanasopoulos (ed.), *Communication Issues, Tribute: Media Education and Media Literacy*, 6, Athens: Kastaniotis, pp. 13–29.

Buckingham, David (2008), *Media Education: Literacy, Learning and Contemporary Culture*, Athens: Ellinika Grammata.

Center for Media Literacy (CML) (n.d.), 'Five key questions form foundation for media inquiry', http://www.medialit.org/reading-room/five-key-questions-form-foundation-media-inquiry. Accessed 20 June 2019.

Costa, Conceição, Car, Victoria and Papadimitriou, Sofia, (2017), 'Chapter 7/ Good practices and emerging trends in media and information literacy', in *Divina Frau-Meigs, Irma Velez, Julieta Flores Michel 'Public Policies in Media and Information Literacy in Europe'*,

London: Routledge, https://www.routledge.com/Public-Policies-in-Media-and-Informat ion-Literacy-in-Europe-Cross-Country/Frau-Meigs-Velez-Michel/p/book/9781138644373. Accessed 20 June 2019.

EMELS (2018), 'European media literacy standard for youth workers', https://emels.eu/. Accessed 30 August 2019.

EMELS (n.d.), 'European media literacy standard for youth workers', https://emels.eu/. Accessed 4 October 2021.

ESR (2019), 'European School Radio', http://europeanschoolradio.eu/6fest/the-competition-make-it-heard/. Accessed 30 August 2019.

European Commission (2009), 'Media literacy: Study on the current trends and approaches to media literacy in Europe', https://tinyurl.com/yb3q2k3e. Accessed 20 June 2018.

GAPMIL (n.d.), '*Global* alliance for partnerships on media and information literacy', http://www.unesco.org/new/en/communication-and-information/Media-development/Media-literacy/global-alliance-for-partnerships-on-Media-and-information-literacy/. Accessed 30 August 2019.

Hobbs, Renee (2007), 'The integration of media literacy in secondary education', in S. Papathanasopoulos (ed.), *Communication Issues*, *Tribute: Media Education and Media Literacy*, 6, Athens: Kastaniotis, pp. 59–72.

Hobbs, Renee (2010), 'Digital and media literacy: A plan of action. The Aspen Institute. Communications and society program', https://eric-ed-gov.proxy-ub.rug.nl/?id=ED523244, Accessed 4 October 2021.

Iordanidou, Sofia (2018), 'De profundis: Reconsidering media literacy from the perspective of communication education', in S. Iordanidou, S. Papadimitriou and L. Valsamidou (eds), *Media Literacy: In search of Its Meaning and Function*, Athens: Metamesonykties Ekdoseis & Advanced Media Institute, pp. 11–34.

Iordanidou, Sofia and Papadimitriou, Sofia (2017), 'Education communication and media literacy: Exploring the merging of media and communication studies with education studies in theory and in practice. Developing a new curriculum for the digital era', in A. T. Kontakos and P. I. Stamatis (eds), *Theories and Models of Communication in Education*, 2, Athens: Diadrasi Publishing, pp. 139–75.

Iordanidou, Sofia, Stamatis, Panagiotis I. and Valsamidou, Lina P. (2020), 'Communication in education and media education: A theoretical and research approach in the field of early childhood education', in A. T. Kontakos and P. I. Stamatis (eds), *Issues of Theory and Research Methodology of Communication in Education*, vol. C, Athens: Interaction, pp. 209–44.

Karpos (n.d.), '*Videomuseums*', http://www.karposontheweb.org/. Accessed 10 November 2015.

Kellner, Douglas and Share, Jeff (2007), 'Critical media literacy, democracy, and the reconstruction of education', in D. Macedo and S. R. Steinberg (eds), *Media Literacy: A Reader*, New York: Peter Lang Publishing, pp. 3–23.

Luke, Carmen (2000), 'Cyber-schooling and technological change: multiliteracies for new times', in B. Cope and M. Kalantzis (eds), *Multiliteracies: Literacy Learning and the Design*, pp. 69–91.

Masterman, L. (2001), *Teaching the Media*, London: Routledge.

Mihailidis, Paul (2018), 'Civic media literacies: Re-imagining engagement for civic intentionality' (trans. Lina P. Valsamidou), in S. Iordanidou, S. Papadimitriou and L. Valsamidou (eds), *Media Literacy: In Search of Its Meaning and Function*, Athens: Metamesonykties Ekdoseis & Advanced Media Institute, pp. 371–94.

MIL CLICKS (n.d.), 'MIL CLICKS social media initiative', https://en.unesco.org/milclicks. Accessed 30 August 2019.

Papadimitriou, Sofia and Sofos, Alevisos (2019), 'Good practices in digital literacy for audiovisual media: Outcomes from an action-research at the University of Aegean', in A. Lionarakis (ed.), *10th International Conference of Open and Distance Learning*, 22–24 November, online, https://eproceedings.epublishing.ekt.gr/index.php/openedu/article/view/2316. Accessed 22 May 2020.

Samaras, Athanassios and Iordanidou, Sofia (2017), 'Exploring the educational capacity of causal inference in the teaching of media theory: A case study analysis of CNN-effect related theories', in A. T. Kontakos and P. I. Stamatis (eds), *Theories and Models of Communication in Education*, vol. 2, Athens: Diadrasi publishing, pp. 87–121.

UNESCO (2011), 'Media and information literacy curriculum for teachers', http://unesdoc.unesco.org/images/0019/001929/192971GRE.pdf. Accessed 30 August 2019.

UNESCO (2014), 'European media and information literacy forum', http://www.europeanmedialiteracyforum.org/. Accessed 4 October 2021.

Valsamidou, Lina, P. (2019), 'Literacies, multiliteracies, media and news literacy: Terms, definitions and conceptual clarifications in the light of a contemporary school', *Journalism*, 19, pp. 14–17.

Valsamidou, Lina, P. (2018), 'The art of communication on school radio in the light of communication and media education: From idea to practice in a classroom with young children', in E. Koltsakis and I. Salonikidis (eds), *Utilization of ICT in Teaching Practice*, Proceedings of the 5th Panhellenic Educational Conference of Central Macedonia, vol. B, pp. 278–92.

Valsamidou, Lina, P. (2017), 'Time for advertisements: Children producers of audiovisual advertisements', in S. Grosdos (ed.), *Audiovisual Literacy in Education*, Proceedings of the 1st Panhellenic Scientific Conference with International Participation, Thessaloniki, June, pp. 88–102, http://www.kmaked.gr/site/images/praktika-synedriou.pdf. Accessed 30 August 2019.

In Lieu of a Conclusion
'Media, Polis, Agora', a Challenging
Exploration Mission

Sofia Iordanidou

This book, as well as the 'Media, Polis, Agora' AMI *Conference on Journalism and Communication in the Digital Era* from which it was derived, reminds one of the exploration missions undertaken in times past – missions toward areas and cultures that played a vivid role in the minds of people shaping public opinion but remained by and large ill-understood.

But do we really mean that speaking of the media, of journalists and journalism today – and getting deeper into the 'crisis narrative' thereof, as well into the 'opportunities promised' – we speak of them as akin to the voyages of discovery of the South Seas or the jungle expeditions in the Dark Continent of earlier centuries?

The option taken, to use the Greek paradigm/the media situation in (financially, economically, socio-politically crisis-ridden) Greece so as to delve into the pathologies of the media in the digital era, then to use the wisdom or at least different views from the great outer world, trying to establish some sort of common discussion ground for academics/ivory tower dwellers and media practitioners/professionals, proved an interesting option indeed.

In a way, nobody could foresee since in Spring 2020 the world experienced a tremendous global crisis. The COVID-19 pandemic catalysed a series of changes, shaking up existing structures and accelerating digital transformation solutions for that are made accessible to all. This profound ongoing crisis has put societies around the world into a VUCA environment – with Volatility, Uncertainty, Complexity and Ambiguity being its main characteristics. At the same time, it changed consumer habits and the relationship between citizens and the media. According to research and surveys, screen time has increased, as well as use of social media and messaging apps and subscription platforms such as Netflix, Amazon, etc. Moreover, there is a vibrant debate regarding the influence of the pandemic to the increased amount of false or misleading information ('fake news'), causing an infodemic with severe consequences.

At the end of the day, the issues faced boil down to a triple inquiry: Is there a problematic situation in media life in the digital era as it has evolved in the work of its professionals, in the social function assumed by the media? If yes, can something be done about this – and what?

Reversing somehow the order of discussion in the book, one immediately sees two problem areas emerging: the one has to do with the media business model followed in the digital era; the other with the work conditions of journalists, that is those venturing – or remaining – at this field of endeavour.

The erosion of the business model of mainstream media goes hand in hand with the stressful search for funding in the new media environment: Could crowdfunding or 'community engagement' approaches serve as convincing and effective alternatives/ways out of the funding impasse? The jury is still out on that crucial issue. The same goes for the disturbing deterioration of journalists' work conditions – both in more structured businesses, where work stress is for quite some time now the main issue of the day, and in freer environments, where the need to self-finance is acquiring central importance.

Talking of business models or of quality-eroding work stress in the media world may sound disingenuous, if not indifferent, to the general public: but given the fact that the media constitute quintessentially labour-intensive and socially directed enterprises, whose influence on public life remains an important issue, one understands that this problem area is here to stay. The absence of credible/ adequate responses should not be underestimated, especially in a period where collective bargaining/union power is at a low ebb.

To go to the heart of the matter of efforts to convert the very modus operandi of the media in the digital era to some sort of solution to issues as described earlier, one has to tackle directly the issue of taxing the value collected by 'web giants' through their own business model and reallocating – somehow – such value back to content producers – that is, journalists. Recent efforts undertaken at EU level or by single countries (France, Spain) show an increasing awareness of the issue. Still, the resistance of web companies along with that of other heavy-weight players (especially the United States under the Trump administration) is an important factor; one further issue that remains open is how any such taxation proceeds would be channeled back to content providers (and how they would be shared) rather than used for general-purpose public spending.

More recently, 2021 saw serious developments in regard to taxation and regulation of the 'web giants' that grew even more gigantic during a year of confinement. The main front of the battle between regulators and big tech shifted to Australia in February 2021. The Australian government passed a bill[1] that would force Google and Facebook to negotiate and come to terms with news publishers on how the tech companies would pay them for the use of their content. The basic idea was similar to the European Union 'link tax' discussed in several Member States, and it did indeed confirm all the criticisms levelled against the idea of the link tax in the European Union: It has proven to be a scheme to force Facebook and Google to share a minimum of profits with large media conglomerates, prominently Murdoch's News Corp, the dominant media company in Australia, with huge political clout. This deal (which Google took, through the conclusion of deals with individual publishers, and Facebook initially declined) has no provisions directly supporting journalists or journalism and left smaller publishers out completely. In any case, even this seemed too much for Facebook which went on to take the unprecedented step of banning Australian news sources from its platform for almost a week before settling with the Australian government. As expected, European news publishers sided strongly with their Australian counterparts, and less expectedly so did Microsoft.

The change of guard in the White House has restarted discussions on big tech taxation between the European Union and the United States. Under the Trump administration, there was very little negotiation possible. French and German government officials felt optimistic they will achieve a deal with the United States on GAFA taxation by the summer of 2021.[2] In the meantime, GAFA companies were making a show of shifting their tax burden to the consumer, by upping their prices of their services. Greece has been following such debates at quite a distance.

Two further fields touched upon by 'Media, Polis, Agora' may seem somehow apart – but in fact they are peculiarly intertwined. On one hand, the possibilities offered by bridging the gap between academia and journalism, thus creating a constant forum for ongoing self-discussion of the media world; on the other, the approach of media ethics in such a way that would integrate ethical concerns to everyday journalistic practice. Where can one find some common ground between building a positive relation (or even an ongoing partnership) of the media world with academia and integrating ethics to the point of establishing a media ombudsman institution, further to any self-regulation practices? The answer is that both approaches reveal a desire of the media world to open up, to self-analyse, to respond to demands of the outside world. But … does there really exist such a mentality?

Last, but by no means least, the issue of media literacy arises. Is it a solution? If yes, to what problem? It was approached under several angles in the 'Media, Polis, Agora' debate, but the most pertinent one may prove to be a reflex of self-protection that is gradually developing in society. In the era of disinformation, fake news, the negative impact the blogosphere has had on twenty-first-century politics, a 'citizens' journalism' turned rogue, the media-audience-changed-to-content-producer (with the role of gatekeeper sadly put to rest), in such moving sands for one to be aware of what one 'consumes' as news, what one digests as opinion, media literacy is of primordial importance. To realize that such a learning process has to start early, even at school age is one thing; to do so is quite another!

Cases of police brutality experienced in Greece, although not remotely as lethal as the ones occurring in the United States (which have given rise to the *I can't breathe*/George Floyd movement in May 2020, which soon widening to the *#BlackLivesMatter* protest/surge) gave the content-producer dimension of the proverbial man (or woman) on the street a potent political capability. In fact, faced with demonstrations even in the middle of a COVID-19 lock-down, demonstrations originating at footage of police excesses, the authorities were forced to provide front-line police forces with cameras to restore some balance to the all-powerful visual language carried over smartphones and social media.

If such is our overview of 'Media, Polis, Agora' in lieu of a conclusion, there is one missing piece – the one concerning Twitter and its interesting (if not disturbing) landing in Greek journalistic, but also political, practice where it has overtaken the dynamic of Facebook. Why leave it as a sort of post-script?

Because, as exemplified by Tweeter-in-chief Donald Trump addressing a world audience from across the Atlantic, but also by the increasing use of tweeting in the very country where Polis and Agora (i.e. places where citizens came to congregate, to trade but also to debate on issues of public interest, or to arrive at political decisions) have their roots, this form of expression shows to its best the enmity potential that the digital era has bestowed upon us. This applies, however a breadth of communication may reside in such a lapidary from of expression masquerading as argument.

The role that Twitter, along with Facebook, has played in the transposition to Greek reality of the *#MeToo* movement offers a further example. While we are looking for solutions, an honest look at the problems arising is fast becoming a public duty.

NOTES

1. Treasury Laws Amendment (News Media and Digital Platforms Mandatory Bargaining Code) Bill 2021, https://parlinfo.aph.gov.au/parlInfo/search/display/display.w3p;page=0;query=BillId:r6652%20Recstruct:billhome. Accessed 26 May 2021.
2. France looks to summer deal with US tech giants over digital tax, RFI 27 Feb 2021, https://www.rfi.fr/en/business/20210227-france-looks-to-summer-deal-with-tech-giants-over-digital-gafa-tax-google-amazon-facebook-apple. Accessed 26 May 2021.

Contributors

NIKOS ANTONOPOULOS is an Assistant Professor in the Department of Digital Media and Communication at Ionian University. He is head of New Media Communication and Usability Lab (NeMeCULab), and he has published books and papers on scientific journals and presented papers in international and national Conferences. For more information, please visit his personal website at http://www.antonopoulo.info.

* * * * *

DESPOINA FOUSKA was born in Athens, Greece, and lives in Larnaca, Cyprus. She studied political science and public administration at the National and Kapodistrian University of Athens. She holds a master's degree in communication and new journalism at the Open University of Cyprus. She is a content writer in the fintech industry and a freelance translator. She has worked as a communication consultant for the Secretariat General of Information and Communication, Greece. Her scientific interests include digital and social media, content management and digital culture and labor. https://advancedmediainstitute.com/en/ami-team/despoina-fouska/.

* * * * *

KATHRYN GEELS is leading the Engaged Journalism Accelerator – a programme accelerating the skills, people, ideas and knowledge transfer of European news organizations working to empower communities and their conversations, and create solutions that can positively impact journalism and society. Prior to the EJC, Kathryn was the policy and strategy lead for creative industries at Digital Catapult – a UK agency driving the adoption of advanced digital technologies. Kathryn also worked alongside Google News Initiative to deliver the Digital Identities programme for journalists in seven countries. And prior to this, she was at UK innovation foundation Nesta, where she led a programme supporting innovation in hyperlocal media. https://engagedjournalism.com.

* * * * *

VALIA KAIMAKI is a journalist. She has been with the National Greek radio-television (ERT) as a radio producer since 1997. She has also been the director of the Greek edition of the French monthly review *Le Monde Diplomatique* since its first publication in 1998. She also contributes as a columnist in various publications. She is the author of the first Greek book about media and the internet (1996). Since September 2013, she has been Adjunct Lecturer at the Open University of Cyprus and Social Media and Journalism at the postgraduate programme 'Communication and new journalism'. In July 2021 she was elected Assistant Professor in 'Digital Journalism' at the Ionian University of Greece. She is a specialist in new media – social media and journalism. https://valiakaimaki.

* * * * *

MINOS-ATHANASIOS KARYOTAKIS is a Ph.D. student at the Department of Journalism of the School of Communication of Hong Kong Baptist University. His research interests include framing theory, hate propaganda and media ethics. https://minoskar.net/.

* * * * *

MATINA KIOUREXIDOU is a Postdoc Researcher at the Aristotle University of Thessaloniki. She received her Ph.D. in medical informatics in Aristotle University. She also has an MSc in cultural informatics and communication at the Aegean University and her BSc in cultural heritage management and new technologies. She has published in numerous scientific journals and conferences about communication, media, multimedia content and virtual and augmented reality.

* * * * *

EVANGELOS LAMPROU is an Adjunct Lecturer in the Department of Digital Media and Communication at the Ionian University in Greece. He teaches journalism, online media and communications courses. His research interests include media economics, online media and contemporary journalistic practices.

* * * * *

ELENI MAVROULI works as a journalist (reporter – editor) since 1994, specializing in international news (Middle East, North Africa, Arab – Muslim world in general and Europe). She has carried out many journalistic missions, including in those war zones. She has worked mainly in written press (newspapers, magazines), in online media and radio as a reporter but also as a radio producer. She received her Ph.D. in political philosophy and political and social movements in the General Department of Law of Panteion University of Athens. She is a post doc researcher at the sociology department of the Aegean University on the subject 'From the newspaper to the internet: Journalists' work and social conscience transformations'. https://advancedmediainstitute.com/en/ami-team/eleni-mavrouli/.

* * * * *

MICHAEL PANAYIOTAKIS received a BSc in physics from the University of Athens and a MSc in theoretical physics from the University of Crete. Over the past twenty years, he has worked as a consultant, an Information Architect and Project Manager in web development and corporate web projects as well as participating as a freelancer in digital research projects. He was a columnist in the Greek Edition of *Monthly Review Magazine* and a journalist and web advisor in the Greek edition of the *Economist*. He is currently a contributor and a member of the editorial team of *Dimosiografia* magazine (Greek affiliate of the *Columbia Journalism Review*). https://advancedmediainstitute.com/en/ami-team/mihalis-panagiotakis/.

* * * * *

SOFIA PAPADIMITRIOU studied mathematics and has a master's degree in computer science from the Athens National University. Her Ph.D. regards the field of open and distance learning in higher education and was developed at the Hellenic Open University. She is the Head of the Educational Radio-Television, and she has been working as a tutor-counselor at the Hellenic Open University and the University of Piraeus in post graduate courses since 2017. She is a postdoctoral researcher at the Aegean University in the field of digital literacy in Audiovisual Media. http://eap.academia.edu/SofiaPapadimitriou.

* * * * *

NIKOS SMYRNAIOS is an Associate Professor of media studies at the University of Toulouse. His research includes the political economy of online media, digital journalism and the political use of social media. He has published *Internet Oligopoly: The Corporate Takeover of Our Digital World*, Emerald Publishing, Bingley, 2018. http://ephemeron.eu/bio.

* * * * *

VASILIS SOTIROPOULOS is a lawyer at the Supreme Court (Court of Cassation) of Greece and holds a master's degree in public law. In 2005, he founded the first Greek legal blog, e-lawyer, in an attempt to generate debate on the protection of personal data and respect for civil liberties on the internet. He was the first elected Ombudsman of the City of Athens in 2012. Alongside a group of co-workers, they created this structure from scratch in Athens for the prompt resolution of disputes between the citizens and the City of Athens. Having been elected Ombudsman of the Region of Attica, his mission was to strengthen the relations between citizens and public services and to achieve the resolution of disputes between them, acting as a mediator, without having to go to court.

*****

JOËLLE SWART is an Assistant Professor in journalism studies at the Centre for Media and Journalism Studies at the University of Groningen. Her research focuses on the crossroads of news use, journalism and citizenship, considering how digitalization affects the way users employ news to connect socially and democratically. Her most recent work centers around media literacy and the question of how people develop user practices, norms and attitudes around news and journalism in digital environments. Her work has been published in several international academic journals, including *Journalism Studies, Media, Culture & Society* and *New Media & Society*. https://www.rug.nl/staff/j.a.c.swart/.

*****

SARA TORSNER is a Postdoctoral Research Associate to the UNESCO Chair on Media Freedom, the Safety of Journalism and the Issue of Impunity, located at the Centre for Freedom of the Media, the University of Sheffield. Sara completed her Ph.D. entitled 'Profiling the civil diminishment of journalism: A conceptual framework for understanding the causes, and manifestations of risk to journalism' in 2019. http://www.cfom.org.uk/about/people/sara-torsner/.

*****

LADA TRIFONOVA Price is a journalism lecturer in the Department of Media, Arts and Communication, Sheffield Hallam University, United Kingdom. She is a former journalist, and her current research is focused on media and journalistic practice in transitional Eastern European democracies. She is examining threats to press freedom such as censorship and self-censorship, media corruption, ethical challenges to journalistic practice and violence and intimidation against journalists. Her recent published work includes chapters in *Critical Perspectives on Journalistic Beliefs and Actions: Global Experiences* (Routledge, 2018) and *Public Service Broadcasting and Media Systems in Troubled European Democracies* (Palgrave Macmillan, 2019). She is currently editing the forthcoming *Routledge Companion to Journalism Ethics*. https://www.shu.ac.uk/about-us/our-people/staff-profiles/lada-price.

*****

LIDA TSENE holds a Ph.D. from Panteion University, Department of Communication, Media and Culture (2010) in the field of social media and social responsibility. Since 2008, she has collaborated with the Advertising and Public Relations Lab of Panteion University as researcher and teaching associate. Since 2012, she has taught at the MA communication and new journalism Open University of Cyprus and since 2013 at the MA cultural organisations management of the Hellenic Open University. She has worked as a journalist, CSR and communication consultant, while since 2005 she has worked as the Public Relations and Educational Programmes Director of Comicdom Press. In 2015, she founded Athens Comics Library. https://advancedmediainstitute.com/en/ami-team/lida-tsene-2/.

*****

LINA P. VALSAMIDOU is a Ph.D. candidate in communication and new journalism at the Open University of Cyprus, holds an MA in communication and journalism, an MSc. in cultural studies and new technologies and an MSc in gender and new educational and labour environments in the information society. She has worked for many years as a journalist, a television producer and as a researcher in research programmes of Greek universities. Her academic articles have been published in Greek and foreign journals, collective volumes and proceedings of conferences. https://advancedmediainstitute.com/en/ami-team/lina-valsamidou/.

Lightning Source UK Ltd.
Milton Keynes UK
UKHW032101160123
415456UK00004B/67